Him 'n Me

The Life Journey of a Very Ordinary Man

7-16-11
To Jon Trimble,
Presently, my best human friend in all the world!

By Bill

Bill Boylan

Life Enrichment Services, Inc.
leservices38@yahoo.com
www.leservices.org

Him 'n Me
The Life Journey of a Very Ordinary Man
by Bill Boylan

Printed in the United States of America

ISBN 9781613796351

All other Bible references are paraphrases and amplifications from the original Hebrew and Greek (and sometimes Aramaic) languages of the Bible.

To order additional copies, call 1-866-381-2665 or go to XulonPress.com

www.xulonpress.com

Also By Bill Boylan

Network Marketing For Christians

LIFEgiving (Clear directions for You to Have A Successful and Prosperous Journey Through Life)

Friends Forever (Available fall 2011)

Dedication

I dedicate this book to a great-uncle, James Boylan, whom I have not met . . . yet; his mortal journey here on planet earth ended long before mine began. Uncle James is buried in the Boylan family burial plot in the little Piedmont, South Dakota, cemetery near the old Boylan family homestead.

Through the years, I've often wondered many things about you, Uncle James: what you were like, how you lived, what your days were like, were you a believer in Jesus, why you died, what your earthly aspirations were . . . And, whether or not you inherited the penetrating blue eyes my grandfather, my Dad, my brother, and my son have. I didn't inherit those blue eyes, but friends of our family tell me I do have that "Boylan look."

On Uncle James' grave marker are inscribed these words—barely readable now: *"Another link is broken in our family band, but a golden chain is forming in a better land."* Uncle James, I look forward to meeting you in person one day in that "better land" and getting to know you, as well as all my other ancestors. What a great Boylan family reunion that's going to be!

I also dedicate this book to my children, their children, and their children. I pray each of them in their mortal lifetimes will know, love, and serve our extra-ordinary God.

Finally, I dedicate this book to other descendants yet to be born and yet to be named who—even though they will not know me in person during their mortal lifetimes—will know a little about their ancestor, Bill Boylan, by reading this book.

I look forward to a grand and glorious Boylan family reunion in Jesus' Kingdom after He returns to earth.

Table of Contents

Introduction

A soft breeze is whispering through the stately Ponderosa pine trees surrounding me—telling me of past generations of my ancestors who have been in this very spot before me. It is a bright, warm summer day. My legs are spread out in front of me on the ground blanketed with fallen pine needles. I am sitting with my back resting against a large sandstone rock atop Boylan's Peak rising abruptly from the floor of Elk Creek Valley, a mile east of Piedmont, Meade County, South Dakota, USAmerica.

Boylan's Peak is part of the original land homesteaded by my great-grandparents in the 1870's. It is now 2011, and I am in my seventies in solar years. My thoughts today carry me back to when I first climbed the Peak with my mother when I was 4 or 5 years old. What a wonderful journey I have trod these 70+ years.

From the top of the Peak where I am musing this beautiful summer day, I look to my right—to the west—and a mile away I can see the small community cemetery where some of my ancestors are buried, laying there asleep, awaiting the summons for them to awaken from the dead and arise from their sleep on a bright, golden morning in Jesus' coming Kingdom.

And now let me begin my life story.

I know, I know . . . "Him 'n me" is a really poor choice for a book title, likely ensuring this will never be a best-seller. And I know my title ain't grammatically correct, neither, having uncorrect punkchewayshun and misuse of the big letters . . . Yes, "me" should be capitalized. And "'n" should be "and." Maybe it should be "Him and Me," or "He and I," or "I and He," or, just "Us" or "us'ns" . . . whatever.

But this is ***my*** life story and I can write it any way I want to. I ain't no dummy; I no how to write rite. My folks din't raise no idjits and I din't just fall off no turnip truck (some people feel I did, however—falling a long way and hitting my head . . . hard). I wrote the title that way to make a very subtle, but extremely important, point: ***My life story really isn't about me; it's about Someone else.***

These are the voyages of the earth-ship Bill Boylan. My mission is to boldly go where no Boylan has gone before . . . Just wanted to see how that would sound if I said the words out loud. Not a bad ring to them, huh? They're based on the old, original Star Trek television series.

WARNING: Throughout this autobiography you will find interspersed a number of my brief teachings. I can't help it; I'm a teacher. *I can't not teach*. If you're not interested in the teaching portions of my autobiography, just skip them and "fast forward" to the main, ongoing, chronological parts of "Him 'n me."

Six lengthier teachings are in the Appendices. I included those six teachings because they are six of my most favorite ones to teach and write about. They also seem to be six of my teachings most helpful to hundreds, perhaps thousands, of my "students" worldwide. In fact, the teaching in Appendix One is included in my book entitled ***Friends Forever.***

Also, bear in mind ***that my memory is just as flawed and faulty*** as everyone else's, and there are probably some events and incidents of my life I write about that are not quite correct, but I've tried to be as honest and correct as possible in writing "Him 'n me."

In fact, some recent studies by behavioral scientists suggest that each time we bring up a memory from our "memory banks," the very act of bringing up a memory alters the memory itself. If those studies are true, it seems that our memories are very fluid and changeable, never "written in stone" as we have previously believed them to be.

Any human who has reached my chronological age has amassed and stored billions of separate, interconnected, and interrelated memories in his or her subconscious "memory banks." I haven't counted them, but I'm sure this book doesn't contain more than a few hundred of my separate memories, if that many.

A few hundred memories out of billions. Thus, this book—any autobiography—is not complete, not in any sense of completeness. Any autobiography such as this contains only bits and pieces of one's life. So, you're going to be reading only the proverbial tip of the iceberg in terms of my "complete" life story.

Maybe some warm afternoon in Jesus' Peaceful Kingdom, we can sit down together on the banks of the River of Life, dabble our feet in its cleansing and LIFEgiving waters, and I can tell you more about me than just the bits and pieces you'll read about in this book. That is, if you wish to know more.

Perhaps we'll be so enthralled by what we're seeing and experiencing in that Kingdom that we won't even want to remember very much about this mortal life. We'll see.

Now I have a "secret" to tell you right at the beginning of my life story. Most adults in many modern societies and cultures read, on average, at about a sixth grade reading level. Also, because of the influence of television and other media, most adults have much shorter attention spans than people did in generations past.

So, what's my secret? *I have written this autobiography at about a sixth grade reading level and with mostly short paragraphs*. I hope that doesn't insult your intelligence if you read at a higher level or have a longer attention span. I **can** use bigger words and lengthier paragraphs, but I simply choose not to; check me out: I will limit most of my paragraphs to ten lines or fewer, and most of my words to fewer than four syllables. Anyway, that's my secret.

Okay, here we go. My life story about "Him 'n me."

Way back, pretty early on in my life story I learned this important truth about us humans living here on planet earth: **We are spiritual beings sent here to have a temporary, mortal human experience on earth, not merely human beings having spiritual experiences.**

Brief Ancestry

Years ago I traced our Boylan family ancestry clear back to County Monaghan in Ireland. From there, some of my Irish ancestors made their way to what is now New Jersey some time in the early 1700's. Later in the 1700's they migrated to Muskingum County in southeastern Ohio. From there they made their way through Illinois to Bristol, Iowa, in extreme north central Iowa, a little southeast of the existing community of Lake Mills, Iowa. Bristol no longer exists as a community. All the information I know about from Ireland to Bristol, Iowa, is sparse and sketchy; I suppose a skilled genealogist could fill in much missing information.

Years ago, after collecting information about our Boylan family history, I packed it all up in a cardboard box and gave the box to my son, Joel. I don't know if he has ever done more Boylan family research . . . or even cares to. Perhaps some day some descendants of mine will find that box, and it will spark their interest in finding more details about our Boylan family history.

I do know more detail about my more recent ancestors from their time in Bristol, Iowa, to my generation. When I was a teenager, Dad's parents told me a little about their parents and grandparents. I have two tiny, faded photographs of my paternal great-great-grandparents, Isaac and Catherine (nee DeMoss) Boylan, who trekked from Illinois and settled in Bristol, Iowa. Catherine was born in Illinois in 1822 and died in Iowa in 1871. Isaac was also born in Illinois in 1822 and died in Iowa in 1907.

To the best of my knowledge, they are both buried in an obscure little cemetery near where Bristol, Iowa, used to be located. Elsewhere in Iowa there even used to be a community named Boylan's Grove, Iowa, but at the moment I cannot recall where that was located.

Speaking of that photograph of Isaac Boylan, my son Joel greatly resembles his great-great-great-grandfather Isaac, especially his eyes and high cheekbones. It's an uncanny resemblance!

Isaac and Catherine had a number of children, one of them being William Marion Boylan, my great-grandfather, born in Peoria, Illinois in 1849. He married Jane (Jennie), born in Ohio in 1853. William and Jennie trekked to western South Dakota (actually Dakota Territory at the time) in the late 1870's from where they had both grown up in Bristol, Iowa.

As best I can recall, my grandparents told me William and Jennie traveled from Iowa in a covered wagon drawn by mules to the Black Hills, homesteading in 1878 about a mile east of the village of Spring Valley (later subsumed into the small foothills community of Piedmont in southern Meade County).

One can cross South Dakota these days in about 5 or 6 hours on Interstate 90. By contrast, I imagine it probably took my great-grandparents an entire summer to cross the state by covered wagon. I'm sure they rode in the wagon as well as walked alongside it. Those wagons didn't have any suspension and could beat one to death if one rode in them constantly. Often, when pioneers walked, they walked barefooted to save shoe leather.

If they traveled across South Dakota on any sort of path, often those paths would be pocked with mud holes deep enough to sink a wagon to the axles. Hard rains in the eastern part of the Territory could have held them up. There may have been terrible thunderstorms—with damaging hail. In those days, often their food supply could spoil with the dampness. To supplement their food supply, I'm sure they ate berries, bird eggs, rabbits, pheasants, turkeys, and other game they killed along the way.

As they crossed the Missouri River dissecting Dakota Territory from north to south, they went almost immediately from rain and dampness in the east to hot, dry heat in the western part of the Territory. As they approached the stark Badlands about 60 miles east of the Black Hills, more than likely they began to encounter huge prairie rattlesnakes, and deer, antelope, and buffalo.

What a relief it must have been to finally arrive at Spring Valley nestled up against the eastern edge of the Black Hills. It was the fall of 1878. About a mile east of Spring Valley, they quickly built their first one-room sod hut in order to survive their first western South Dakota winter. That sod hut was later destroyed in a flash flood.

They homesteaded 160 acres each, for a total of 320 acres, acres still owned by my brother, John, who continues to work on the ranch raising cattle. John still has the original land "patents" (certificates) signed by the then President of the United States granting William and Jennie Boylan their 320 acres of homestead land.

Later—in 1879—they built an imposing two-story stone house nearby, using huge sandstone blocks taken from the nearby butte—later named Boylan's Peak. The old stone house was occupied until the 1960's, and stood until the late 1970's when it was torn down because the deteriorating mortar made it unsafe to be around. My brother John's home is located right where the old stone house used to stand.

Conception

Dad and Mother were married in 1933; he was 22, she was 19. Mother had previously attended the South Dakota State Normal School (teacher's college) in Springfield, South Dakota, and had begun teaching her first year of school in a one-room school house near Viewfield, South Dakota, about 20 miles east of where Dad lived near Piedmont.

Mother often recounted how cold she had been that winter, and most of what she had to eat that entire school year were potatoes. In those years, one of the few types of social events people attended were dances in the various small communities in the area. Dad and Mother met at one of those dances. Once, she disclosed to me that the only reasons she married Dad were because he was such a good dancer, and he could take her away from the miserable conditions she endured teaching school that winter.

It's true—Dad was a great dancer. I saw him dance many times through the years. He was very smooth and graceful, seeming to glide around the dance floor. It was a delight to watch him dance.

Me? That's another story. As you'll read later, when I was a teenager I *thought* I was a good dancer, but being drunk most of the time, in reality I was probably very clumsy and awkward on the dance floor.

After I married my present wife, I actually took "Basic Ballroom Dancing" lessons four times, but still I'm not a decent dancer. I've kept telling Anne that I honestly can't hear and feel the beat of the music. Now I have proof of that. As I write these lines, a report came out recently from the University of Montreal in Canada. Scientists there have discovered that certain people have "Beat Deficit Disorder" (BDD) and really can't hear, feel, or follow the beat of dance music.

Yep, I now have incontrovertible, scientific proof I'm a klutz and can't dance and chew gum or talk at the same time. So there!

Now I want to continue my introduction about who "me" is by telling you about an interesting experience I had a few years ago.

I was in my mid-fifties of my earthly pilgrimage. Our family was gathered at my parents' home for a typical Sunday dinner—my parents, my "branch" of the family tree, some of my brother's family, my sister's children, and various grandchildren.

While we were all engaged in typical Sunday afternoon conversations around the dinner table, my mother looked across the table at me and exclaimed: *"Bill, it's time you knew about when and where you were conceived!*

I just gaped at Mother with my mouth wide open. Where did that come from? Did I really need to know that? Why? She proceeded to tell me in front of everyone present in the room exactly where, when, and under what passionate circumstances I had been conceived. I didn't really feel a deep-seated need to know about my conception, but my mother was a very outspoken woman and she obviously felt I needed to know right then and there; maybe she felt I was finally old enough and experienced enough to know about such a thing!

The building where my conception occurred still stands in the same location—even the same dirt floor where the moment of passion happened many years ago. I'm still waiting for someone to erect a statue of me in front of the building.

Chapter One

Ages Conception To Four

After that moment of passion in early June of the previous year resulting in my conception, I was born nine months later at 8:09 a. m. on the cold Monday morning of February 28th in the old Black Hills General Hospital (formerly Black Hills Methodist Hospital) near the corner of Rushmore Road and South Street in Rapid City, South Dakota. Part of that hospital building is still standing as I write these lines; it's an office building now. I'm still waiting for a statue of me to be erected there, too, but so far that hasn't been done, either.

My name is William Edward Boylan, named after the first name of my great-grandfather, and the middle name of my grandfather. I was sent here to live in a family already consisting of four living grandparents (William Adolph Sloan and Harriette Eva Sloan (nee Rowland), Charles Edward Boylan and Helen Marie Boylan (nee Schreckenghaust), my parents, Basil LaVerne and Maxine Harriette Boylan, and my older sister by four years, Barbara Lee. Four years later, the four of us in my immediate family were joined by my brother, John Gerald Boylan.

As stated previously, our local family history goes back to the late 1870's when my great-grandparents, William and Jennie Boylan, homesteaded on land near the tiny town of Piedmont, South Dakota, now a bedroom community a few miles north of Rapid City where I was born. As mentioned previously, they came here by covered wagon to homestead on 320 acres about a mile east of Piedmont; they immediately built a one-room sod hut on a gently sloping hillside.

Also as mentioned in my Introduction, my brother John still lives on the original homestead land and still has the original land patents issued by the then President of the United States. Our family is the oldest family in the Piedmont area still living on the original homestead land in an unbroken succession of generations. A mile east of Piedmont is a peak jutting up from the surrounding prairie lands; it is named Boylan's Peak (or Piedmont Butte).

Traveling north on Interstate 90 as you pass Piedmont, look to the right (the east). You'll see Boylan's Peak just a mile away. Over the years I've spent many days on Boylan's peak—doing everything from playing guns and hunting rabbits as a child, to chasing cattle, hunting for petrified wood, to removing large boulders, to building barbed wire fences, to simply hiking up and down its slopes for pleasure.

The first few years of my mortal life were spent living near Piedmont where my father built, owned, and operated a Texaco franchise service station on Highway 14-79, at the junction of Elk Creek Road. The day I was born, Dad planted a tree near the station. That tree stood there for many years until it recently died and was chopped down for firewood; looks like I've outlived that tree. The building Dad built as the service station was later moved a few miles away to the community of Black Hawk, and is now a private residence.

We were a close-knit family, with my grandparents closely involved in our day-to-day lives. In some ways it was an idyllic life in my infancy and early childhood; in other ways some very negative lifestyle patterns were beginning to emerge, especially when my dad began to be more and more angry and brutal with my sister and me.

On one occasion when I was about two years old, in a fit of rage, Dad actually threw me down a flight of stairs; fortunately, I was unharmed, but an early life of brutality and physical beatings for my sister and me was beginning and would grow in intensity.

My earliest good memory, however, was sitting on Dad's lap in the old Elks Theater in downtown Rapid City, eating popcorn out of a bag he held. Our combined memories place that early event when I was about 18 months of age. The Elks Theater is still in use as a discount movie theater, and occasionally I attend a movie there and sit up in the balcony, perhaps in the same seat where I had sat on Dad's lap as an infant. As you'll read later, during my teen years the theater remained much in use.

Photos of me at various locales in and around Piedmont during my first four years show me looking somewhat like a ragged little urchin in bib overalls and a strange looking little striped cap that I must have been obsessed to wear most of the time. But I seemed to have a smile on my face much of the time as I appeared in photos standing alongside various family members, friends of the family, farm animals, and butchered livestock, deer, and antelope.

I was also obsessed with carrying around with me everywhere I went a raggedy little Teddy Bear. Years later, when I was an adult, Mother gave me back my Teddy Bear she had saved for me all those years; I have since passed it on to my son.

It was during my first four years that Mother's mother, Grandma Sloan, began the tradition of baking "from scratch" an angel food cake for me on my birthdays—covered with delicious "sugar frosting." Right up until the year before my mother died, she continued that tradition, as did my former wife, Sharon, while we were married.

We don't have angel food cake anymore on my birthdays simply because of the high sugar and calorie content, but occasionally we'll have a "store bought" angel food cake with strawberries and whipped cream. Not often, but whenever we do I remember those delicious, "made from scratch" angel food cakes my grandmother, mother, and former wife made for me on my birthdays.

I am compelled now to write about something that happened on the main street of Piedmont when I was only three or four years old. This is pretty raw; don't let small children read it.

My grandfather Boylan took me one weekday afternoon to Piedmont. On the main street in front of the old red brick building (formerly the Homestake Mining Company general store), a wooden platform about five feet high had been erected. Quite a crowd was gathered and milling around the platform—men, women, children. Some men forced a struggling young man up the steps to the platform. Some of them carried pistols and rifles.

Two of the men quickly pulled down the pants and underpants of the struggling young man. Another man quickly grabbed the young man's genitals and with one stroke of a sharp knife cut off his testicles—castrated him! Immediately afterwards a man rushed from the nearby blacksmith shop with a red-hot iron and held the iron where the knife had severed the young man's testicles, thus cauterizing the wound. I'll never forget the "sizzling" sound it made!

Right away, a number of men grabbed the young man who had been castrated—he was unconscious—and carried him away down the street. The crowd dispersed and the event was over. I was traumatized by what I had witnessed, not even being able to speak for a couple of days. Weeks later I asked my grandfather to explain what had happened.

He replied, *"Billy, I will only tell you this once. After that, we must never speak of it again."* He proceeded to explain to me that the castrated young man had raped a young girl in town; of course, I didn't know what "raped" meant. Caught in the act, he was immediately captured and held captive somewhere in Piedmont while that wooden platform was hastily erected. You know the rest of the story.

Many years later, I did break our vow of silence and asked my grandfather if, in fact, that event had really occurred or had it simply been a bad nightmare of mine. Grandpa responded that it really had happened, but never said another word.

I guess what I witnessed that day was simply a matter of some type of vigilante justice in a small western town. I'll never forget it as long as I live!

World War II

The United States of America entered World War II in December, 1941. Meanwhile, during the decade preceding America's entry into the War, Dad had taken some classes at the local South Dakota

School of Mines and Technology, a college rated very high nationally and internationally.

He proved to have such extraordinary mathematical and engineering talents that the school couldn't offer him many classes after his first year in attendance there; he simply knew more than they could teach him. So he left school because of that and because of the Great Depression of the 1930's.

I remember as a child watching Dad sitting at the kitchen table many evenings with a slide rule, some books, and paper working on mathematical equations just for fun . . . as a hobby. And not just simple mathematics, but algebra, geometry, and calculus. To him, such evenings were fun and exciting. When Dad died, we found a number of the papers he had worked on . . . and a couple of old slide rules he had saved for years.

Chapter Two

Ages Four To Eleven

In the early years of the war, the very secret Manhattan Project was initiated by the federal government's War Department to develop and build the first atomic bomb. The War Department established and built three "Atomic Cities" at remote locations around the nation—Hanford, Washington, Los Alamos, New Mexico, and Oak Ridge, Tennessee. The newly created Atomic Energy Commission scoured the nation's schools of engineering and technology seeking young mathematicians and engineers to work in those cities.

When they were scouting at the South Dakota School of Mines and Technology in Rapid City my father had attended earlier, the professors remembered my Dad's mathematical and engineering skills and abilities and recommended the Atomic Energy Commission scouts locate Dad, who, at the time was working at a radio store in Rapid City, as well as operating the Texaco service station in Piedmont, which my mother helped operate when Dad was working at the radio shop.

The scouts located Dad and gave him an ultimatum. Remember these were war years . . . Dad could either join the Atomic Energy Commission voluntarily or be drafted into the US Army as an infantryman "foot soldier." Dad wisely chose the Atomic Energy Commission.

During the latter part of 1942 and early 1943, our family was first relocated to Denver, Colorado, where Dad took "crash courses" at the Union Carbide and Carbon Company before being moved to one of the three Atomic Cities, Oak Ridge, Tennessee.

I have only a few vivid memories of those months in Denver: my brother being brought home after he was born; having my tonsils and adenoids removed (I can still smell the ether used as an anesthetic!), running away on my tricycle and being found after hours of searching, playing on the banks of a river—and being severely punished afterwards.

I remember attending a Christmas party with friends of my parents and receiving a real orange as a gift, a rarity in those war years; being sexually abused in the boy's bathroom by my kindergarten teacher; with a friend eating some raw oats from a horse's feed bag in a nearby barn—and being deathly ill for days; sitting on our living room sofa being read to by my sister.

Good and bad memories combined, mixed, and mingled.

One incident from those years haunts me to this day. I was walking to school (kindergarten) one day with a little girl from my neighborhood. As we passed under a bridge, I pulled a safety pin out of my pocket and told her I would stick her with it if she didn't show me her private parts (meanness and brutality were already beginning to emerge in me, having seen it "modeled" by Dad); she was terrified and sobbing and showed me her private parts.

I remember thinking at the time, *"Okay, now I know; that's what little girls 'have.'"* As we continued walking together to school that day, I remember the horrible shame, remorse, and guilt I felt for having threatened to hurt her, for scaring her, and for making her cry. We didn't laugh, or play, or visit as we had been doing. After that day, we never again walked together to school.

Just for your information, years later—even though I didn't remember the name of that little girl under the bridge, or whether or not she was even still alive somewhere—I reached out across the miles and the years of time and "asked" her forgiveness for what I did to her, especially that it didn't somehow traumatize her for life.

I know, I know, many little boys and girls play "doctor and nurse" and show their private parts at some time or another, but for some reason that incident plagued me for years until across time and space I asked the little girl's forgiveness. I expect to meet her again some day and apologize again, this time in person.

Oak Ridge, Tennessee

Early in my 5th year, we were relocated by the War Department from Denver to Oak Ridge, Tennessee, (near Knoxville) one of the three "secret cities" built by the Manhattan Project. Dad became a supervisor in one of the huge factories operated there by Union Carbide and Carbon. The factory where he worked was so huge that Dad went about his supervisory tasks on roller skates!

Being a "secret city" (you can't even find Oak Ridge on a map of those years), Dad was never able to discuss with his family exactly what type of work he did. It was only about 30 years later that he was permitted to disclose that he had helped design and build the trigger mechanism for the first atomic bomb.

My years in Oak Ridge were almost idyllic. Because the city was a critical part of the war effort, it was completely surrounded by a six-foot high chain-link fence with armed guards and guard dogs patrolling the area night and day. For us children living within the city, we were absolutely safe. There was no safer place on earth for children to live and play.

And play we did! We roamed the city, playing in the woods and on playgrounds throughout our neighborhoods. Bus travel within the city was free, and unaccompanied children got on the busses at bus stops everywhere throughout the city, riding to playgrounds, to stores, to school, to shopping centers, to theaters, and the like.

We caught "crawdads" in flowing streams, swung Tarzan-like on numerous tree vines scattered here and there in the woods, played cowboys and Indians, played "house" in old farm homes emptied by local residents when the city was built, and picked blackberries and ate them on the spot with bowls of cream and sugar.

Years later, I returned to visit Oak Ridge and located one of the actual vines we used to play on; in fact, the day I located the vine, children were still swinging on it over 50 years later! As a child, it seemed like that vine swung out over a very deep and wide ravine. When I visited it later, I was surprised and amazed to learn that ravine was only about four feet deep and eight feet wide. Perceptions do change with age.

Even though Dad had an excellent income while we were in Oak Ridge, he was too frugal (cheap?) to buy bicycles for us kids, so at lunch time at school I gave my homemade lunch to a friend named Dick Culver for which, in exchange, he let me ride his bicycle around the neighborhood during the lunch hour; years later, when that memory returned to me very vividly one day, in some mysterious way across the miles of time and space, I "thanked" Dick for sharing his bicycle with me during all those lunch hours.

I loved school in Oak Ridge, their schools being some of the best and most progressive in the nation, with many of the nation's finest teachers having been recruited by the school district; as I recall, their pay was higher than any other school district in the nation. We had the "cream of the crop" for our teachers.

Years later—while in my early sixties—I returned to visit Oak Ridge. The school where I learned to read was still standing, but it was then a children's museum. Actually, I'm not sure that's where I first *learned* to read, but it was where *my eyes were first opened* to the wondrous possibilities of books—beginning my lifelong love of reading.

When I returned years later to visit the school, I broke down and wept with joy in the very room where books began to open a wondrous world to me! I've read thousands and thousands of books since then. And will continue to do so right up until the day I die. And even after that.

Yes, my years in Oak Ridge were wonderful, but they were mixed with some bad situations at home. The brutality by Dad continued unabated. It was so bad that my mother even ran away for a few months, only to be located when my grandmother let slip accidentally to Dad where she had run away to—Phoenix, Arizona.

I don't know whether or not she had an affair during those months, but I suspect she did. Those few months were among the very few in our young lives when Dad was nice to the three of us children, even giving us allowances and buying us a few toys as gifts—just to impress and win back Mother.

When Mother returned at Dad's pleading, things were never quite the same again between them; even at my young age I could sense that my mother sort of gave up on life ever thereafter, taking joy only in us children and in the rest of our family. She and Dad remained distant and aloof from one another until the very day Mother died at age 86. I'm sure there were never again any moments of passion such as resulted in my conception!

I know you've been waiting breathlessly to read about (Ta Da!) **Spam.** During the war years, in Oak Ridge (as well as throughout the entire nation), because of rationing of meat and other essentials, Spam was the meat of choice for most families. I learned to love Spam during those years (but please don't tell me the ingredients; I don't wanna know).

We had fried Spam, barbecued Spam, Spam kabobs, Spam sandwiches, Spam casseroles, broiled Spam, and, as I recall, Mother even made roast Spam with carrots, onions, and potatoes; I never did figure out how she did that. To this day I still love Spam, but my wife, Anne, won't let me eat it. Occasionally—rarely—I'll buy a can of it and have Spam sandwiches for a few days. Bread, Spam, mayonnaise, lettuce, and sweet pickles: food of the gods! Somehow, before I exit this mortal journey I want to undertake a sacred pilgrimage to visit the Spam museum in Minnesota (just kidding about the visit, but there really is a Spam museum!).

While in Oak Ridge, I first began to smoke cigarettes at the age of 6 (quite common in the tobacco-growing South) and smoked until age 18, consuming 4-5 packs a day my last few years of smoking. Can you believe that cigarettes were only 19 cents a pack then?

Speaking of tobacco, some of my most vivid memories of my years in Oak Ridge are of *women* chewing and spitting tobacco. I was fascinated by one neighbor woman (a rather chic, sophisticated appearing woman) who chewed tobacco and carried a tin can around with her to spit in. And when she spit on the ground, she could even aim at and hit crawling bugs about ten feet away!

It was in Oak Ridge that I also became a fledgling "businessman." At age 6 I built my own shoe-shine box and earned money shining shoes at Grove Center, one of the two modern shopping centers in Oak Ridge.

Since those days when I ran my own "shoe shine business" I have always kept my own shoes carefully shined. Just this morning, I was shining three pairs of my shoes that had gotten dirtied from the slush after a recent snow. There I was with my little shoe shine kit, shining away—when I began thinking back to age 6.

I kept my shoes shined all through my childhood years, my teen years, my years in the Air Force (naturally, because we had to keep them "spit shined"), all through my adult years, right up to this very day. You'll very seldom find Bill Boylan without shined shoes. I even joke with Anne that if I should die first, I "order" her to make sure I have nicely shined shoes while I lay in my casket! Unless she decides to have me cremated.

Oak Ridge had a huge man-made lake for swimming by the local populace. I "learned" to swim by my Dad taking me out to a large raft in the middle of the lake about mid-morning one summer day and simply leaving me there to find my own way back to shore.

With a horrible sunburn, hours later just as the sun was going down, I jumped off the raft and clumsily dog-paddled back to shore—terrified I was going to drown—there to find my own way home late in the evening. Not a word was ever said about the "method" Dad used to teach me how to swim. It was a horribly traumatic experience in my childhood.

I don't know that I was any "badder" than other kids my age during those childhood years in Oak Ridge, but I remember one incident involving Mother and a spanking by Dad that really stands out vividly in my memory. I must have done something wrong (I can't remember right now what it was), but I flew out the front door of our house on West Outer Drive with Mother running after me with a spanking stick in her hand.

Across the street from our house was a gently sloping hillside about a half mile in length. Mother was chasing me down that hillside and I remember laughing at the top of my voice, daring and taunting her to catch me. I was gaining on her and quickly slipped from the path into a hidden fort my friend, Bruce Cline, and I had dug into the side of a little hillock. Mother whizzed right on by me and never did find me that afternoon.

That posed a real dilemma for me; I was no longer laughing, because I knew I would have to go home sooner or later, and would most likely get a serious "lickin'" from Dad. I stayed hidden in our fort as long as I could until it began to get dark and I began to get hungry. Sure enough, when I got home I got that lickin' from Dad with his belt! It just seems to me today—years later—with hindsight that I got into a lot of trouble during that era in my life.

Speaking of my friend, Bruce Cline, I have attempted repeatedly through the years to try to locate him, all to no avail. I hope he's still alive somewhere on the planet and that I might finally locate him. It'd be nice to be back in touch with him after all these years. Except for one other friend, Wayne Coon (whom I'm still friends with because he lives here in Rapid City), Bruce was one of my earliest "best" friends.

A very unpleasant memory I have of our family's years in Oak Ridge is that Dad always seemed to be angry: at Mother, at us kids, at his job, at life in general. I don't remember seeing him smile very much.

The only times I remember Dad seeming to be happy are when he played on softball teams in Oak Ridge. I can still picture him smiling a beautiful smile as he gathered with his teammates and engaged in camaraderie and laughter with them.

Dad and his brother Keith had apparently been very skilled at the games of softball and horseshoes during their teen years and young adulthood, playing in many tournaments throughout South Dakota. Dad even had some trophies he had won in state horseshoe tournaments; I wonder whatever happened to those trophies.

Anyhow, I can still picture my Dad with happy smiles on his face as he played in various softball tournaments in Oak Ridge. He was a southpaw (left-handed) pitcher. I can still picture him wearing an old tattered "lucky" green T-shirt as he would wind up a pitch and release his special "fast ball" toward the batter. As I recall, he was both a good pitcher and batter. But that's the only time I can remember him happy and smiling.

One other very painful and traumatic matter stands out in my bad memories of Oak Ridge. My sister, Bobbie, and I were at the age where we began needing dental checkups, care, and treatment.

I mentioned previously that Dad was very frugal (cheap? stingy?), so he located a very inexpensive dentist who practiced in the front room of his home in a nearby town, Norris, Tennessee; looking back, I have wondered on occasion whether or not the man was even a licensed dentist, but be that as it may, that's the dentist who treated my sister and me.

All I remember more clearly than I want to is that Dad would not pay for the dentist to use any pain-killer (or, in Dad's defense, perhaps the dentist simply chose not to use it when we were there alone without our parents) when he did our dental work. Yes, all of our dental work—tooth pulling, drilling, filling—was all done without any pain medication! There were times when I honestly felt I was going to pass out from pain as that man worked in my mouth. Not good memories.

Another incident stands out. My parents and my sister took a brief vacation to Florida, leaving my brother and me with some family friends named Mr and Mrs Farmer. While staying with the Farmers for two weeks, we were given very little to eat, and Mr Farmer fondled me sexually; he also brutally beat my brother and me. We never told anyone, knowing we would most likely be beaten again by Dad for having allegedly done whatever it was Mr Farmer beat us for doing.

So, I have mixed memories and feeling about our years in Oak Ridge, Tennessee. Years later, I recall some of them with joy and a sense of peace; some of them I recall with terror and pain. You'll read later in my story about how I completely forgave my Dad for his meanness and brutality during my childhood. He was simply repeating what had happened to him and his brother as children. I thank God I was able to break that cycle with my own three children!

Oh, here's one other pleasant memory of my years in Oak Ridge. Much long-distance travel in those days was by train. Each summer, my sister and I were put on a train in nearby Knoxville and traveled unaccompanied—through connections in Chicago—back to South Dakota to spend much of the summers with our grandparents living in and near Piedmont.

Those times traveling on the trains are very precious memories. We needed no escorts; again, overall life was much safer for children in those days; the conductors looked after us, and many servicemen and servicewomen befriended us and looked after us on the trains. I have wonderful memories of falling asleep in the Pullman berths to the clickety-clack of the train wheels and eating our meals like grownups in the dining cars.

When we lived in Oak Ridge, Dad would often sit at the kitchen table in the evenings and on weekends, drawing pictures of houses. When I asked him what he was doing, he told me that he had always wanted to build his "dream home" east of Piedmont on the gently sloping hillside near where his grandparents had built their sod hut upon arriving there in 1878. The pictures of homes he drew all the time were his "dreams" about how his dream home would be configured.

Later when we had returned to Rapid City in the early 1950's, sometimes on Sunday afternoons Dad would drive our family around town looking at houses for Dad to get more ideas for when he finally built his dream home.

I didn't mind driving around and looking at various homes from our car, but sometimes Dad would stop in front of a home, walk up to the front door, knock, and ask the people living there if we could come in and look at the inside of their home. You have no idea how much that embarrassed me in my early teen years! I was mortified when Dad did that, so much so that I even quit going on rides with the family . . . even though I liked the rides themselves. I just didn't understand how Dad had the gall to ask people if we could come in to their home unannounced and look through their home.

Dad finally built and completed his dream home in 1955 shortly after I left for the Air Force. I've never felt it was much of a "dream home," but we all have different tastes. To me, it was just a plain little house—nothing at all remarkable about it.

Oak Ridge was located in the South where in those days there was still a lot of racial discrimination and segregation. Even as a small boy I wondered about "black" people and "white people," but whenever I tried to ask my parents or teachers about the differences in the two races, I was always given the runaround.

The "blacks" in Oak Ridge were hired for menial tasks such as janitorial work and the like, and lived in a separate enclave in town, with their own stores, laundromats, bars, and social halls. I did see them on busses occasionally, but they always sat toward the rear of the busses. I also noticed there were separate restrooms for blacks and whites at various places around town, as well as separate drinking fountains. As I recall, the signs said "Whites" and "Coloreds."

Having moved to Oak Ridge from the northern United States where there were very few blacks at the time, I just kept wondering and asking about the differences between "them" and "us," but after being shushed repeatedly by my parents and teachers, I finally stopped asking questions. Inwardly, however, I remained troubled at the discrimination and segregation. One or twice when I attempted to talk with a black child my own age, I was quietly whisked away from them by my parents.

One other thought about blacks in Oak Ridge comes to mind. I don't know when or where Aunt Jemima pancake mix and syrup originated, but I remember as a young child in Oak Ridge seeing the Aunt Jemima logo on boxes and syrup bottles. The logo was of a portly, smiling black woman with a bandana on her head, and a long dress covered with an apron.

Imagine my surprise one day when I stepped into a grocery store and there stood Aunt Jemima live and in person! I just stared at her with my mouth open. I didn't imagine there was actually a "real" Aunt Jemima. Of course, I know now that it was an ordinary black woman dressed up to represent Aunt Jemima as a promotion for their products. I think I stood nearby for an hour or so staring at her, completely fascinated as she demonstrated various products.

As I'm sitting at my computer right now inputting these thoughts about Oak Ridge, I'm wondering if our younger brother, John, ever knew that my sister, Bobbie and I consistently robbed his piggy bank to buy candy? Ooops. Now he knows. John, I'm sorry. Please forgive me.

We got "paid back" for stealing from John one day. We used the money we stole from him to buy some black licorice. It turned out to be medicinal licorice instead of licorice candy, and Bobbie and I were sicker'n dogs for a couple of days.

Summers In Piedmont

I have some other vivid memories of those years in Oak Ridge, but they actually involve my grandparents back in Piedmont whom my sister, Barbara ("Bobbie"), and I visited for a few weeks almost every summer when we lived in Oak Ridge. I don't recall whether or not my brother John visited them, too. He may have been too young at the time.

For an example of such memories of our summers in Piedmont, to this day I love cottage cheese and eat it from time to time at home and in restaurants. Why my love for cottage cheese? One of my grandmothers used to make homemade cottage cheese; I remember days when her entire kitchen would be filled with large cheesecloth bags full of cheese hanging from ropes suspended from the ceiling.

I didn't quite understand the process of making cottage cheese, but the memories of those bags filling the kitchen, the smell of the processing cheese, and the wonderful taste after it was processed still come to mind whenever I eat it. The cottage cheese we buy in the grocery stores doesn't even come close to comparing with the taste of that homemade cottage cheese my grandmother made.

My grandparents had a large walk-in pantry in the old original stone homestead house. One day, my grandmother returned from shopping at the little store in Piedmont with a cardboard box of *Rice Krispies* cereal. It was the first such box I had ever seen; what a novelty—dried cereal in a box! Whoda thunk it? Before that, cereal was always home-cooked Cream of Wheat . . . or oatmeal . . . or something called Farina. I recall holding the *Rice Krispies* box to my ear and trying to hear the little "elves" in the box "snap, crackle, and pop" as the printing on the box advertised.

Cows And Chickens

Oh yes, the old family barn. My grandparents always kept a few milk cows around the ranch and I learned to milk cows at an early age. There's not much in life more exciting than milking a cow and having her slap you in the face with her twitching, manure-filled tail while you're milking her!

I know this may sound gross to any health conscious reader, but as a child I loved warm, fresh milk from the cow with the foam still on top, pouring it directly into a drinking glass from the bucket into which we squirted the milk while milking. Who cared if there were some flecks of cow manure or other debris in the milk!

The watered-down liquids called "low fat" or even "2% milk" many people drink these days shouldn't even rightly be called milk when compared to "whole" milk right from the cow. Then, of course, these days one can purchase soy milk and almond milk, both a far cry from "real" milk I learned to love in my childhood. I don't quite understand how one can "milk" soy beans and almonds, anyway.

After milking, we would carry the buckets of milk to the house where my grandparents kept a "separator" in the front entryway. I was fascinated by the separator. You would pour the milk into the top of it, crank a handle, and from two spigots would pour milk and cream . . . separated. What a wonder to me!

Then once a week on Saturday mornings, my grandparents would transport the milk in 5-gallon cans to the Fairmont Creamery in Rapid City where they would be paid cash for their milk and cream, the money to be used for shopping in town the remainder of the day. Meanwhile, there was nothing quite like using real cream on cereal for breakfast; sometimes it was almost as thick as sour cream we purchase these days.

Also, once a week my grandmother would get out a big wooden butter churn, pour sour milk or cream into it, crank the handle for approximately a half hour . . . and the white cream from a brown cow which ate green grass turned into yellow butter; I never did figure out how that happened. Oh, such good butter it was! Then, of course, the remaining milk would be buttermilk and we would drink large, cool glasses of it throughout the week as a beverage treat.

While milking, it was fun to direct a stream of milk at the faces of the barn cats who always hung around during milking time; they would move their heads and mouths in an effort to catch the stream of milk, and then afterwards sit regally licking the milk off their faces.

Speaking of the Fairmont creamery where we took the milk, today the building houses some offices and shops with a wonderful specialty restaurant in the basement. Whenever I go there to eat, I am immediately transported back in time to my childhood when I made those Saturday morning trips to the creamery with my grandparents.

During the week, it became the responsibilities of my sister and I to "hunt" for eggs in the "hen house" and at various places around the barnyard where the hens might have laid their eggs. It was sort of like a perpetual Easter egg hunt.

Each day, my grandparents washed the outside of the eggs and then stored them by placing them in wooden, stackable egg crates. Each Saturday when they drove into Rapid City with the milk, they would take the crates of eggs, too. After being paid for the milk at the Fairmont creamery, the next stop would be the old Safeway store in downtown Rapid City. There, they would trade the eggs for groceries, using the money paid for the milk as well. In case you're interested, the old Safeway store was on the southeast corner of Main and Eighth Streets; the building currently houses a sports bar.

Speaking of eggs, I probably shouldn't tell you this . . . I don't want word to get out about some of my childhood escapades. One time, I took a large bottle of my grandfather's whiskey from the house and poured it in the chickens' drinking water. As I recall, my grandparents were gone that day; I was bored and simply trying to amuse myself. Not only did the chickens get drunk, but it killed them! Boy, did I ever get a beating. Fortunately, they got some more chickens (from a neighbor, I think) and we were back in the egg business.

On Saturdays, after purchasing groceries in the morning, my grandmother spent the remainder of the day shopping in other downtown stores. My grandfather would spend most of the day at one of Rapid City's downtown pool halls. I never realized until years later that my grandfather gambled at pool, and usually lost a lot of money each Saturday—much more than he won. They didn't have the money to lose during those lean years of World War II! Incidentally, that pool hall was in a building on Main Street directly west of the building now housing the *Rapid City Journal* newspaper offices.

While my grandmother shopped and my grandfather played pool, my sister and I would often attend an afternoon matinee at one of the three downtown theaters. That made Saturday an exciting day for us while we visited our grandparents in Piedmont during the summers.

Saturdays were then "topped off" by my grandparents going to a dance at the local I. O.O.F. (International Order of Oddfellows) hall in the evening. While the adults danced, all the kids played and ran around the dance hall. As the evening wore one and we became tired and sleepy, we would crawl underneath some of the chairs and go to sleep.

It was so comforting to be carried to the car after the dance ended, laid down in the back seat, covered with a blanket, and then sleep all the way back to Piedmont to the humming of the tires and the drone of our grandparents' voices. Then it was even more comforting to be carried into the house and put to bed while we were in sort of a "twilight zone" . . . half asleep, half awake.

Now I must tell you about carbide lamps in the old stone house—because when I tell the story today, most people don't even believe me because they've never heard of such a thing. When I was still quite young, my grandparents illuminated the old stone house with carbide lamps. Here's how they worked. In front of the house, there was a large pit in which they would mix bags of some substance (I don't recall what it was, or that I ever even knew what it was at the time . . . maybe lye) with water.

The substance mixed with the water would fizz and hiss and create carbide gas under pressure (as in carbide lamps miners used to wear), and the gas would then flow through copper pipes into the house into lamps arranged around the walls of each room. To light the gas, they would twist a handle to release the gas, put a lit match to it, and the lamps would light. Looking back, I wonder if that wasn't a very dangerous type of lighting.

Another memory surfaces right now: the ballpoint pen. During the first four years or so that I attended school, I remember that we learned to write using wooden pens with a metal point called straight pens we would dip into ink bottles, nestled in "inkwells" located at the upper right hand corner of our wooden desks.

One summer day while staying with my grandparents, my grandmother brought home a new ballpoint pen to show to everyone. I was fascinated that one could write with it without dipping it into an inkwell or without filling the "ink cartridge" of a pen. It's funny how such little, insignificant memories will surface from time to time.

Oh yes, I mustn't forget the *Grit* magazine and *The Saturday Evening Post*. They came in the mail regularly each week to my grandparents' mail boxes. It was such a delight to sit down in the evening by the old round heating stove and read both magazines from cover to cover. Once read by the entire family, both magazines were then "converted" into toilet tissue; more about that later.

During the War, both sets of grandparents had to work at extra jobs in order to make a living, but both of them kept their tourist attractions open on the off chance that an occasional tourist would travel through the area.

My mother's parents, Gramp and Grandma Sloan, owned and operated a "cabin court" with a "rock garden" and retail rock shop and museum out front near the highway. Their one-room cabins with outside running water and outdoor toilets cost fifty cents a night. I loved helping Grandma clean the cabins, wash the sheets, hang them to dry, and then iron them with a "mangle ironer."

I remember many summer days listening to Gramp spout his "canned spiel" in the rock shop in the hopes that visiting tourists might purchase a souvenir, agate, piece of petrified wood, or a fossil. Just by osmosis, I learned his spiel, and on those days when he and Grandma would take an afternoon nap, I could go through his entire spiel by memory.

I've often wondered what tourists might have thought when they heard that little kid telling them about fossils and dinosaurs, and agatized petrified wood, and calcite crystals, and geodes, and agates, and geologic ages, and local Native American history and lore . . . like he knew what he was talking about!

I remember that I would voice the spiel like I really did know what I was talking about—not like it was something I had memorized. I was beginning to hone my "gift of gab" that would surface in later life as my "con artist" skills would develop; more about that matter later. To this day, many years later, I can still recite that spiel almost word-for-word.

Mother's parents kept all sorts of children's books at their home (I remember, for example, *Mother Goose Nursery Rhymes*), and

Dad's parents kept games for us kids to play with; for example, they kept a set of Lincoln Logs, an Erector Set, "Jumping Jacks," and Pick Up Sticks.

Both my grandfathers smoked cigarettes—hand-rolled ones. I remember being fascinated by how each of them would roll their cigarettes. The cigarette papers came in little orange packets from which you could remove individual papers (like thin tissue papers) one by one; they would hold the cigarette paper in one hand in the shape of half a cylinder lengthwise and then shake the tobacco from a can or bag onto the paper, distributing it in a little pile evenly on the paper.

After the tobacco was distributed evenly, they would then roll the paper containing the tobacco into the shape of a cigarette, lick all along one edge with their tongue to "seal" it, twist both ends, put one end in their mouth and light it. They were both so expert at the process that they could complete each cigarette and have it lit quicker than it probably took you to read these two paragraphs.

I recall that their tobacco most often came in red metal cans labeled *Prince Albert Tobacco*. When the cans were emptied, they were then used to store all sorts of small items in their homes and shops; it seemed like everywhere one looked there were things stored in *Prince Albert Tobacco* cans.

Both grandfathers were adept at lighting wooden matches by striking them on their trousers where the friction of rubbing the match briskly against their trouser leg would ignite the match. It seemed that denim jeans worked the best, and I can still see my grandfathers sort of lifting one of their legs and briskly rubbing the match against the trousers.

For a while when I smoked during my teen years, I hand-rolled my cigarettes, too, but it wasn't considered "cool" by my peers so I didn't do that for long; I even perfected the process of lighting my matches on my trouser legs like I saw my grandfathers do. Wonder if I could still do that today? Hmmm. I'm gonna have to give it a try one of these days when I think of it.

Dad's father, nicknamed "Baba," chewed tobacco, too. He carried it around in a "plug" about the size of a candy bar and cut off pieces of it to chew. Only once did I ever try chewing tobacco when

I asked Baba to "give me a taste." Within about 30 seconds after I bit down on it I began vomiting violently and was sick for hours. Never again did I try chewing tobacco!

I can still see in my memory Baba holding the plug of tobacco in one hand, cutting off a piece with his knife in his other hand and then inserting the piece in his mouth from the knife blade—all in one swift, practiced motion.

During those years, when my sister, Bobbie, and I would return to South Dakota to spend much of our summers with both sets of grandparents, I have a couple of very pleasant memories of evenings spent in the old stone homestead house where my dad's parents were then living.

On Saturday nights we would gather around their old upright console radio and listen to the Grand Ole Opry from Nashville, Tennessee. I can still hear the squawking of the radio and hear the music fade in and out due to changing atmospheric conditions. Grandma "Hon," as we called her, would make a batch of popcorn on the old wood-burning kitchen stove and we would eat popcorn out of a large bowl while listening to the radio.

And, on occasion, Hon would make homemade doughnuts fried in bacon grease or lard in a large iron pot. I have never tasted better doughnuts; even today's popular Krispy Kreme donuts are tasteless in comparison to those homemade doughnuts.

Speaking of lard, I guess I didn't realize at the time how poor my grandparents were. For example, often for lunch during the summers we would have only lettuce or cucumber sandwiches: two slices of homemade bread slathered with lard and filled with lettuce or cucumbers. I loved them!

And, my grandmother made the best pancakes in the morning, fried in a big, black skillet in bacon grease or lard, and then covered with lard and homemade sugar syrup! Wow, I can still taste them to this day!

Also speaking of lard, I remember the day that Grandpa Sloan made a trip in his old pickup across the state line to Alladin or Hulett, Wyoming, to purchase the new type of oleomargarine, just new on the market. He purchased it in Wyoming because for some reason or another it could not be purchased legally in South Dakota at that time.

Anyhow, the oleomargarine came in one pound plastic bags with a little "button" or capsule of a red dye in the bag. We would first make sure the margarine was soft, and then we would pinch the bubble, releasing the red dye into the soft margarine. We kids would fight over who got to pinch the bubble and then knead the coloring throughout the margarine while it was still in the bag. I was fascinated how the red coloring would turn into yellow as we kneaded the margarine. Strange little memory, huh?

"Pebble Puppies"

Since both sets of grandparents were in the tourist business from the 1930's to the late 1950's, our entire family would often go on rock, agate, petrified wood, and fossil hunting expeditions throughout western South Dakota and in various places throughout Montana, North Dakota, and Wyoming. The adults were called "rock hounds," and we kids were "pebble puppies."

In those days, we could still go to places such as Eden Valley in Wyoming, the Badlands of both South and North Dakota, and Hell's Canyon in Montana, all of which are now closed to the public for rock hunting. In Eden Valley, Wyoming, near the Little Popo Aggie River we found tons of Eden Valley petrified wood, now a very rare type of petrified wood. In Montana, we found large quantities of agates.

I remember one time in North Dakota while we were hunting a certain type of agatized petrified wood, we entered a farmer's field and there strewn out before us for about ¾ of a mile were huge broken petrified logs, each almost the size of a railroad car. I've often wondered through the years if those huge logs are still there, or, if not, how they possibly could have been moved.

Most of the petrified wood, agates, fossils, and various other types of rocks we found and brought back to South Dakota—tons of them—during those years are still in the possession of my brother, John. We both hope that one of his sons, Stuart, will go into the tourist business so that all those items can be displayed, some of them to be cut and polished.

At one time, Dad's collection of such items was featured in the Oak Ridge, Tennessee, newspaper and even garnered some national attention as being one of the finest private collections of cut and polished petrified wood, agates, and fossils in the entire United States. That beautiful collection is in a very safe place these days awaiting Stuart's decision whether or not to go into the tourist business some day there on the old Boylan family homestead.

Speaking of rock hounds and pebble puppies, I am compelled to tell you about Levi and Fern Zink. They were a husband and wife, living on a small farm a few acres east of Tilford, South Dakota, located about five miles north of Piedmont. Apparently, their land contained some petrified wood worth hunting for because often we would go to their land for brief rock hunting excursions.

Do any of you, my readers, remember a movie series from the 1940's and early 1950 about "Ma and Pa Kettle"? Well, if you can visualize Ma and Pa Kettle, you can sort of visualize Levi and Fern Zink. When we hunted rocks on their land, Levi and Fern would come with us to show us where some likely places might be to find petrified wood and agates.

When people were out hunting rocks like that, naturally there were times when one would have to hunt for a private spot to relieve oneself. Fern was an honest-to-goodness female, but she exhibited a lot of masculine qualities. One day when she needed to urinate (thinking that everyone else was off in the distance and not knowing I was nearby), she stood facing the left front wheel of one of the pickups. Well, as a small child I already realized that men stood up to urinate and women squatted.

Not Fern! She dropped her trousers and underpants right there and proceeded to urinate against the tire while standing up just like a man! I was absolutely dumbfounded; I couldn't believe my eyes. I didn't think that was possible. I don't think she ever knew I was watching her. Later, when I told my parents about the incident, they responded: *"Oh, that's just Fern. She's a little different. That's the way she does it."*

You might not even believe this next story I write about. In Piedmont lived a young housewife and mother everyone called "Mad Mary." She seemed to live a normal life . . . most of the time.

Two or three times a year on Monday washdays, after washing the clothes she would hang them out on the line in her yard to dry . . . while she was naked! Well, you can imagine what happened next; somehow through the childhood grapevine in Piedmont word spread quickly that naked Mad Mary was hanging her clothes to dry.

Hiding behind anything nearby that was large enough to hide behind, it seemed like every child in town was there to watch Mad Mary hang up her clothes. Once the clothes basked was empty, she carried it back in the house and that was the end of if . . . until next time.

To my knowledge, nothing was ever done to Mad Mary by any authorities. It was just one of those strange things that happened in a small town in western South Dakota. I wonder whatever happened to Mad Mary. The house she lived in is still occupied today. I wonder how many other small towns had things like that happen in them.

Outhouses

One more rich memory. Remember, it's my autobiography; I can write it and put it in any format I choose to.

Let me tell you about some outhouse incidents during those war years. Remember, my sister, Bobbie, and I often spent much of our summers with our grandparents in Piedmont. Those were the days of outhouses in many regions throughout the United States, primarily in rural and semi-rural areas. During the Great Depression of the 1930's, the federal Works Progress Administration (WPA) hired hundreds of thousands of out-of-work men to travel all over the nation working at many "make work" projects. One of those projects was to build outhouses—hundreds and thousands of outhouses.

They weren't just plain old jerry-built outhouses, either. Most of them were built on concrete slabs, roofed with asphalt shingles, had solid doors with sturdy latches and locks, etc. One distinctive feature of many of the WPA-built outhouses was that **they were two-**

seaters! Yep, many of them had two sturdy seats—an adult seat, and beside it, a child seat.

Another distinctive feature of those WPA outhouses was they were built with 1" x 6" boards for siding, placed horizontally. I've never been able to find out why (and I've talked to hundreds of old-timers who had such outhouses), but those boards were always placed so there was about a ¼" to ½" crack between the boards. So . . . one could sit in the outhouse doing one's "business," while looking out through the cracks to see what was going on around the outhouse!

I remember many mornings sitting in the two-seater with my grandfather, just visiting and watching through the cracks all that was going on in their backyard. We also laughed a lot about certain bodily noises. See how extremely normal and ordinary I am! I know you really wanted to read about such matters.

Oh, and those were days before toilet paper rolls came into vogue—and there was paper rationing during the war, too. So our "toilet paper" of choice was at first corn cobs! Yep, corn cobs. Hey, use your own imagination. Later, we graduated to using the inner pages of the Montgomery Ward's and Sear's catalogs; the covers were too firm for such delicate use.

And, *The Saturday Evening* Post and *Grit* magazines made good toilet paper after everyone in the family had read them cover to cover. I think many people in those days picked up catalogs from the stores just for use in their outhouses, never having any intention of making any purchases from the catalogs.

Back in Oak Ridge we had indoor bathrooms, so it was actually kind of a fun treat to use the old backyard WPA outhouses when we visited our grandparents in the summers.

Of course, if a home had an outhouse, then most often they had chamber pots which were kept under the beds to be used at night and emptied in the mornings—usually by the youngest child in the household. And, in addition to chamber pots, many homes used "slop buckets" they kept in the kitchen to dispose of kitchen scraps to be later fed to the hogs and chickens.

I remember many nights when I would hear my grandfather get out of bed to urinate in the slop bucket in the dark. Often, he would miss the bucket, and if it was a cold winter night, then the urine would freeze in a puddle on the floor near the slop bucket. That was back when many people didn't heat their homes at night.

Kinda gross memories, but fond ones of life on the old ranch during the years of World War II. For years after Dad built their new home on the ranch during my teen years, Mother pleaded with Dad to build her an outhouse—even though they had a nice "inhouse"—just to be available for emergency use and to sit in during the summers and watch what was going on outside the outhouse. Dad never did build one for Mother, but she went to her grave still wishing he had.

School Clothes

Each fall, just before school began, Mother took us kids to the J.C. Penney's, Sears, or Montgomery Ward stores to purchase our "school clothes" for the upcoming school year. My school clothes usually consisted of two pairs of jeans, two long-sleeved shirts, some socks, a couple of changes of underwear, one pair of shoes, one belt, and a new winter coat, hat, and mittens (only older kids got to wear gloves with fingers).

Speaking of shoes, it's funny how memories can come to our consciousness in just an instant of time. When I wrote "shoes" in the paragraph above, I immediately had a memory surface of the types of shoes both my grandfathers wore. They both wore ankle-length, black, soft leather shoes when dressing up to go to town, for example.

Otherwise, they wore brown calf-length leather boots that laced partway and the rest of the way there were little "hooks" through which they wound the laces. I haven't thought of their shoes in years, and I know it's not an important matter in the grand scheme of the universe, but somehow those memories just surfaced. I wonder if a person could even buy such "dress shoes" these days?

Of course, everything newly purchased for us kids in the fall was always about two sizes too big—so we would grow into them. That's it, that was my school wardrobe for most of my childhood years—not a varied and colorful wardrobe, but I didn't mind; most of my friends wore pretty much the same things. Sometimes I'm envious when I see all the myriads of styles and colors of clothing that young people wear today.

It wasn't until my teen years when I began buying my own clothes that I began to get a little daring in my clothing styles; I even purchased a bright red, high-topped, soft leather pair of shoes once to wear to school; not even the girls wore such fancy shoes.

My Ninth Summer

"Backward, turn backward, O time in your flight . . ." Those were some words from a popular song during my teen years. But, let's take a look now at an event which occurred before my teen years—during my 9th summer—a few years before I became a teenager. My family was still living in Oak Ridge, but as I mentioned earlier, my sister and I spent much of our summers back in Piedmont, South Dakota, staying alternately with both sets of grandparents who lived in and near Piedmont.

Almost every Saturday night, dances were held in the old Piedmont school and town hall, attended by almost every family within a 10-15 mile radius of Piedmont. They were great social occasions, not only with lively dancing to the music of local bands, but lots of visiting and gossiping—and playing games by all the children attending. Warm Saturday summer nights were great fun for my sister and I as we played with many of our friends at the dances.

One Saturday night the summer I was 9 years old, an older teenaged boy asked some us who were younger if we would give him some money so he could buy some liquor for us to sample. We thought that would be great fun, so off he went to a liquor store in a nearby community which sold liquor to minors. I was later to learn that many liquor stores would sell liquor to minors, some as young as nine years old!

Back our friend came with a "fifth" of some type of "hard" liquor and about 3 or 4 of us boys chugalugged and drained the bottle all too quickly. The next thing I remember was waking in the old stone house about noon the next day with a horrible headache and very nauseated. But I had learned the sheer delight of the numbing and forgetting effects of alcohol, and I was addicted to alcohol from that Saturday night for the next nine years of my young life.

From that night on, I and a gang of same-aged boys and girls I ran around with stayed either stumbling-down-drunk or at least with a light alcoholic "buzz" almost every day of our lives! When I could, I would purchase my liquor. When that wasn't possible, I stole it from various stores and liquor warehouses right up until the summer of my 18th year of my mortal journey here on planet earth.

Two Important Discoveries

That summer of my 9th year I simultaneously discovered two things about myself: 1. I loved the numbing and forgetting effects of alcohol, and 2. I realized I was fairly intelligent (mentally, not morally) and could easily skate through school without almost any effort—which I proceeded to do right up until my high school graduation. In short, from my 9th to my 17th year I stayed drunk almost continually, was a clever thief and liar—kind of a fledgling "con artist"—and didn't do much studying in school. Later, I felt very badly that I had wasted those years, but I came to understand that in the great, eternal scheme of things nothing is ever wasted.

I just wrote that I realized for the first time that I was fairly intelligent. Here's why that was significant. First, I was very, very shy and withdrawn during my early childhood. I didn't interact well with others, especially adults. I even recall one occasion in my early childhood when I happened to be sitting on Mother's lap with my mouth open, sucking on my thumb (which I did until I was about 10 years old); another woman Mother was with asked Mother point-blank if I was retarded.

That question registered in my young mind. I also stuttered in social situations until I was approximately nine or ten years old. My Dad and his father repeatedly referred to me as stupid and dumb. Taken together, such incidents caused me to believe for a number of years in my childhood that I really was retarded, stupid, and dumb.

So that "revelation" in the summer of my 9th year that I was somewhat intelligent was quite a revelation for me; I won't go into the background of how and why that revelation occurred, just that it did. Later, during some IQ testing I took during the military service I learned that I actually had quite a high IQ, which encouraged me to obtain and pursue more and more education in later years.

No God, No Religion, No Church

You'll notice I haven't written anything so far about God or religion or the like in my life. That's because there weren't any such things to write about. Until age 18, I knew next to nothing about God, religion, church, or the Bible. Oh, by simple osmosis I was exposed to some of that in the ordinary course of living in a nation with a strong Judeo-Christian heritage, but I knew nothing personally about such matters.

I suppose I was reared as a "practicing" atheist or agnostic, a "modern pagan," so to speak. On occasion as a child I remember going to something called "Midnight Mass" with Grandpa Sloan, but that's about the extent of my exposure to anything religious. And, on occasion I think Dad's mother would attend a Methodist church in downtown Rapid City. Other than that, I don't remember much—if any—churchgoing in my childhood and teen years.

Later, in my early adulthood, I learned that my parents had me baptized in an Episcopal Church in Lead, South Dakota, when I was a year old. Later in life, when I asked my parents why they had done that, they just mumbled something like *"it was the thing to do."* That baptism had no ongoing significance in my life that I am aware of.

For example, for a period of time while living in Oak Ridge, my sister and I were sent (not taken) to Sunday School, but we didn't go; instead, we went to the nearest school and played on the playground until Sunday School was over and then returned home. We kept the coins Mother gave us to place in the Sunday School offering, and spent them later each week for candy.

Until age 18, I had never opened a Bible or read anything from one. I didn't believe in God; I heard about something called "God," but had no clue what that concept meant.

Enough about my years in Oak Ridge. Mixed memories, but good ones for the most part.

Chapter Three

Ages Eleven To Seventeen

Now I want to continue this rather lengthy, convoluted stroll down memory lane and write about my 11th to 17th years.

These were the years I was a "rebel without a cause"; do any of you reading these lines remember the movie by that name—starring James Dean? I was rebellious against good, the right, and truth, and decency, and honesty—and God (if there was such a being). Later, you will read that I became a "rebel *with* a cause."

I later learned that I was so rebellious because I had contracted a fatal disease while still in my mother's womb, and that disease began to kill me slowly and surely. We're all infected with that fatal disease; it's part of our DNA; it's part of who we are. More about that later.

Return to South Dakota

A few years after World War II had officially ended, we returned to South Dakota, first to live for a few months in the town of Lead in the northern Black Hills, where after the War Dad readily found employment with the Homestake Mining Company as an electrical engineer. We lived there only a few months in the winter and spring of the 11th year of my mortal sojourn on planet earth.

A couple of memories about our time in Lead come to mind: I had a newspaper delivery route for which I trudged through horribly deep snow drifts from house to house to deliver the early morning papers; all I remember is being so very cold that winter!

While we lived in Lead, I suffered a mild bout of dreaded polio, but Dad wouldn't let Mother take me to a doctor; my back is permanently "humped" as a result and my right leg is a little shorter than my left. Thank God the bout with polio wasn't more serious!

I fell in love for the very first time while attending the sixth grade in Lead; her name was Patty, and I didn't feel I could ever live without her. They call it "puppy love," but it's real to the puppy! A few years later while attending high school in Rapid City, I talked with Patty while she was in Rapid City as a cheerleader for the opposing Lead high school basketball team. Can you believe it, she didn't even remember me after having been the love of my life! How was it possible that she didn't remember such a "studly hunk" from the sixth grade?

It was in Lead that I began a few years of thievery and continued serious lying which began in Oak Ridge. It was common in those days for kids around town to exchange comic books with one another: one comic book for one comic book. I learned how to cleverly stuff comic books inside one another so that sometimes I would end up getting two or three comic books for the one I traded.

Once when my theft was discovered, I cleverly lied my way out of the situation; I was so proud that I was able to do so and I think that's where a few years of crime began that became very serious in my 15th to 17th years. More about that later, too.

Back to Rapid City

In the summer of my 11th year, my family moved from Lead back to Rapid City where my Dad used his savings to make a down payment on a new and used furniture store in downtown Rapid City. He hoped to earn enough from that store over the next few years to buy back some of the old ancestral homestead land near Piedmont that his dad had lost for failure to pay taxes during the Great Depression and years of World War II.

The Federal Building in Rapid City is now located on the site of the old furniture store. The Texaco Service Station on the corner to the north across main street is now a pizza restaurant. While having lunch there the other day with my wife and a friend, I casually pointed to the northwest corner of the restaurant and—tongue in cheek—mentioned that I used to "pee" in that corner! It greatly puzzled my wife and our friend until I told them that corner was where the men's restroom had been located when it was a service station.

I was eleven years old that summer and quickly heading down a slippery slope to moral and emotional ruin. My conscience was becoming "seared" and numbed. I wanted what I wanted, and didn't care much about what anyone else wanted. I became pretty mean, foul-mouthed, and obnoxious.

During those years, our family lived alternately in a tiny, crowded one-room apartment in the back of the furniture store and in the old original stone house built by my great-grandparents on the family homestead land. For the most part, my parents and brother and sister lived in the old homestead house most evenings and weekends, only occasionally staying overnight in the one-room apartment in Rapid City. For all practical purposes, I had that apartment mostly to myself. Again, more about that later, too.

During the summer of my 11th year I worked as a tour guide in a "petrified forest" tourist attraction near Piedmont owned by my paternal grandparents and managed by Dad's brother and wife, Keith and Helen.

Some memories about that summer surface into my consciousness as I write these words. First, I continued honing my skills as sort of a young "con artist." When I guided groups of tourists through the petrified forest I could readily pick out the members of the tour group whom I could most easily influence by my "spiel" to later give me larger tips than usual at the end of the tour.

I would sort of focus on them, "butter them up," so to speak, and, sure enough, I would usually get a larger tip from them. Of course, more tips meant more money to buy liquor; I learned that if I maintained just sort of a "low level alcoholic buzz" throughout the days I would be glib, humorous, more talkative, a better liar, and the like. Of course, I chewed a lot of gum to mask the smell of alcohol on my breath. Daily consumption of alcohol just became a way of life for me lasting until June of my 18th year.

My uncle Keith was even more brutal and mean than Dad. Case in point: on one occasion while he and I were manning the ticket booth leading into the petrified forest, the driver of a carload of tourists decided they couldn't afford the fee to tour the forest. Uncle Keith flew into a blind rage, grabbed the hardwood pick handle he kept nearby in the ticket booth, and proceeded to break all the windows in the tourist's car. Naturally, the tourist and his family in the car were terrified and sped away as quickly as they could. I don't know whether or not they ever reported the incident to local authorities.

My uncle and his wife, Helen, lived in a beautiful, but small, log home they had hand-built near the entrance to the petrified forest. One day for a reason they later said was simply to do their summer house cleaning, they emptied everything—I mean everything!—from their house and placed all its contents—furniture, appliances, personal items, etc.—outside in the front yard. By mere coincidence (!), that night the house burned completely to the ground, they collected the insurance, and built a new, larger home. Hmmmm.

On another occasion while I was guiding at the petrified forest that summer, I had an argument with my aunt, a rather portly woman. During the argument, I became blindly enraged and pushed her through the screen door of the building outside of which we were arguing. (Incidentally, that was the very same building where years earlier I had been conceived.)

I heard my uncle rummaging around inside the building and I had a feeling I knew what was coming next. I took off running as fast as possible down the long, steep, gravel road leading up to the petrified forest.

While running down the hill as fast as my legs would carry me, I began to hear loud popping noises in the distance behind me, followed by what sounded like bees or wasps rapidly whizzing by my head. They were bullets! I never learned whether or not my uncle was shooting at me or around me, but I was absolutely terrified!

Often, during my early teen years, I would spend the weekend with one or the other sets of my grandparents. When I spent weekends with my mother's parents, in the evening if the tourist cabins were full, Grandpa Sloan would pile himself and Grandma, me, and some other Piedmont kids into his pickup (kids in back), and he would take us for a cool evening drive.

Often, he would drive up Little Elk Canyon, the entrance to which was a mile or so north of Piedmont. The canyon was always beautiful and serene on summer evenings, with deer and other wild animals grazing in the Canyon's meadows. At the other end of Little Elk Canyon was the small community of Nemo. Sparkling Little Elk Creek ran down the canyon.

In Nemo, Gramp would buy us all hamburgers and malts before we would turn around and drive back down the canyon. Those were the world's best hamburgers and malts! I think they cost a dime each. I'll never forget those evening drives to Nemo.

During a devastating flood in 1972, the road in Little Elk Canyon was almost totally washed out and has never been rebuilt. Instead, it has remained a very scenic walking and hiking area where the road had been before the flood.

One of our favorite pastimes these days is to spend a few hours hiking up Little Elk Canyon. Every time we hike there, I am reminded of my early teen years when we would drive up the canyon to Nemo for hamburgers and malts. The restaurant in Nemo is still there, but hamburgers and malts no longer cost a dime each.

Just as I wrote the previous paragraph, a memory of something my dad told me years ago rose to my conscious mind. Dad said that that when he was in his late teens and early twenties, on many Saturday evenings (in all seasons) he and some of his male friends would often walk from Piedmont to Nemo through Little Elk Canyon to attend dances in Nemo. That's about an eight-mile trek!

After the dances ended at midnight or one o'clock Sunday morning, they would then walk back to Piedmont in the dark, and have only a couple of hours of sleep before having to get up early to do their farm chores. They must have really loved to dance!

Another memory of Little Elk Canyon comes to mind. For as long as I can remember, about one third of the way up the canyon an old rusting car body is partially imbedded in the canyon wall. Many parts of the automobile are missing, but one can readily see from its visible parts remaining, it was from the 1920's; there's no way to determine the make and model, however.

My dad and grandfather told me at various times through the years that the wreck has been there since the late 1920's. It's riddled with bullet holes. Over the years, I checked with the Sheriff's records to see if they had any information about the vehicle. I have also talked with many old-timers, seeking information about the wrecked vehicle. So far, no one has been able to shed any light on it—who owned it, how it was wrecked, when it was wrecked, whether or not anyone was killed or injured in the wreck . . .

There it lays imbedded in the bank of the Canyon, a silent witness to a wreck which occurred over 80 years ago!

My "Corral Experience"

At the beginning of the summer of my 12th year, I had my "corral experience." One Saturday, Dad and "Baba" were doing some branding and castrating of that year's calf crop. I was assisting. It was raining that day. There I was, standing in the corral, up to my ankles in mud mixed with manure, soaking wet, feeling lower than the mud and manure because Dad and Baba kept calling me stupid and telling me I was doing everything wrong. I remember thinking to myself, *"I don't want to do this anymore; I don't want to be a rancher. I don't want to live in the country. I hate this!"*

The very next day I moved permanently from the ranch at Piedmont to the one-room apartment in the back of the furniture store and never looked back. From that day forward I never returned to the ranch except to visit. I was on my own living in Rapid City, supporting myself with various odd jobs and selling newspapers in downtown Rapid City.

People ask me if that was legal for me to leave home and move into town, if my parents didn't object, if it was dangerous to be completely on my own at age 12? Hey, that's just the way things were. It was western South Dakota many years ago, a different way of life back then.

With hindsight, I think Dad was glad to be rid of me, and Mother was grateful I was out from under my Dad's beatings, fury, and blind rages toward me. It wasn't as though I never saw them again or had moved to another planet. Even though I was roaming the streets of downtown Rapid City and selling newspapers throughout the day, I saw them from time to time when they were at the furniture store and on those few occasions when they stayed overnight in town.

But I was pretty much on my own: supporting myself, buying all my own clothes and most of my food, getting myself up for school in the mornings, maintaining my own personal hygiene, paying to go to the doctor or dentist when I needed to, etc. I did all the drinking I wanted to. And I finally purchased my own bicycle!

During my teen years after I had moved into Rapid City, Dad finally built his dream home he'd hoped for years to be able to build. He built it only a few feet from where the original sod homestead shanty built in 1878 by my great-grandparents was located on a sunny hillside. Dad's house is still there, now being lived in by one of my nephews. As mentioned previously, the big stone house later built by my great-grandparents in 1879 was razed in the 1970's, and my brother's home is located right on the site of that house.

Selling newspapers in downtown Rapid City was quite an experience. There were six paperboys who worked the streets and business establishments downtown. It was traditional that the six paperboys engaged in fist fights to "win" the best locations to sell the most newspapers—business establishments, apartment buildings, hotels, restaurants, and bars. I was thin and wiry, but fought pretty dirty, and for the next few years had the best locations to sell newspapers. I honed my skills at lying and conniving and became very skilled at "rolling drunks" in the bars and saloons.

For example, if one of them gave me a $20 bill, I had an instinct to know just how drunk he was, and if he was drunk enough, I would give him change for only a $1 bill. I stole a lot of alcoholic beverages from the backrooms of many downtown bars and stores—and other types of goods I was later to get arrested for. I knew how to sneak into almost every building in downtown Rapid City, especially into the grand old Alex Johnson Hotel which is still Rapid City's downtown landmark. More about my sneaking and thievery later.

When I started selling newspapers, each cost five cents. When the price was raised to the astronomical sum of seven cents, my customers were outraged and at first I lost a lot of business.

I Fell In Love With Movies

While living in downtown Rapid City and selling newspapers on the streets, I had occasion to attend a lot of movies. There were 3 theaters downtown and 3 drive-in theaters on the outskirts of town. It was during those years that I fell head over heels in love with movies. Any movies, just as long as they were movies. As I recall, I attended 4 to 5 movies each week. I developed a lifelong habit of enjoying movies. To this day, I love it when a full-length movie is shown on television and I can spend an evening just getting lost in the movie.

I especially fell in love with science-fiction movies during those years, a love which continues to this day. Just the other evening I watched the recent remake of *The Day The Earth Stood Still*, the original of which I saw at the old State Theater downtown when I was 14 years old. And, it was during those years I fell in love with reading science fiction books, and I think I've probably read everything written by the well-known, major science fiction authors since those days.

Years ago, I even wrote a "Sci Fi" short story for my grandson, Christopher, when he was only 5 or 6 years old; the story was about him and our cat, Panda. I think I still have a copy of that story somewhere in my Journal; I should dig it out one of these days and re-read it, or maybe send a copy to Christopher who is in his mid-twenties now! The years do fly swiftly by.

I was also 14 years old when I saw my first horror movie at the old State Theater in downtown Rapid City. It was *The Thing*. In the scene where the alien *"thing"* leaped out of a cabinet in which it had been hiding, I was absolutely terrified and I've never watched another horror movie since! Recently, my wife wanted me to watch *Silence of the Lambs* with her and we even got into an argument because I refused to watch it. I know my fear of horror movies is irrational, but I just can't watch them.

Previously I wrote about an early memory I had about sitting on Dad's lap in the Elks theater. In my teen years The theater became a rendezvous for most kids in town, and we often sat in the back row of the balcony, smoking, drinking, and necking. Are any of you, my readers, old enough to remember when most theaters were filled with a blue haze from people smoking cigarettes? And when all movies were still in black and white?

When I was a teenager, on Saturday mornings for fifteen cents we could see a double-feature at the Elks Theater, including a weekly serial feature, a cartoon, and the weekly news; five more cents would purchase a soft drink; popcorn cost another nickel. A wonderful way to spend a Saturday morning for only twenty-five cents!

Attending drive-in movies during those years was an experience altogether different than attending the downtown theaters. We would usually pile six to eight of us kids in our gang into one of our cars, load the trunk with a case or two of beer, and then proceed to get drunk and make fools of ourselves during the movie. Or, sometimes we took two or three cars, parked them side-by-side, and proceeded to make ourselves pretty obnoxious. A number of times management called the police and we were kicked out of the drive-in area.

In cooler weather, we would keep the windows closed and the cars would fill with thick cigarette smoke while we necked and "swapped spit" as we called it in those days. Those were actually horrible experiences, but we must have felt we were "cool," because we usually went to one of the drive-in theaters and did the same thing every weekend they were open.

I had many girls who were friends during high school, especially the ones in our little gang. But I did have two actual "steady" girlfriends, Margo Johnson and Kay Kertzman. Margo died of cancer in her forties; I stayed in touch with Kay Kertzman for years, but somewhere along the way I lost contact with her. Recently, I even sent a brief note to her last known address, but it came back marked "addressee unknown." I've also tried to locate her on FaceBook, to no avail so far.

Speaking of cars, I purchased my first one the day after I turned 16 and obtained my first driver's license. It was a 1941 four-door Plymouth, and I thought I was king of the world after I bought that car. I sold it later to one of my buddies just before I left for Air Force Basic Training. A week after I sold it, the engine blew and the friend to whom I sold it blamed me for selling it to him "in that condition." I had no knowledge that the engine would be blown.

My second car was a sleek, bullet-shaped, Maroon 1949 Nash Rambler, a very comfortable, smooth-riding car, but it really wasn't much of a "chick magnet!"

My third one was a beautiful, light green, 1951 Studebaker Land Cruiser with many extra features in place long before other vehicles had them. It was a smooth-riding, almost-luxury vehicle which I drove from Rapid City to Spokane, Washington, where I was stationed with the United States Air Force; I drove that car right up until the day I left Spokane to be transferred overseas.

I first learned to drive at about six years of age when I began driving tractors and pickups on the ranch. I remember my grandfather affixing wooden blocks to the brake, clutch, and accelerator pedals on an old pickup so I could reach the pedals and drive the vehicle. I could barely see over the steering wheel, but it was exhilarating to be able to drive at that early age.

And, speaking of things around the ranch, I have a couple of very vivid "bad" memories. One was when my grandfather barred a huge hog inside a farm building and then shot it with a rifle in preparation for butchering it for meat. I was inside the building with him at the time, and I remember the hog in it's death throes seeming to chase me around the interior of the building, blood streaming from the hole where the bullet had entered.

I was terrified, and my grandfather just stood there laughing at me! I don't know whether or not that large boar hog was actually chasing me, but it seemed so, and I was traumatized for days after that event.

The other bad memory is this. We stacked hay in those days by pitching cut and mowed hay on the ground onto a hay rack pulled by horses. When the hay rack was full, it would then be taken to the "stack yard" where people standing on the hay rack would use pitchforks to pitch the hay up to the person building the stack.

Often, when we would pitch a forkful of hay up to the stacker, rattlesnakes would fall out of the hay we were pitching! I grew to just dread when it came time in the spring and summer to start building the hay stacks. I don't recall that any of us were ever bitten by the rattlesnakes, but I nevertheless dreaded haying season.

Back to my years on the downtown streets of Rapid City. Let me tell you about my Boy Scout membership and movies—just to illustrate how I was always conniving and scheming about something. The local Boy Scout troop held their weekly meetings in the old Elks Building in downtown Rapid City upstairs from the Elks Theater. I devised a scheme where I joined the Boy Scouts and then attended their meetings every Thursday evening; about midway through the meetings I would excuse myself to go to the bathroom.

Near the bathroom, there were some emergency exit stairs leading down to a storage area adjacent to the theater's men's room. I found a way to "jimmy" that bathroom door so I could sneak in and see (for free, of course!) whatever movie happened to be playing that evening. Until some years later, I never realized the "disconnect" between Boy Scout *honesty* and sneaking *dishonestly* into the theater. Hey, it's just who I was in those days.

Meanwhile, I attended school regularly, all the while earning excellent grades with very little study and effort. I didn't engage in many extracurricular school activities because I spent so many hours selling papers and drinking. To this day, I don't remember much about school or other activities during those years because I generally lived in sort of an alcoholic fog. I remember getting into a lot of fights—my nose was broken 7 times during those years! I even broke a window at school one time by throwing a chair through it, and one time I hit a teacher with a chair while in a blind rage.

One of the few good memories I have of my time in high school was taking a typing course during the ninth grade; I took it only to get out of another course I felt wouldn't be very interesting. Taking that typing course was one of the best things I've ever done for myself. I have typed all my adult life and even now that typing course I took years ago helps me with using my computer keyboard for word processing; I can still type about 50 words a minute without looking at the keys.

Of course, I learned to type on an old manual typewriter which took a lot of finger strength and dexterity to type properly. How excited I was when years later, I got my first electric typewriter; it was one of those IBM Selectric typewriters with the font "ball" which spun and whizzed around and around as my fingers hit the keys. What a wonder that was! And then, when I got my first word processor, that was even more of a wonder.

Way back in the "olden days" of manual and electric typewriters, to make copies one had to use those old flimsy, black (or blue) sheets of carbon paper placed between the sheets of typing paper; I don't know how many things I smudged—including myself—with sheets of carbon paper. For some reason or another I kept a packet of carbon paper for years and years and finally threw it away only a couple of years ago; I guess it's true that "old habits die hard."

I didn't get into much trouble with school authorities as a result of such angry escapades because I had become such a consummate liar and exhibited a winsome "con artist" personality. I could talk my way out of just about any negative situation. I ran with an "outlaw" gang of about six boys and six girls which got into a lot of trouble in school, at various Saturday night dances throughout the region, and the like.

On many weekend evenings even though I was under the legal age to purchase and consume alcoholic beverages, my three favorite hangouts were a bar in New Underwood, east of Rapid City, a bar in a general store in the small community of Pactola in the Black Hills north and west of Rapid City, and a pretty seedy bar in Hermosa, now a bedroom community a few miles south of Rapid City. The little community of Pactola is now buried hundreds of feet under the waters of Lake Pactola. There were a number of other establishments which sold alcoholic beverages to minors, but those three were my favorite places.

No one in any of those three drinking establishments every questioned my age or refused to sell liquor to me. I was small for my age and was clearly a minor, but I was never asked to show my identification.

Back to my times in school. I did a weird thing one spring day while in study hall during the 10th grade. I was just sitting there at one of the tables and decided I no longer liked to write using cursive letters. I made a decision right then and there that I would no longer ever use cursive writing when I wrote. From that very day in study hall, I have never again written cursively; actually, I can't anymore—I've forgotten how. I always print when I "write."

I just wanted to tell you about that, because many people through the years at various times have asked me why I don't use the cursive style of writing. Maybe that matter doesn't interest you at all, but I wanted to include it in my autobiography just in case someone might be interested.

I wore traditional garb popular during those years and had sort of a "James Dean" look: black engineer boots, low-slung jeans, black leather jacket, cigarette pack rolled up in the sleeve of my T-shirts, greasy "duck tail" haircut; you get the picture. Not a pretty sight, but it's who I was in those days.

Holidays during those years? Not good! I remember vividly one particular New Year's holiday when I was 15 or 16. West of Rapid City, there is an area called Dark Canyon. It's . . . well, a very dark, remote canyon. In those days it contained only a few summer cottages and cabins. One New Year's Eve I learned of a party going on in one of the cabins. It was a very cold, snowy evening. I arrived there already halfway drunk and proceeded to drink even more as the party progressed.

The last thing I remember about the evening was going outside to urinate behind an evergreen tree. The next thing I knew it was early dawn, I was laying in a snow bank, very cold, very chilled, nauseated, vomit all over the front of me, my nose broken and covered with dried and frozen blood, my new engineer boots missing. Yep, those were the good ol' days alright!

For whatever weird reason during those years, I came to really loathe and detest any classmates who appeared to be authentic Jesus-believers; I didn't waste my time with just the church-going, hypocritical kids—only those who appeared to be "real" Jesus-believers. I made fun of them, picked on them, shoved them down stairs at school, slapped their books out of their arms, humiliated them, swore at them, and just generally harassed and hounded them. The Jesus-believer kids hated to see me coming their way.

I remember snatching Bibles out of the hands of some of my Jesus-believer classmates and then proceeding to rip out some of the pages and strew them on the hallway floor. I have no clue why I did such things; there was just something inside me that seemed to compel me to engage in such activities.

I also developed a strange notion that I didn't like church buildings, and so I began a "mission" to vandalize churches in town. I recall breaking out at least one window in most of the church buildings in Rapid City—just to be mean, just because I didn't respect or like what I felt they represented. I never got caught for that particular obsession.

Years later when I finally attended one of my high school class reunions (the 40th, I think), I sought out some of those classmates who were Jesus-believers and apologized to them for the way I had treated them back when we were in high school. Without exception, each of them readily and freely forgave me. That felt good!

During those years I also developed a horribly foul vocabulary. In fact, I even developed sort of a strange "cult following" of other kids who hung around me to see what new foul words I would come up with from day to day. My favorite foul word was the "F" word, and I became skilled at using it in almost every sentence I spoke and putting humorous twists to the word. More about that later when I tell you about the events of the 18th year of my mortal journey here on planet earth.

I just continued on with my "modern pagan" lifestyle, not having a clue—or a care—about how it affected others or how it was warping and destroying my own life.

I Fell In Love With Music

While growing up in South Dakota and Tennessee, I don't remember hearing much music in our home. Maybe there was music, but, if so, I don't remember it. I don't remember hearing much music on the radio. I can't remember Dad ever singing, humming, or whistling. I do have some faint memories of Mother singing or humming occasionally, but other than that I simply don't remember hearing much, if any, music before I became a teenager.

When I became a teenager, I discovered jukeboxes in cafes, restaurants, bars, and saloons while selling newspapers on the streets of downtown Rapid City. And did I ever love the music I discovered!

Before discovering jukeboxes, however, I do have some very, very faint memories of three songs which were popular during

World War II: *Pistol Packin' Mama, Praise The Lord And Pass The Ammunition,* and *Coming In On A Wing And A Prayer*. There were probably other songs and music I heard during those years, but I just don't remember much in terms of music. Oh wait, a couple of other songs are coming to mind just as I write these words: my grandfather, Ed, Dad's dad, loved *Pretty Red Wing, Tumbling Tumbleweeds,* and *Cool Water.*

My first vivid memories of music are when I began to sell newspapers on the streets of downtown Rapid City. As mentioned above, I discovered jukeboxes. I even remember at first carefully observing grownups using the jukeboxes, watching carefully to learn exactly how to put money in them, how much money, and how many songs I could hear based on how many coins I put in the little slot.

Later, while I was consuming so much alcohol, I would often get in fights if people didn't "shut up" and let me hear my music on jukeboxes.

The first real music I listened to on the jukeboxes was old-fashioned "hillbilly" music—not what is called country and western music today. I learned to absolutely love that type of music—Hank Williams, "Cowboy Copas," Eddie Arnold, Webb Pierce, Faron Young, Roy Acuff, and others of that genre of music. That's about the only type of music I listened to from my early teens to age 18.

After I became a Jesus-believer, I then began to fall in love with Christian music, particularly Southern Gospel music, and I've loved that type of music ever since—along with old-fashioned hillbilly music and earlier country and western music.

When I attended Moody Bible Institute in Chicago after I was honorably discharged from the United States Air Force, I took an introductory course in "Music Appreciation." That course introduced me to a broad range of music, ranging from classical, to big band, to popular, to country and western, to Gospel, and everything in between. I learned to appreciate all types of music, but still have my favorites.

Today, I do appreciate all types of music, and we have in our home cassette tapes and CD's of many varieties of music. The only kinds I really don't like to listen to are Hip Hop and Rap music; to me, those are not really music—just disconsonant, loud sounds, but I do respect them as types of music others listen to.

Recently, I discovered YouTube. Oh, I've known for years that it was available on my computer, but I simply assumed it was too technical for me to learn how to access it. Wow, has it ever been great to learn to look up and listen to music on YouTube. I've been able to find everything from old hillbilly music to contemporary Christian music . . . and everything in between.

Occassionally, I'll take an hour or so, shut the door to our home office and just listen to all types of music on YouTube. It's really a great way for me to spend an hour or so of relaxed listening to some of my all-time favorite music going clear back to some from the 1920's!

I know, I know you're sitting on the edge of your seat right now waiting with bated breath to know which songs are my very lifetime favorites. Okay, here they are:

My favorite Gospel songs are ones I want played and sung at my memorial service after I die: *Zion's Hill, It's Real,* and *My Savior First of All*. My favorite secular songs are: *Rose of Tralee* (reflecting my Irish heritage), *Caledonia* (reflecting my love of Scottish things), and *Shenendoah* (my favorite American song of all time). There you have it—everything you always wanted to know about Bill Boylan's love of music.

Oh, there are other songs which are sort of my lifetime "secondary" favorites, but I won't bore you with all of them; most of them are what is called Celtic Gospel music, reflecting the all-inclusive love of God for all humankind. I also love American patriotic music and music from the Civil War era . . . all right there in front of me on YouTube. Will modern technical marvels from "somewhere out there" in cyberspace never cease . . .

Band Of Thieves

During my last two years of high school, in order to have more money for alcoholic beverages, good clothes, my car, etc., I began a theft ring operating in the more upscale neighborhoods of Rapid City, breaking and entering, stealing radios, electrical appliances, jewelry, car parts, furniture, and the like. The downtown Alex Johnson Hotel also became a target of my thievery. We also broke into the backs of bars and saloons and into liquor warehouses.

That finally proved to be my downfall. One evening in early September after I had graduated from high school in June, two others in my gang and I were breaking and entering a liquor warehouse near downtown Rapid City; as we exited the building each carrying a case of beer, all of a sudden I heard running footsteps about a half block behind us.

I stopped dead in my tracks because I knew what the sounds were. They were made by the new German Shepherd guard dog which had just been put into use in Rapid City by a private "merchant policeman." The second I stopped, that dog was on me.

I didn't dare move or even breathe; he had his massive paws on my chest and was staring at me with his muzzle only inches away from my face. I could feel and smell his hot breath. I knew I had been caught red-handed and was in bad trouble.

I spent the night in jail and was arraigned in juvenile court the next morning. In brief, the judge gave me two options: 1. I would either be imprisoned in the state Reform School, or 2. I could immediately enlist in the military. I was just smart enough to know that enlisting in the military was the best choice, so I got my parents' signed permission, stepped into the Air Force recruiting office only a few doors up the street from my apartment, and on September 7th of my 17th year I boarded a train bound for the Military Entrance Processing Station (MEPS) in Sioux Falls at the other end of the state.

During all those troubled years from about age 6 to age 18, I was filled with blind rage, anger, frustration, brutality, and hostility—all very much a part of my "family DNA," at least on the male side of my family. It was manifest in my paternal great-grandfather, my grandfather, my father, and in my brother and me.

Fortunately, I was able to break that DNA chain at age 18. Again, more about that later. I see a tiny bit of that anger and frustration in my son, but not near to the extent it was down through past generations to my own generation—and I see no brutality or blind rage in him at all; he has a very gentle, warm, and generous spirit—he's a gentle-man in the truest sense of the word, and his son, Zane, my grandson, exhibits that same gentle, cheerful spirit.

Zane also has a very witty sense of humor. Years ago after I had major surgery and was showing him my scar from the surgery, Zane (who was about six years old at the time) remarked *"Hey, Grandpa, don't worry about your scar; chicks dig scars!"*

Oh, I've seen Joel feel and display "righteous indignation" at dishonesty, injustice, and foolishness displayed by others, but, overall, I think that generational cycle of rage and brutality has been broken for good on my branch of the Boylan family tree.

The United States Air Force

We are now at early September of my 17th year. I sat in jail overnight. The very next day I enlisted in the United States Air Force. On September 9th I was enroute to my basic training base near Pleasanton, California, near San Francisco. My 16 weeks of basic training is a story in and of itself, but I won't bore you with it. One thing I did during basic training was kind of weird, however.

Having been raised in kind of a middle class family during the years of World War II and thereafter, most of the food I ate was standard fare—the traditional meat and potatoes diet, so to speak. I had never eaten any sort of ethnic, gourmet, or "fancy" foods. On my first 48-hour leave after my 10th week of basic training, I took a bus into San Francisco, checked into a cheap hotel and proceeded to get drunk.

I stayed just sober enough, however, that I knew I wanted to try some of those "fancy foods" I had only heard about previously. Here's what I did. I first went to a Chinese restaurant, ate a full meal, and then went outside in an alley and made myself vomit it all up. Then I proceeded to an Italian restaurant and repeated that scenario. Then to a Russian restaurant. Then to a Japanese restaurant, Then to a Middle Eastern restaurant. And so on. I ate lots of great food, stayed fairly sober with just a "slight buzz on," and had a great time enjoying all those exotic foods and them vomiting them up immediately afterwards. Pretty weird, huh?

Chapter Four

Ages Seventeen And Eighteen

This brings us to January, late in my 17th year. I was dispatched to my first assignment after basic training, assigned to the Base Education Office at Fairchild Air Force Base near Spokane, Washington. I was an Education Clerk . . . AF 17438817 . . . AFSC 75B10. They say veterans never forget such numbers.

I was housed in a 50-man barracks—everyone sleeping in one big room on single cots. Another room served as the latrine with many showerheads, and urinals and commodes lined along one wall facing rows of sinks on the opposite wall. In basic training there was no privacy and for the first few months at Fairchild Air Force there was no privacy either until I was moved a few months later into another building that contained double and single rooms depending upon one's rank.

I was excited; I had completed basic training successfully, had gained some weight, had a neat "butch" haircut, and looked sharp in my new uniform and spit-shined shoes. I was earning big bucks (all of $69 a month!). Free food and housing. Life looked good.

Only one problem: nothing had changed inside me; I was still that drunken, foul-mouthed, conniving, angry, hostile, chain-smoking modern pagan who disliked authentic Jesus-believers.

Back up a few months first. I just thought of something else I want to write about my months of basic training. During basic training, for some reason or another due to my bodily configuration and bone structure, I was physically unable to position my feet properly while standing at attention and parade rest. A kind, gentle, mild-mannered drill instructor thought he would tenderly assist me in that endeavor by repeatedly stomping hard on the arches of my feet while I was standing in those positions. The end result was that he crushed both my arches. Later, you'll understand why I am telling you that.

(Hey, in case you've been keeping track, very few of my paragraphs have been over 10 lines in length yet. And, I haven't used many words over four syllables in length, either)

Later, while stationed at a US Air Force Base in Newfoundland, I was exposed to numerous chemical, environmental, and nuclear pollutants. As a result, I developed very severe environmental allergies. Those two matters (my bad feet and allergies) combined resulted in my receiving a permanent disability designation when I had my discharge physical exam, and I've had health challenges in both those areas my entire life. For example, without sturdy, custom-made arch supports I can stand or walk only for a few moments without experiencing severe foot pain.

I'm a lifetime member of the Disabled Veterans of America (DAV), and feel deep sympathy and empathy for any veterans permanently disabled to any degree.

Five Young Men Slaughtered

Back again to my first assignment at Fairchild Air Force Base, near Spokane, Washington. After a few weeks there I began to get quite bored. There was still lots of inexpensive alcohol to drink off-duty, but otherwise it was work, eat, back to the barracks, hang out, play cards, drink before curfew and lights-out, a pretty boring first few weeks. One evening, just to kill a little time before joining my friends at the airmen's club to begin our usual evening's drinking, I visited the base library.

Most of our national headlines and news stories on the radio were then broadcasting the heartbreaking story of 5 young American missionaries who had been cruelly slaughtered January 8th on the banks of the Curaray River, a serpentine, creamed-coffee-colored, jungle river in Equador. I picked up a current copy of ***Life*** magazine from the periodicals shelf of the library and read a lengthy article about the "martyrdom" of those 5 young men. I had no idea what that word meant, but I was somehow deeply touched by their deaths.

A few days after those young men were slaughtered, rescuers found the journal of one of the missionaries. In it, the young man had written these words: *"He is no fool who gives what he cannot keep to gain what he cannot lose!"* Those words haunted me day and night for 3 months until they became part of God's means of bringing me to surrender my wasted, meaningless, empty life to Him a few months later on April 26th of my 18th year.

NOTE: If you're interested in reading a full account of the lives and deaths of those five young missionaries, I highly recommend the book, ***Through Gates of Splendor*** by Elisabeth Elliot; be sure to get the updated 40th anniversary edition. The title of the book comes from the words of a song the young men sang together a few days before their death as recorded in the journal of one of the young men:

> *"We rest on Thee, our Shield and Defender,*
> *Thine is the battle, Thine shall be the praise*
> *When passing* ***through the gates of pearly splendor,***
> *Victors, we rest with Thee through endless days."*

Another great book about the slaughter of those five young men is ***Jungle Pilot*** (subtitled *The gripping story of the life and witness of Nate Saint, martyred missionary to Ecuador*). Both books contain lots of photographs and updates, and can be inexpensively purchased in paperback editions.

To the world at large, the deaths of those five young men were a sad, cruel waste of their young lives. But, God used the deaths of those young men to transform the lives of hundreds, even thousands, of people around the world! And, most of the savage tribespeople (and their children and grandchildren) who slaughtered the young men are Jesus-believers today, carrying God's Good News to other tribes and people-groups throughout the jungles of South America!

No life lived for God—and given for God—is ever truly lost or wasted. The ancient saying is true: *"The blood of martyrs is the seed of [the worldwide spread of the Good News about Jesus]."*

Meanwhile, in mid-February of that year (just before my 18th birthday) a young Sergeant (nicknamed "Duke") who had just returned from Japan awaiting discharge, was assigned as our Barracks Chief, putting him in charge of curfews, barracks cleaning, maintenance of our personal space, cleanliness and proper wearing of our uniforms, etc. We nicknamed Duke "House Mother."

There was something inexplicably different about Duke. I couldn't put my finger on those differences at the time, but whatever they were, they irked me. I didn't like him at all, and resented his being able to tell me what to do by virtue of his assignment as Barracks Chief and the fact that he outranked me. On top of that, I felt he was just too f— — —g nice to all of us in the barracks who were under his charge.

For example, since he was the only one who owned an automobile at the time, he would take some of us to the on-base airmen's club where we did our drinking, but he wouldn't drink alcohol with us, only soft drinks. I resented that. Did he think he was better than us? Also, he didn't swear and curse and use foul language like the rest of us did. And, he went to church somewhere in Spokane. I was beginning to figure out that Duke was one of "those." He wasn't pushy about his Jesus-faith, however, just different. Who did he think he was?

I want to go back a ways now to sort of recount what my life had been like before that January evening when I read about those 5 young slaughtered missionaries and the events of February that year involving Duke.

Please understand very clearly that **what I am about to relate to you hereafter is not about me; it's all about God!**

What I have written about my life so far is just the way things were. I don't blame God, or life, or my family, or society, or a failed school system, or anyone but myself for who I became—a modern pagan; I accept full responsibility. That was just the way life was for me during the first 17 years of my mortal pilgrimage. I was just one of many teenage pagans in mid-20th century USAmerica, thinking that's just how life was meant to be lived. I was just being who I thought I was supposed to be. I was simply "doing what comes naturally," as the words of an old song state.

By the way, when I use the word "pagan," I'm using it in the dictionary sense of one who simply has no religion.

I didn't realize that my self-centered, self-focused, self-indulgent, self-absorbed, self-seeking, self-filled, self-consumed life was "sinful." I didn't realize living that type of life instead of a God-filled life made me a sinner needing salvation from my sin and from death as the result of my sin.

Okay, back to late February, just days before my 18th birthday.

Although I didn't openly accept it or admit to it, Duke was actually turning out to be a pretty decent guy. He had an aura of peace surrounding him that none of my foul-language accusatory barbs and taunts could penetrate. My verbal "persecution" just rolled off him like water off a platypus's back. He never condemned our pagan behavior, just did things for us, ate with us, visited with us, but it was clear he wasn't one of us.

He lived in another world, "marched to a different drummer," and was driving me crazy! Everywhere he went, he either sang, hummed, or whistled the words to a religious song, ***It's Real!***

Those words lodged in my mind and "stuck in my craw"; I couldn't get away from them. I even began to sing and hum them myself just by osmosis or by some sort of weird association with Duke. Here are some of the words and chorus to that song that was driving me crazy through February, March, and April that year:

"O how well do I remember
how I doubted day by day,
For I did not know for certain
that my sins were washed away.

When the Spirit tried to tell me,
I would not the truth receive;
I endeavored to be happy
and to make myself believe.

Chorus:
But it's real, it's real!
O I know it's real!
Praise God, the doubts are settled,
for I know, I know it's real!

. . . Then at last by faith I touched Him
And, like sparks from smitten steel,
Just that quick salvation reached me
And I know, I know it's real!

My First Shower Experience

This section is not about the first shower I ever took; no, it's about something that happened to me in a shower. Let's "fast forward" to April 26 of the 18th year. I was standing in the shower in my barracks; actually, I wasn't just standing there; that would be weird. I was naked, the water, was on, and I was taking a shower; I wasn't just standing there. No one else was is in the barracks building at the time. All of a sudden I begin weeping rivers of tears, wetting me almost as much as the shower. I was sobbing uncontrollably for no apparent reason.

I shook my fist above my head and screamed out:

"God, if you really are real like Duke claims you are, then, damn it, make yourself real to me, too!"

Little did I realize that in that atomic moment suspended in space and time, a silent, but very real, transaction occurred inside me in my young life. A silent, tectonic shift had occurred inside me. Everything around me was unusually hushed and still; I couldn't even hear the water of the shower cascading down my body and splashing on the floor. An amazing peace washed over, encompassed, and filled me. I finished showering, got dressed, and went to my work assignment for the day, not having a clue what that incident was all about.

I just knew something "weird" had happened inside me while showering that morning; I just knew some type of inner transaction had occurred inside between me and "Someone" who instantly became very real to me. My thoughts, attitudes, and behavior were rapidly changing throughout that very first day. What in the world was happening to me? I was quickly morphing into a new person. When I looked into the mirror in the next few ensuing mornings, it was me, but it really wasn't. A tectonic shift of some sort had occurred inside me.

Two weeks later one of my buddies in the chow line asked me: ***"Boylan, what in the hell has happened to you? You haven't sworn, or cussed, or used one word of foul language for two weeks. And I haven't caught you lying or exaggerating."***

SIDEBAR about my lying: Yes, God did clean up my foul mouth almost instantly, and the lying and exaggerating went away almost instantly, too. However, to this very day many years later I still have a propensity for lying. Well, maybe not lying so much as exaggerating, especially when I get excited about something and start babbling. God really uses my wife, Anne, to catch me when that starts to happen; she jumps right on top of me with both feet and almost instantly points out what's happening, bringing it to a bloody, screeching halt! She helps keep me brutally honest, to say the least. Do I necessarily like it when that happens? No. But I appreciate it.

When my friend mentioned that my cussing and foul language had stopped . . . at that atomic second in time and space, in my "knower" I knew that I knew that I knew something very real had occurred within me in that shower two weeks earlier. I ascertained a short time later that in that shower on April 26th of that year, I had been born[2] (meaning born again, born twice, born from above) by God, and had begun to become a brand-new creation in and through Jesus.

I didn't know it that day, but a lifelong—and eternal—process began that moment in the shower to transform me back into the clear image of God through Jesus. Someone inside me began to transform me that very day. And that Someone has continued to transform me daily for many years since.

All I knew was that somehow I had become a new creation in Jesus that moment in the shower. Somehow I knew in my "knower" that I was embarking upon a brand-new life that was going to be unlike anything I had ever dreamed of or imagined.

I immediately had this strange, inner urging to begin attending church, so the very next Sunday I showed up bright and early at a little neighborhood church I had spotted one day while I was driving around Spokane near the Air Force base where I was stationed.

I didn't know what "brand" of Church it was or what people did in that building, but I just felt that was where I should be the next Sunday morning. Only God knows how hard it was for me to walk into that building that morning, but I summoned up some kind of new, inner strength, parked my car, walked up to the front door, and stepped inside.

My H-u-g-e Bible!

Meanwhile, I had even purchased a huge Bible (I mean h-u-g-e!) a few days after that moment in the shower; I just felt inside myself that's what I should do; no one told me I needed a Bible or should begin attending church services. I just knew that I should. About that huge Bible, I reasoned that if I was going to be a "good" new believer in Jesus, I should have the largest Bible I could afford to buy—to show people how serious I was about my new life.

As I remember, that Bible measured approximately 12" wide, 16" long, and was about 4-5 inches thick!

I carried that huge Bible into that little church that Sunday morning and everybody looked at me and at my huge Bible very strangely. I learned later the huge Bible I purchased was called a "Pulpit Bible" or "Family Bible." The man who sold me the Bible from a carnival booth at a fair in Spokane conveniently neglected to tell me it was that type of Bible.

To this day, I wonder what they were thinking that Sunday morning upon seeing this skinny, 112-pound kid (in low-slung jeans, a T-shirt with a pack of cigarettes rolled in the sleeve, black leather jacket, and engineer boots) walk into church that morning carrying that huge Bible that weighed almost as much as he did. But they were very gracious, greeted me warmly, and invited me to have coffee with them after the service.

The Pastor even came up to me and talked with me for quite a while; I figured he was sort of checking out who I was and why I was there with my huge Bible. I was overwhelmed that he would deign to visit with me; I didn't know whether to bow or kiss his ring or call him "Sir," "your highness," O great one," or whatever.

By the way, I gave away that huge Bible a couple of months later to a large family in the church (I figured they needed a large family Bible since they were a large family), and bought another Bible that was a lot more portable and easier to carry around.

Those were the first few days of the beginning of my new-creation life after I had been born[2]. And I've been letting Jesus live His own eternal, uncreated, self-existent, abundant LIFE **in** me, and **through** me, and **as** me for many years since that moment in the shower.

A couple of weeks after I began attending that little church (I was there for every service they had—even mistakenly walking into a "Board meeting" I shouldn't have been at; hey, I figured a "good Jesus-believer" should be there every time the doors were open!), the Pastor approached me one Sunday morning after the worship service and said he wanted to ask me something.

First Teaching Experience

He said there was a small country church of their denomination just a few miles outside of town that had recently lost their part-time Pastor by transfer to another church. He asked me if I would consider going there for a few Sundays (until they got another Pastor) and teach their adult Sunday School class with about a dozen adults in regular attendance.

I gulped and replied *"Sure, I'll be glad to,"* even though I was shaking and almost ready to faint because I was so scared and weak in the knees.

Almost the "Number One Greatest Fear" of all adults worldwide is the fear of public speaking! In fact, a comedian once joked: *"Studies reveal people fear speaking in public more than death, which means that if you have to be at a funeral, you would rather be in the casket than doing the eulogy."*

Perhaps my new Pastor saw something in me that caused him to think I could do that, even though I had been a new believer in Jesus for only a few weeks. I was scared to death, but I respected my Pastor and figured he wouldn't have asked me if he didn't think I could do it. I had never attended Sunday school, but I reasoned it must be like regular school . . . except on Sundays.

I was up late every night in my barracks for the next week, poring through the pages of my huge Bible and putting together extensive notes for what I would teach, as usual in those early days of my new life not really having a clue about what I was doing.

I even remember the subject of my "lesson" to this day, but I don't remember any of the details. It was about the young man, David, in the Bible, and five smooth stones he selected to go into battle against the giant Goliath. I even thought I had over-prepared, believing I had prepared enough notes for about 3 hours worth of teaching just so I couldn't possibly run out of material.

I arrived at the little country church the next Sunday, was warmly greeted by the people there, and I launched into my "lesson." I had even purchased a new suit—my first ever—for the occasion; it was a light grey sort of "zoot suit" with dark blue specks in it; I wouldn't be caught dead in it today. Hey, I wanted to do this new "Jesus-believer thing" right—with a new suit and my huge, new Bible.

No one except God will ever know how nervous and frightened I was that Sunday morning, especially just the raw fear of speaking in front of people for the first time in my life. Well, I went through all my 3-hours' worth of notes in about 15 minutes and there I stood with nothing more to teach.

I gulped and asked the people if they wanted to talk about what God was doing in their lives. Fortunately, they responded well, and before we knew it the Sunday School hour was over, and we were having coffee. Most of the adults in attendance even patted me on the back and congratulated that skinny, 112-pound young man with the new suit and huge Bible for presenting such a great lesson. As the saying goes, the rest is history.

I knew that I knew in my "knower" from that very Sunday many years ago that God was "calling" me to be a teacher. To "confirm" that call, two weeks later a very strange thing happened to me.

My Second Shower Experience

Once again, I was standing in the shower in my barracks. I heard a real, audible voice saying these words to me: **"Bill, I have called you and will equip you to be a teacher of the Bible and related subjects in and to the worldwide Body of Jesus, without any exclusiveness!"**

Can you imagine what was going through my mind at that moment in time? First of all, I had heard an actual voice right out of thin air; that alone just about did me in, but somehow I knew in my "knower" it was God's voice. Second, to hear those exact words (which are forever emblazoned indelibly on my mind) just about fried my brain cells. What in the world was that all about? I could scarcely believe the words, much less understand all they meant. Again, no clue at the time.

And then I had this weird thought: *"What is it about me and God and showers!? Does He speak to everyone this way?"* In the years since, God has "spoken" to me many times while I have been showering (never again in an audible voice, however). Maybe He "speaks" to me in the shower because I'm "naked and open" to "hear" from Him.

Anyhow, from that very day forward God has kept me involved in a lifelong "project" to equip me to be a teacher. I was very humbled and privileged to have been able to attend the world's premiere (and very difficult and arduous) Bible School right after my enlistment in the Air Force ended, to graduate from college a few years later (the first one in my family for generations), to earn two difficult master's degrees from a leading Christian university, and even to be awarded a "lifelong learning PhD" degree.

I don't really count that last one, however, because it's not an "earned" degree like my others; not many people even know it was awarded to me; don't tell anyone else, okay? I don't want to be called "Doctor Boylan"; it just sounds too pretentious. Hey, I'm just a very very ordinary human who happens to serve an extra-ordinary, super-human God! And, I've been able to earn many other graduate hours of credit in various subjects in addition to my master's degrees. Yes, in respect to just sheer formal academic education, God has been very gracious to me—far beyond anything I could have ever imagined while standing in that shower years ago.

Yes, I'm grateful for all my secular and Christian education, BUT I'm even more deeply grateful that God has allowed me through the years to read and study my Bible all the way through many, many times. I don't tell many people this (because I don't want to sound like I'm bragging, but now my secret is out): I've been deeply privileged to have read and studied the Bible completely through over a hundred times—and I intend to continue reading and studying it as many more times as I'm able to. Why am I telling you that?

The simple fact is that people cannot be teachers of the Bible and related subjects without knowing their Bible! Period!

If you ever have occasion to teach the Bible, no matter the situation or venue, don't ever presume to tell anyone that you are a "called and equipped" teacher of the Bible and related subjects if you do not read, and read, and re-read, and study, and study, and re-study your Bible daily! It just doesn't work without that kind of commitment to daily reading and studying (and attempting to obey!) the Bible, God's Living, printed Word, day after day, week after week, month after month, year after year, and applying it to your life daily—letting it and the Holy Spirit transform your life.

Those are seemingly harsh statements, but it's true! ***Don't read books about the Book, read the Book!*** I'm not saying that books about the Bible and related subjects aren't good, but they're only secondary to reading and studying the Bible. Books about the Bible are good. Sunday school teachers' manuals are good. Christian magazines and periodicals are good. Denominational teaching publications are good. Theology books are good. ***But, the good is always the enemy of the best!***

Yes, read and study your Bible. ***God's Word, the Bible, will keep you from sin, or sin will keep you from the Bible!*** Those are just pithy sayings, but they're true, dear reader!

I've had many, many Bibles through the years since I bought that huge Pulpit Bible. I've had many different versions of the Bible in English. Just last week I purchased a copy of a new paraphrase of the Bible entitled ***The Message.*** I've begun reading through that version as well as continuing to read and study my regular Bible each day.

Rebel With A Cause

Earlier, I wrote how I was a rebel without a cause. Actually, I did have a cause. I wrote that I later found out I had contracted a fatal illness while still in my mother's uterus. What fatal illness? It's called **SIN** (that's the cause for my rebellion!), and it has brought death to every human ever born since Adam and Eve.

It'll kill you, too, unless you let God "inoculate" you with salvation through Jesus. That's all I'm going to say about sin in this entire autobiography except every human ever born has been infected with it, every human will die from its effects; some people deny they have it, but that doesn't alter the fact that they have it and that it will kill them. You know you have it. I know I have it. It's killing us. God's the only one who can reverse its fatal effects in us.

As mentioned earlier, here's the best definition of sin I know of: ***"Sin is for me to make a conscious choice or decision to live a self-filled, self-centered, self-focused, self-absorbed, self-indulgent, self-seeking, self-centered life instead of a God-filled life."***

As I began to earnestly read, study, and attempt to obey the Bible, I started to become a ***rebel with a cause***. What do I mean by that? I began to see that many Jesus-believers were more interested in what their particular "brand" of church teaches, what their particular church doctrine is, what their church teaches that's correct—and other churches don't teach, what they've "always believed," who's right and who's wrong, *ad nauseum*.

I began to see many people were boxed in by their own thinking, religious tradition, and history, often ignoring the clear teachings of the Bible—*taken together as a whole*. Many Jesus-believers were enslaved by what they **thought** the Bible teaches, not by what it **actually** teaches—again, taken together as a whole. I began to hear such expressions as *"That's how we've always done it, that's what we've always believed," Our denomination teaches it this way," Our church believes what's written in our prayer book."*

Well, just as I had earlier been a rebel without a cause, now I became a rebel with a cause, that cause being to learn and understand what the Bible—taken together as a whole—clearly teaches about certain matters, topics, and subjects, no matter what the cost of that type of learning and understanding. I began a lifelong quest to learn and teach what the Bible—taken together as a whole—clearly teaches. That has gotten me into a lot of trouble through the years.

I've been branded as an apostate (whatever that is), as a false teacher (whatever that is), as a heretic (whatever that is), an unorthodox believer (whatever that is), and many similar epithets. What can I say? I'm a happy heretic! And, I'll just keep digging through the Bible and searching for truth therein as long as I have breath—and then later after I awaken in Jesus' Kingdom when He returns to earth. I'm never going to stop learning and teaching the Bible.

Did you notice how I wrote a few times above these words about the Bible: ***taken together as a whole.*** Dear reader, that's the key to reading, studying, understanding, and obeying! the Bible. Never, never, never, never take certain "proof-texts" about various subjects, topics, and principles in the Bible. Always ascertain what the Bible—**taken together as a whole**—teaches before arriving at a conclusion about any subject, topic, or principle. That's the only "safe" way to read, study, and obey! the Bible. We must read it as a whole.

Since I heard God's voice in the shower many years ago, God has been very faithful in letting me teach *"in and to the worldwide Body of Jesus,"* as He promised me that day in the shower. I have been privileged to teach all over the United States one-on-one, in home groups, churches, and auditoriums; in the jungles and villages of Central and South America; in a large city in China; and in the world's largest Church in South Korea (700,000 members at the time!).

Yes, I have been privileged to teach, ranging from one person, clear up to teaching many hundreds and even thousands of people; I once taught an audience of 25,000 people! Young and old. Rich and poor. Educated and uneducated. Literate and illiterate. Handsome and homely. Large crowds. Small groups. One-on-one. Well-dressed and poorly dressed. To this day, I can scarcely believe how a very, very ordinary man named Bill Boylan has been able to teach so many people in so many places throughout the world.

And now, in the past few years **by means of our ministry's web site**, my teachings are being studied by thousands more students throughout the world: Russia, Africa, Indonesia, Europe, Australia, New Zealand, Malaysia, all over USAmerica . . . wherever.

And I'll be able to go on teaching by means of our web site long after I'm dead—as long as someone maintains and keeps up the web site. I like a reference in Hebrews 11: 4 in the Bible that *says " . . . Though he died, yet he is still speaking."* Isn't modern computer technology amazing? Even after I die, I'll still be able to go on teaching.

In addition, I now write and publish a free, monthly e-mail teaching publication entitled ***The Traveler.*** When I e-mailed the first issue, it was received by about 65 – 70 people. Now—as of this writing—it's being read by thousands of people on 6 of the 7 continents of planet earth! It's just a God-thing that it's being received and read by that many people. It's not something I could have done all by myself. Just a few days ago I received an inquiry from a reader in Norway. I have no clue how I obtained his e-mail address.

God has been s-o-o-o faithful to me. To this very day, I remain overwhelmed with his love, grace, and mercy that have allowed me to teach the Bible and related subjects for many years now—just as He told that skinny, uneducated, young 18-year old in that shower many years ago! In the words of an old song: *"Great is Your faithfulness, O God, My Father; morning by morning new mercies I see. All I have needed, Your hand has provided. Great is Your faithfulness, Lord, unto me!"* To God be the glory; great things **He** has done! It's not about me.

My lifetime teaching credo is found in one of the Old Testament books of the Bible, Deuteronomy 32: 2 – 4: (paraphrased):

"let my teaching fall like gentle rain, my words be like nurturing morning dew. Let it be like spring showers on a garden, like abundant rain on new grass. For it's God I'm teaching about. Praise the greatness of God, our Firm Foundation. His works are perfect, and the way He works is fair and just. He's a God you can depend upon—no exceptions, a trustworthy God.

In those early months after becoming a Jesus-believer, I continued to teach in various settings here and there throughout the Spokane area. I continued to read, study, and attempt to obey! my Bible. I was privileged to be part of a young peoples' "revival" through the local Youth For Christ ministry. I helped out at our church. I shared what I knew about God and Jesus at the local Servicemen's Center in downtown Spokane.

I shared the Good News about Jesus with others in my office and barracks. Sometimes, I was in-your-face overly zealous, but God was teaching me and transforming me all the while. I went door-to-door in various neighborhoods of Spokane sharing the Good News about Jesus. It was a wonder-full time for me as God continued transforming me into a "new creation," displacing and replacing the "old me" with an entirely new me.

But I continued to drink and smoke heavily all the while through May and June that year; God must have known I was not yet ready to give up those two pursuits.

That changed on June 30th of that year. I had been home on a 30-day furlough commencing June 1st, all the while continuing to drink and run with my old gang in Rapid City, but telling them at the same time about the new me God was rapidly transforming me into. I was blind to the obvious incongruencies and inconsistencies between what I was doing and what I was telling them. I wasn't "walking my talk."

On Thursday evening of the Monday before I was to leave home and begin the drive back to Fairchild Air Force Base, I began drinking very heavily with my old gang. The next thing I remember was awakening the next Sunday morning slumped down behind the steering wheel of my car, with a horrible headache and a complete blackout of where I had been and what I had done since Thursday evening.

My car had 600 additional miles registered on the odometer and I had no clue how they got there. The car smelled like vomit and there were numerous empty beer cans and bottles and empty wine bottles strewn all over the floor of the car. That blackout scared me dry-mouthed, and it was many years before I ever again had a beer or a little wine now and then.

As to my smoking, when I approached the main gate of the Base after having driven back from South Dakota in a hazy, smoke-filled car, I lit up one final cigarette, threw the rest of the pack in a waste container, and I haven't had another cigarette since; I thank God I was able to quit "cold turkey" and instantly. I know many people aren't able to quit that easily, and I feel for them.

An important thing I did while I was home on that 30-day furlough—even though I was pretty drunk and still smoking "like a chimney": I sensed down in my "knower" that I should go around to the various businesses and homes I could remember having stolen from and tell them what I had done, offering to repay them, and asking their forgiveness. I had never yet heard about restitution or reparation or anything like that; I just knew it was something God wanted me to do.

I received varying responses. In some instances, the people who had lived in some of the homes when my theft had taken place were no longer living there. In other instances they were. Some thanked me for admitting my wrongdoing, told me they were pleased I was "turning my life around," and didn't feel I needed to make restitution. Some thanked me for my honesty and did want me to repay them; I made arrangements with them to do so over time. And I did pay them back in installments.

Some thought I was just a kook trying to "con" them out of something else and asked me to leave before they called the police. Some did call the police and that led to some other interesting situations I won't bore you with.

Anyhow, during that 30-day period I went to as many homes and businesses as I could remember I had stolen from, and met with those various responses—and more. I have felt good all these years since that I did that, although I'm sure I didn't remember at the time all the homes and business I had stolen from.

What about the churches, the windows of which I had broken while I was still a pre-believer? Without exception, the Pastors or other people in charge the day I visited each church, told me I didn't need to pay for the windows to be replaced and that they would be praying for me as God continued to launch me into my new life! Wow, was I excited about that!

To this day, sometimes when we are driving here and there in Rapid City, I find myself pointing to a home or church and telling my wife that I remember having stolen from that home or having broken a window in that church. It's not a morbid recollection at all; rather, I am at peace that I made a serious attempt at restitution and repayment all those years ago.

Back to Spokane. That same summer, I received orders that I was to be transferred to an Air Force base in Newfoundland, Canada, in early January of the next year. So I spent from April 26th to early January of the next year as a new Jesus-believer being transformed by God there in Spokane, Washington. I have so many precious memories of those months in Spokane, and I'm still in touch with a few of my Jesus-believer friends I hung out with during that time.

Spokane was the place of my spiritual "nativity," and I always thank God for those early months of my new life I spent there. Years later, I drove through Spokane on a vacation trip and was overjoyed to be able to visit that first church I attended there, some other places I hung out, and Fairchild Air Force Base. I wept with joy like a baby at various times throughout the entire two days I was in Spokane. Great memories!

Here are a couple more of those memories I still treasure. Some friends and I went one summer evening to hear a "tent evangelist," whose name I don't even recall. I was still sort of new at this "new creation thing" and some of my old ways would surface now and then in those early months.

We actually went to that tent evangelist's meeting to mock and find fault with him and what he was doing. It turned out he was not merely an evangelist, but he was a "healing evangelist." At the time,

I couldn't stomach that kind of stuff so I went there to really check him out, mock him, and learn how he "faked" the healings.

I seated myself on a seat at the end of a row near the center aisle of the tent, only a few rows from the front—so I could really check things out and prove to myself that so-called healings by God were completely faked—just so the evangelist could bilk people out of their money.

When the evangelist called for people needing healing to come to the front, I was watching very closely every one who came forward down the center aisle. A little girl about 7 0r 8 years old wearing sort of a sundress walked past me as she was heading down the aisle; I noticed that the entire right side of her face, her arms, and her legs were horribly scarred from what I assumed were burns. I remember thinking to myself how was the evangelist going to fake her healing. A few moments later he laid his hands on the little girl and asked God to heal her.

From where I was sitting, I couldn't see clearly that anything at all was happening. But a few moments later as the little girl walked past me returning to her seat somewhere behind me, her skin—over every part of her body I could see—was as smooth as a newborn baby's skin! She passed by only 6-8 inches away from me. I was stunned! I couldn't deny what my eyes had seen. She had been completely healed! That shut up my mockery and fault-finding forever after, although I'm fully aware there have always been some healing charlatans around.

I was earning a little over $70 a month (in addition to my food, housing, free medical and dental care, uniform allowance, etc.) The first Sunday after my new birth experience the previous week, I walked into that church and something (SomeOne?) inside me told me to give 10% of that $70+ to God. I placed $7 in the collection plate and ever since that day I have given 10% (and sometimes more) of my income to God.

Nobody told me I had to, nobody taught me about tithing, no one coerced me to give. I simply "knew in my knower" that I should give God that $7. It was a joy and pleasure to do so that first Sunday morning in church, and it's been a joy and pleasure to do so ever since that very first Sunday I ever attended a church meeting as a new Jesus-believer.

Heart For Missions

Another memory surfaces just now. As mentioned previously, I had become an authentic Jesus-believer on April 26th. Only a few weeks after that happened, the church I had begun attending hosted and held an event called a "missions conference." I had no clue what that was. Having been reared as an atheist/agnostic, modern pagan, I hadn't even considered that there were other people in other parts of the world who needed to hear the Good News about Jesus' salvation from sin and death.

But since I had been so impressed by those 5 young missionaries slaughtered (I still didn't know what "martyred" meant) a few months earlier in January, I was excited to be able to attend something called a "missions" conference. I wasn't disappointed. It gave me a "heart for missions" that hasn't diminished to this day, many years later.

I've supported missionaries one way or another since then. Presently, Anne and I help support a young woman in Cambodia, providing some of her living and educational expenses and those of her family in a small fishing village in that nation.

We help support a man and his wife who work with believers in the underground church in the great nation of China and have opened up a medical clinic and a number of orphanages. We send some monthly support to an "underground seminary" in China.

We also support a Chinese national and his Canadian wife who work, serve, and minister to the Chinese people in central China. Anne and I were privileged to go to China a number of years ago to teach English there and minister and serve the Chinese people in various ways.

We also support some Jesus-believers who work in Israel, and send a small amount of support to the famed Wycliffe Bible Translators. I'm not trying to impress anyone by writing about our support for missions. We simply have a heart for missions that began many years ago at that missions conference at my first church in Spokane.

During that missions conference so many years ago, many missions-oriented songs were sung. One of them contained the words, *"Little is much when God is in it . . ."* I have found that to be true all these years. We cannot outgive God. We are never diminished when we give to God.

God always gives back to us at our points of need when we maintain a rhythm of sowing and reaping, giving and receiving, planting and harvesting. In fact, my second book I wrote a few years ago is all about giving to God; it's simply entitled **LIFEgiving.** Yes, I learned much from that missions conference I attended a couple of months after God had implanted his new, eternal LIFE in me and began transforming me into a brand-new person.

Another great memory of those months in Spokane is just now surfacing from my memory banks as I input these lines. I had occasion to attend for the first time what was billed as a "Christian" movie, being held in a large downtown church. I decided to check out the movie because I had seen plenty of the other kind. The movie was titled "Seventeen." It was a horrible movie. The actors were all amateurs, the acting was atrocious, the sets and lighting were very poorly done.

"What a waste!" I was feeling as the movie progressed. But then the main female actress—a young woman seventeen years old, hence the title—began to sing a song as part of the plot; I don't remember much about the plot—something about that girl being "called" to be an overseas missionary and all the struggles, loneliness, and hardships she would face on the mission field, but all being worthwhile because of so much Jesus had done for her. Something like that.

The words and music to the song the actress sang entitled *"Follow Me"* absolutely "broke" me inside. My heart just broke apart with compassion for "lost" people and for the harsh conditions under which many missionaries served in those years (for that matter some serve under even worse conditions to this day). Ever since I viewed that movie I've had a "soft spot" in my heart for missions and missionaries.

Years later, I attended another missions conference on a little island off the southern coast of Alabama. The missionary speaking at the conference all of a sudden burst out singing *"Follow Me,"* and once again my heart was *"broken with the things that break the heart of God!"* I keep the words and music to that song in my Daily Planner and often break out singing them while I'm writing, showering, or driving.

Okay, another memory has surfaced about those months in Spokane while God was rapidly at work in the early stages of transforming me to be like Jesus. While volunteering at the Christian Servicemen's Center downtown, the director, a young Marine veteran named Ron York, got me started memorizing Bible references using a method called the Topical Memory System developed by a man named Dawson Trotman who had recently established a worldwide Christian outreach ministry called The Navigators.

Speaking of the Servicemen's Center, I first encountered a phenomenon there that I've encountered only a few times since. A former Marine named Ron York was the Director of the Center. He was a very godly young man whom I came to greatly admire. He took a lot of time simply to be with me, to mentor and disciple me, to pray with me and for me.

I noticed something unique about Ron. I know this may sound a bit weird, but I could actually "see" Jesus in Ron, even to the point where he had a different "odor" about Him—like I could somehow "smell" Jesus on Ron. It was a sweet, kind of muted flowery scent he exuded. I can't explain it and I know it sounds weird, but it's true. I'm not writing about "seeing" and "smelling" Ron with my physical eyes and nose; it was a vague, hard-to-define spiritual reality that Ron exuded because He spent so much time with Jesus and much time spent in praying and fasting.

I've noticed the same phenomenon in only about a dozen or so other people I've met through the years—and, of course, I've met hundreds, even thousands, of Jesus-believers. But only a few of them have had that unique spiritual quality I'm attempting to describe. I could just tell immediately upon meeting them that they "had been with Jesus" in a unique way known by only those few I have run into here and there in my travels.

I have secretly prayed through the years that I might be one of those unique individuals who simply exude and "exhibit" Jesus in that kind of way. I don't know if I do exhibit Him that clearly or ever will during this mortal stage of my journey, but I can at least hope that in some inexplicable way other people can see Jesus in me in a unique manner. I pray daily for people to see Jesus wrapped in his "Bill Boylan skin."

Since that time I began memorizing Bible references under Ron York's tutelage and guidance, I have never stopped memorizing them, and right in front of me on my desk as I input these words into my computer is a box filled with 3 x 5 index cards on which I have written biblical references I'm currently memorizing.

Early every Sunday morning before I got to church, I go to a nearby McDonalds restaurant just as they open for business for the day, take my "memory box" with me, have a decaf latte with caramel or vanilla sauce, and spend a couple of hours reviewing my memorized biblical references—and any new ones I'm working on. So far, my old memory continues to serve me well, for which I am deeply grateful to God.

It all started many years ago during those early months of my new life in Spokane, Washington. The first Bible reference I ever memorized was Psalm 119: 9 – 11, very appropriate for those early days of my new life as a young Jesus-believer. Incidentally, both Ron York and Dawson Trotman died many years ago, but their ministries to military personnel and of memorizing Scripture references still live on in me. Thank you, Ron and Dawson for helping launch me into my new life!

Okay, okay, you talked me into it; a couple of more memories about Spokane and then I won't bore you anymore. But, this is my life story so I can write whatever I want to.

Mrs Lunde. What can I say? A plain, almost non-descript, "frumpy" woman who had something wrong with her eyes that drove to distraction anyone who was talking with her; her eyes bounced back and forth from side to side very rapidly, a medical condition which she was unable to control. She and I volunteered together at various times at the downtown Christian Servicemen's Center and for whatever reasons she sort of "adopted" me into her family, especially having me come to their home for dinner many Sunday afternoons after church.

They had an absolutely gorgeous daughter named Andrea who was a couple of years younger than me. No, I wasn't in "puppy love" with Andrea. But she was gorgeous—oh not physically, but something radiated from within her that reached out and captivated anyone who happened to be in her presence.

Truth be told, she was actually kind of homely, wore no makeup, kind of frumpy clothing, but that light radiating from within her compensated for any physical beauty she lacked. She was the first girl I ever looked at without lust. Years later, I found out that type of light radiating from within people was the "manifest presence" of God the Holy Spirit living within them and emanating from them.

My Love For Christian Music

The Lundes were a musical family. Every Sunday afternoon after a delicious home-cooked meal they would gather around their old upright piano and sing Christians songs, mostly in what I later learned was a "Southern Gospel" genre of music. At first I didn't like most of the music they sang and played because I felt it was sort of "hokey," but because I learned to love and appreciate the Lunde family's kindness to me, I finally began to listen—really listen—to the words and music.

The first Christian song I learned to appreciate and sing was the old southern Gospel song, *"I'll Fly Away,"* and I still sing it to this day. The second song I learned was entitled, *"When God Dips His Love In My Heart,"* and still sing it to this day, too. Neither of those songs are very theologically "correct," but I love them, nonetheless.

For that matter, much Christian music is theologically unsound, but it still ministers to me deep in my spirit in very profound and meaningful ways.

It was at the Lunde's home on those wonderful Sunday afternoons that my lifelong love for all types of Christian music began. Oh, there are a couple of types I really don't like, but I will listen to them . . . sometimes. Along with learning to memorize biblical references in those days, I also began a lifelong memorization of

Christian songs, ranging from medieval Gregorian chants, to the most recent types of worship and praise music.

I have a cassette tape and CD music library in my home that would rival that of a small Christian radio station. And I've memorized the words and music to hundreds of Christian songs through the years.

I even have the songs all picked out to be sung and played at my memorial service after I have died and gone to sleep in Jesus. Thank you, Mr and Mrs Lunde and Andrea, for introducing me to Christian music. Mr and Mrs Lunde died years ago and I have no clue whether or not Andrea is still alive or where she might be; nevertheless, on occasion I find myself praying for her—just for her wellbeing and ongoing growth and development as a Jesus-believer.

Female Jesus-Believers

Maybe, just maybe the following might be my final recollection about Spokane. Without going into any detail about my relationship with females in my old, B.C. (before Christ) life, suffice it to say that I did some things I probably shouldn't have done and certainly didn't respect females as I probably should have. After I had my first new-life "shower experience," something shifted inside me regarding my perceptions of females and I began to think of them much differently.

At church and at the Youth For Christ offices and meetings there were a number of physically attractive females my age who were Jesus-believers. They were different, and I was almost fearful of them as though they were too good to be true. Oh, I knew they were just human like everyone else, but there was something different about them; they seemed "clean" and "pure" without being "holier than thou." At first, I honestly didn't know how to relate to the Jesus-believer females my age.

But then I began to develop a brother-sister relationship with three of them: Bonnie Chamberlain, Carol Lohoefer, and Denise Olsen. I fell in love with Bonnie as a Christian sister—a brotherly love, not a man-woman type of love. It was so great for the first time in my life to have a female friend who was just a friend, not an object of my lust.

Bonnie and I and another airman friend, Bob McDonald, sort of hung out together and had lots of great times during those months in my 18th year—especially roller skating at the Wandermere Roller Skating rink outside of Spokane. I wonder if the place is still there. I did some pretty fancy roller skating there. Wonder if I could still skate as well?

I lost touch with Bob McDonald through the years, but finally located him about 25 years after we had first known one another. It turns out that Bob, although a Jesus-believer, had fallen prey to the disease of alcoholism and had almost destroyed his life for many years—until He returned as a "prodigal son" to his heavenly Father.

Years later, when I met and visited with him for a few hours, Bob was very withdrawn and non-communicative and it was not a very joyful reunion; I don't know why he was that way. I've again lost track of him and would love to get in touch with him again and renew our acquaintance and "fellowship" as Jesus-believers. Bob was a very significant person in my life during my months in Spokane; I know I'll see him again "over there," but I'd love to see him again here before that. I'll keep searching for him.

Bonnie always wore Estee Lauder perfume, and I had recently discovered the wonders of Old Spice After Shave Lotion! To this day, whenever I smell a particular Estee Lauder scent on a woman or the smell of Old Spice on a man, I am instantly drawn back to those wonderful days in Spokane during the early months of my new life.

And, during my childhood years being around my grandparents so much, my paternal grandfather, "Baba," used Bay Rum After Shave Lotion each morning after he shaved (with a straight razor!). Whenever I smell Bay Rum even today—years and years after the fact—I am reminded of Baba.

I still correspond with Carol Lohoefer mentioned above, but in her late teen years she was diagnosed with acute schizophrenia and it's been hard to communicate with her through the years. I tell her I love her as my Christian sister and pray regularly and consistently for her; hmmm, it's time I wrote to Carol again.

Denise Olsen was another matter. I fell in love with her—real boy-girl, man-woman love—and she with me. If circumstances had been much different or if we had been a few years older it's possible that Denise and I might even have married. We kissed and hugged a little, held hands, but nothing more than that. It was so nice to have a good friend like Denise whom I also loved in the normal manner—without the downward pull of illicit sex (what the Bible prohibits and terms "fornication").

Of necessity, Denise and I severed our relationship later that year when I received orders that I was to be transferred overseas. Through the years I lost track of Denise, but Bonnie and I (and Carol) have kept in touch all these years now and I just recently sent Bonnie and her husband, Eli, an e-mail updating how I'm faring. Bonnie's been a great friend all these years.

One other incident I want to relate about my time in Spokane is about a young man named John Birdsong (I've tried to locate him for many years, so far to no avail). John and I shared a two-man room together in our barracks for a few months and he became a Jesus-believer after I introduced him to Jesus. When I was promoted, making it possible for me to move into a one-man room, John became angry that I was "deserting him."

A few days after I moved into my new room, John knocked at my door. When I invited him in, he declined to enter and just said, *"Bill, I'm mad at you for deserting me, and I quit believing in Jesus!"*

That was my first encounter with Jesus-believers who (for whatever reason) simply decide to quit believing in Jesus. I've seen it happen again many times through the years and I simply don't understand how people can do that. I don't even believe "theologically" that it can be done, but I simply can't account for it and it remains one of my unanswered questions in this life.

Chapter Five

Ages Eighteen To Twenty-One

Transferred To Canada

As noted earlier, in the summer of my 18th year, I received notice that I was to be transferred to a new Education Office on an overseas base; it would involve a promotion for me so I was eager to go. But I had mixed feelings about leaving Spokane, the place of my "spiritual nativity."

Nevertheless, in early January of that year, I was transferred to Ernest Harmon Air Force Base, Newfoundland, a busy base for military aircraft flying back and forth to Europe; it was a stopping-off base for rest for the crews and refueling for aircraft flying to and from the United States and Europe. I arrived there on a cold, snowy day in January, just a few weeks before my 19th birthday. I remained there from early that year to May 23rd of my 21st year, when I was flown to Patterson Air Force Base, New Jersey, to be honorably discharged from the Air Force after almost a 4-year enlistment.

I enjoyed my work at the Education Office at my new base of assignment. Not only did I begin taking some college courses from the University of Maryland overseas program, but I also began teaching some remedial courses for personnel who were studying for their high school GED test and some other types of courses such as typing.

Meanwhile, I continued teaching the Bible from one-on-one, to classes that were held as part of the Base Chapel church school program. I continued my ravenous reading of the Bible—and attempting to obey what I was reading!—and memorizing various biblical references. God continued transforming the "new me," a process He had begun on April 26th of the previous year that morning in the shower.

We had a very active Jesus-believer chapel group at Ernest Harmon AFB—fellowshipping in the various barracks on base, studying together, praying together, being witnesses for our faith in Jesus, and volunteering to help people in the little village of Stephenville near the base.

Our little chapel group of Jesus-believers sort of "adopted" a large fishing family in Stephenville consisting of one mother, one father, and 29 children still living at home; 2 others had grown up and left home!

Yep, it's true—29 children still at home, in a little two-room cottage in the village. We took them food and clothing, introduced them to Jesus, helped them out in various ways when we had the time and ability. It was with them that I first began to learn and practice selfless service as a Jesus-believer, a practice I've tried to continue in various ways throughout all the years of my mortal pilgrimage.

An "older" Jesus-believer named Phil Baer, a higher-ranking sergeant, sort of took me under his wing to disciple and mentor me while I was in Newfoundland. I thank God for Phil! I lost track of him about ten years after I was discharged from the Air Force, but years later (in fact, only a few months ago) I finally got in touch with him through FaceBook on my computer. I was overjoyed to be in touch with him again; I had prayed for him all through the years and now to be back in touch with him is really exciting. Phil telephoned me just yesterday.

Let me tell you about Frank James and Kenny Wright. Frank was assigned to be my roommate a few months after I arrived in Newfoundland. One evening while we were just resting in our bunks, Frank looked at me, pointed his finger in my face, and said: *"Sergeant Boylan, I know you're one of those weird Jesus freaks. I don't like you. I don't like Jesus-believers. You're all as phony as a three–dollar bill. I'm gonna be watching you like a hawk day and night and you better be who you say you are!"*

Frankly, that sort of scared me that he would be scrutinizing my behavior that closely. I'm happy to report to you that a few months later, Frank had a "real" personal encounter with God like I had had a couple of year earlier in the shower. Frank became a growing, thriving Jesus-believer, and a welcome member of our little base chapel group of believers. A couple of years later, we met again at a famous Bible school in Chicago we were both attending. Frank was a tremendously gifted artist and he was using that gift from God in very creative ways as an illustrator for Christian literature.

Now I'm introducing you to Kenny Wright. He, too, was transferred into my barracks about the same time Frank James had been. Kenny was a tiny little fellow; just barely tall enough and heavy enough to meet the minimum physical requirements for enlisting in the Air Force. He seemed very frail and fragile—not a real "man's man" in the eyes of most people. Kenny had an encounter with Jesus similar to what Frank James and I had experienced, and he began to grow so "huge" spiritually that it was just awesome to see it happening right before our eyes.

That tiny, frail little guy became a "spiritual giant"—and what a delight it was to watch it happen and to be part of his transformation. I lost track of Kenny, but I understand he later became a very influential Presbyterian Pastor somewhere in New Jersey where he came from originally. I still pray for Kenny, too. And from time to time I type his name into Facebook's search engine to see if I can locate him.

While in Newfoundland, I had my first encounter with non-believing "believers." The Chaplain of our little chapel group arranged for us to go on a "retreat" (I've always felt they should be called "advances," instead) to a conference grounds at a remote radar site somewhere on the north end of the island of Newfoundland. We arrived there very excited, looking forward to the speaker who had been invited to be in charge of the retreat. He was another Chaplain flown in from the United States mainland to be our retreat leader.

The more he spoke to us and taught us, I began to perceive in my spirit that something was wrong, that something was missing, that his teachings were sort of "one bubble off level." I later learned that even though he was a Chaplain he was not even a Jesus-believer and did not believe the Bible was God's written revelation of Himself.

Actually, toward the middle of the Retreat, he disclosed that he was an agnostic and wasn't even sure he believed in God. Why he chose to be a Chaplain, I'll never know. That was my very first encounter with a "false teacher." He almost fooled us because we were mostly young Jesus-believers, but some of the more mature, older believers in the group knew what was going on and challenged what he was teaching us. Actually, they ran him off, and about midway through the retreat, he boarded a small aircraft and flew back to the States.

Thereafter, for the remainder of our retreat, the fifty or so airmen who were there had a great time reading, studying and sharing transforming truths and insights from the Bible all by ourselves under the leadership of some of the more mature Jesus-believers; we shared what God was doing in our lives, sang great Gospel songs, ate great food, and prayed together. Yep, it was really a great time after we got rid of that non-Jesus-believer Chaplain.

Overweight

I'm going to reveal something about me now that most people don't believe. I have a propensity to gain weight very rapidly and to be greatly overweight, almost morbidly obese.

When I tell that to people, their reaction is that I'm lying to them or joking, but it's no joke. When I enlisted in the Air Force at age seventeen, I weighed 112 pounds. While in the Air Force, I gained some weight and maintained it at about 140 pounds. The last six months or so before I was discharged from the Air Force at age 21 I experienced a very rapid weight gain and once weighed close to 200 pounds.

I am slight of frame and build, so 200 pounds is very heavy for me. As I was working hard to lose that weight before I was discharged, I found the only way I could do it was not to eat—or to eat very little. Later, one time I experimented with eating all I wanted to eat, and again my weight shot up very rapidly.

At that time I realized I must have some sort of metabolic health challenge that caused me to gain weight rapidly. What to do? I made a commitment to God at that time that I would simply stop eating all I wanted to—generally eating only one meal a day, sometimes two, rarely three. It's the only way I've ever found to maintain my weight at approximately 150 pounds which seems to be my "ideal" weight.

When I tell people this about me, most of them respond with, *"Bill, don't you get hungry eating so little food?"* My response: *"Yes, I'm hungry all the time; every waking moment of my life I'm hungry!"* But the only way I can deal with this weight challenge is not to eat . . . or eat much less than I desire.

Right now as I'm inputting these words into my computer, it's early morning. For breakfast in an hour or so, I'd like to eat a half dozen large pancakes, 4 or 5 big sausages and 3 or 4 eggs, with 3 or 4 slices of toast slathered with real butter and heaped with jam. That's what I'd like to eat. What will I really have for breakfast? A 10-ounce fruit smoothie! That's certainly not want I want to eat, but that's what I'll have.

Starting today, if I let myself eat anything I craved, I could easily weigh 225 pounds within 3 or 4 months. Honestly! So, I just don't eat. Throughout the remainder of my day today, I will probably have no lunch at all or perhaps a small piece of cheese and some dried apple slices. Then for supper ("dinner" to you sophisticates) we'll probably have fish, some vegetables, and a tossed salad.

That's not at all what I want to have—what I crave—but I made a commitment to God many years ago that I would not be obese, and not eating—or eating very little—is the only way I've been able not to become obese. In addition to eating very little, I often fast from time to time, but that's another story.

What would I like to have for supper today? A 10-ounce, one inch thick filet mignon, a huge baked potato slathered in butter and sour cream, a heaping helping of vegetables, two or three dinner rolls, and a huge bowl of ice cream smothered in caramel and nuts for dessert.

That's my weight story, and I'm stickin' to it!

Chapter Six

Ages Twenty-One to Twenty-Four

Let's now move forward to May 23rd of my 21st year. As mentioned above, I was transferred to Patterson Air Force Base, New Jersey, to be honorably discharged. That happened very uneventfully and I returned to South Dakota to spend the summer as a tour guide at a small, working gold mine, a tourist attraction in the Black Hills, before heading to Chicago in September to attend the famed Moody Bible Institute (MBI), billed as the "West Point of Christian Service."

Moody offered a three-year "General Bible Studies" program, but I only attended the program for a year and a half. It was s-o-o-o enlightening and refreshing to study all about the Bible under learned and gifted men and women professors.

The very first thing every incoming student had to do—no matter what program they were enrolled in—was memorize within one week the names—in order—of all 66 books of the Bible and spell them correctly! If we didn't memorize them within one week of beginning our studies at Moody, we were "washed out" of the West Point of Christian Service. It was a challenge, but I completed the task of memorizing them and I can still rattle them off to this day.

I wonder if Moody still maintains that policy; I hope so. I am s-o-o-o disappointed at the numbers of Jesus-believers I've known through the years who haven't memorized the names of the books of the Bible so they can find them readily, but that disappointment is my own little idiosyncracy.

Just last evening, one of the many traveling musical groups from Moody Bible Institute appeared in Rapid City for a concert during their nationwide spring tour this year. It was so great to just bask in the rich, familiar music they presented and to remember back to my brief time studying at MBI.

During the concert, my thoughts roamed far afield. First, I mused about my friend, Jon Trimble, sitting next to me in the audience. He was sixty years old; he had received God's salvation into his life just three years before. I have spent the last two years teaching him a Bible overview course similar to that I had learned so many years before at MBI. I wondered what Jon's life might have been like had he attended a school such as MBI in his younger years.

As I looked at all the "bright, bushy-tailed" (as one of my grandfathers used to say) young musicians, I wondered if there might be another Bill Boylan in the ensemble. A couple of the young men even looked similar to how I looked when I had studied at Moody. I wondered if one of them might have a wonder-full life ahead of them similar to mine. If one of them who looked a little like me might have a worldwide teaching ministry some day . . .

I wondered if in lighter moments the students still sat around in the library, cafeteria, and in their dorm rooms calling the school "Insty Mible Bubitute"? Yes, many wonderful memories surfaced about the rich time I spent at Moody Bible Institute.

After the concert, I visited with some of the young people in the musical ensemble. While visiting, I asked them if they still sang the old school song written almost a hundred years ago by one of the early presidents of MBI. I had loved that song then, and still sing it on occasion to this day. They responded that they not only continued to sing that grand old song, but one of the black students in MBI's music program had re-written the song as a modern rap song! They told me to look it up on YouTube.

Wow, YouTube and rap music! MBI has come a long way since I studied there years ago, writing my lessons on slate, using chalk . . . and in the flickering, dim light of old, smoky oil lamps, I read and studied the Bible written on parchment scrolls. And students had to kill our own game, butcher it, and cook it over campfires while warding off marauding natives . . .

Some of the words to that old school song are surfacing as I write these words:

"God, bless the school that D. L. Moody founded;
Firm may she stand though by foes of truth surrounded.
Riches of grace bestowed may she never squander—
Keeping true to God and man her record over yonder.

Glory over yonder, over yonder;
When Jesus comes in glory we shall part no more!

Glow In The Dark

I must back up a little now and tell you my "glow in the dark story," to show you a few, very strange events that have occurred in my life. First, I remind you that as a child I had lived in Oak Ridge, Tennessee, one of the three "atomic cities" in the War Department's Manhattan project tasked to develop and create the first atomic bomb.

Not very much was known in those days about the harmful effects of prolonged exposure to nuclear radiation. Thirty years or so later, when previously secret, classified records were released to the general public, it was disclosed that almost all the family members living in Oak Ridge during those years had been exposed to various amounts of radiation; in fact, family members were nicknamed "Downwinders."

Now fast forward to the time I spent at Fairchild Air Force Base near Spokane, Washington. Spokane was located not very far from another of those three atomic cities, Hanford, Washington. We didn't think much about it at time, but on occasion some "scientific looking" people would come to our chow halls and put some sort of red liquid substances in our drinking water; we assumed it was some sort of water purification experiment. Once, one of the officers in charge of the chow halls let it slip that it was some sort of radiated substance they were placing in our drinking water to test its effects on human beings.

Years later, when I submitted a claim for partial disability related to those experiments, the records of such activities had been sealed and I could never find anyone who would admit to such experiments. I even joined a class action suit against the government in an attempt to get the records unsealed, but it all came to naught.

Fast forward once more. I was now stationed at Ernest Harmon Air Force Base in Newfoundland, Canada. All administrative personnel such as I was at the time, were constantly placed "on alert" to go to the flight line at all hours of the day and night to stand guard over the unloaded contents of large aircraft, including the formidable B-36 Bomber.

Remember, this was during the early years of the very real Cold War. When we were on the flight line guarding those aircraft and their cargoes, we were exposed to all sorts of weird junk such as liquids that leaked from big drums, some sort of gaseous substances, and, most likely, some degree of nuclear radiation from the nuclear bombs being loaded and unloaded. I remember many nights on the flight line standing in leaked liquid chemicals right next to huge nuclear bombs, crates, barrels, and pallets containing items that were sort of "rumbling" and "hissing." It was very strange and almost surrealistic.

While I was stationed in Newfoundland I began to develop all sorts of weird environmental allergies that plague me to this day. Upon my discharge from the Air Force, when I attempted to submit a disability claim, I was "warned" to back off from pursuing my claim and not stir up any trouble, although to mollify me, the Veterans Administration did grant me a token disability percentage, stating that my immune system has somehow been compromised, but they would not admit that it was possible exposure to nuclear radiation that compromised my immune system.

When I tell people this story about my possible exposure to radiation on at least three occasions, I tell them that in the dark, I glow bright green! I have never been able to prove a case that my severe environmental allergies have anything to do with possible exposure to CBR (chemical, biological, and radiological substances) on those 3 occasions beginning when I lived in Oak Ridge as a child "downwinder."

I feel my propensity to gain weight very rapidly is also related to such exposure, but I have never been able to prove it.

Back to my time at Moody after my discharge from the Air Force; it was challenging, to say the least. Every student was required to perform various Christian service projects while a student there. I preached in parks, went door to door sharing Jesus with people, taught Sunday School at the famed Pacific Garden Mission (we had to go around on Sunday mornings to the housing projects and actually get our students out of bed, feed them, dress them, and take them to and from the Mission on busses), and shared Jesus at the huge downtown Christian Servicemen's Center.

That year and a half was a time of tremendous spiritual growth and development for me as God continued his work of transforming me and restoring me into his clear image as best seen in Jesus, the perfect image of God.

During that time I was also highly privileged to attend the world-famed Moody Memorial Church, pastored by noted Scottish theologian and orater, Alan Redpath. Once again, I was also exposed to Christian missions, both at church and at school, meeting missionaries serving Jesus all around the world. Also, it was my first exposure to what was later termed "Incarnational Theology," a generalized view of God and his loving, eternal relationship with all humanity I've espoused ever since.

I was also exposed to noted teachers and theologians from around the world who came to teach short-term at Moody. In addition, students at Moody came from all over the world and from every possible denomination, theological persuasion, and background. I began to learn how "huge" the worldwide Body of Jesus—the Church—was, transcending all denominations and theological and geographical limitations and boundaries.

Speaking of "theology," let me give you a "down and dirty" definition of the word so you'll know what I mean by the word. *Theology is a person's understanding about God.* In one sense or another, everyone is a "theologian," even atheists and agnostics.

Ever since my attendance at Moody, I have been very eclectic—yet orthodox (whatever that means)—in my own theology and beliefs, realizing how extremely diverse the Body of Jesus is, yet how much true unity there is in such diversity. Okay, I admit to it—you found me out: I am a little unorthodox, too, as well as being eclectic.

Okay, okay, actually I'm pretty much a "happy heretic" (whatever "heresy" is). My time at Moody was great and I thank God almost every day that I was so privileged during that time. Thereafter, I have felt at home in almost any church or denominational setting you can imagine—from grass huts to great cathedrals.

Sharon Lee Smith

Now the "biggy" during my time at Moody. I met a beautiful young classmate named Sharon Smith, from Oak Forest, Illinois, a suburb of Chicago. I was completely smitten by her and it wasn't long after I finished my studies (and then worked at Moody in their printing department for a year or so) that Sharon and I got married in her home Baptist Church in Oak Forest, Illinois, a suburb south of Chicago.

After our wedding, we moved into a second-floor apartment in Oak Park, another suburb west of Chicago. Our few months living in Oak Park, attending a nearby Baptist Church, sharing Jesus together in various settings—including teaching an adult Sunday School class at our church, were idyllic years I will treasure forever. We visited zoos, museums, and nice restaurants and just fell in love with Chicago and its environs.

Chapter Seven

Ages Twenty-Four to Twenty-Seven

It wasn't long, however, before we began to believe that God was leading us back to South Dakota for me to earn a bachelor's degree at the University of South Dakota in Vermillion South Dakota, at the opposite end of the state from my ancestral home in Piedmont and Rapid City. We arrived in Vermillion in August of the 24th year of my earthly pilgrimage. Right away we got settled into our little on-campus married students' apartment housing, and I buckled down to my studies in history, psychology, language arts, and secondary education. Sharon worked in the Business School office on campus, only a brief walk away from our apartment.

We found a little church out in the country about 10 miles north of Vermillion, Dalesburg Baptist Church, where many on-campus Jesus-believer students attended. We were warmly received there as well as by various families in Vermillion. Right away, we met Ronnie Sampson, a young man from Vermillion who had recently fallen from an electrical pole and was recovering on Worker's Compensation.

Ronnie and I became dear friends and we've stayed in pretty close touch through the years; in fact, we spoke on the telephone just yesterday morning. We both quipped at how we're "old'ern dirt" now, but still hanging in there, still moving "deeper" into our relationship with God, still awaiting Jesus' return to earth to establish his peaceful Kingdom. I still take joy in the fact that I was able to help

Ronnie study for and pass his high school GED test and complete at least one college course while we lived in Vermillion—something he felt he would never be able to do.

Friends Who've Died

I keep in my Bible next to a text in the book of First Thessalonians, chapter 4, verse 13 (you'll have to look that up) a list of various Jesus-believer friends who have died since I became a believer myself. I began keeping that all-too-lengthy list while I was at the University of South Dakota; the first two names on the list are Elvin Hoeg and Kenny Lindstrom. As noted, that list is all too lengthy these days; I've added four more names in just the past 3 months.

I don't like the fact that list is growing so lengthy, but, on the other hand, it simply means I have that many more friends on "the other side" to greet me and welcome me home when I finally arrive at my true home—a wondrous land of beauty no mortal eye has ever seen.

I was graduated mid-term from the University of South Dakota in January, late into my 27th year here on planet earth. I spent the remaining spring semester taking graduate courses in psychology and behavioral science.

Death Of Heather Lee

Also, late that January our first baby was born. She lived only a few minutes, but we had time to name her Heather Lee and I fell instantly and deeply in love with her, although I was able to hold her only for an instant. I have missed her all these years and pray for her almost daily. I am assured she is in Jesus' Kingdom with him and is likely now a beautiful young woman appearing to be in her mid-thirties by our solar time reckoning.

I look forward to seeing her again so much that sometimes I can hardly stand it. I continually picture her in my mind and wonder what she's doing. She was my firstborn, and I love her deeply and dearly. I long to see the look on her face when she finally meets her two younger sisters, Robin and Rachel, and her younger brother, Joel.

A few other memory highlights come to mind about my time at the University of South Dakota.

First, while we were at the University an old-fashioned "revival" broke out among the student body, and, as a result, hundreds of students became new Jesus-believers. One of the results of the revival was that we officially formed and incorporated the University Christian Fellowship (UCF), with a Jesus-believing faculty member, Dr Howard Coker, becoming our faculty advisor, with me as the president of the fellowship.

The revival also resulted in teams of Jesus-believer students fanning out within about a 150-mile radius to carry the good news about Jesus to homes, community centers, churches, and schools throughout eastern South Dakota, northwestern Iowa, northeastern Nebraska, and southwestern Minnesota, resulting in an even greater "harvest of souls."

Another thing to come out of the on-campus revival was that I was invited on various occasions to debate some of the professors about the theory of evolution. By God's grace and imparted wisdom I was able to "win" most of those debates and sharply hone my skills at debating.

The Death Of My Best Friend In All The World!

On March 18th of that spring semester in 1963 while I was taking graduate work, we received news that my sister Barbara Lee (Bobbie) had been killed in a car wreck deliberately caused by her former husband. Bobbie had been my best friend and confidante for 25 years and I was deeply saddened and pained by her death. To this day I think of her almost every day and still miss her terribly.

I still find myself often asking what Bobbie might think about this or that question or situation. As with my firstborn daughter, Heather Lee, I have full assurance from God that I will meet and greet Bobbie again when I am awakened from the sleep of death upon Jesus' return to earth to establish his Kingdom. Sometimes, I get very, very homesick to go to my true home to be with Bobbie as well as Heather.

I just visited Bobbie's grave a couple of days ago. I go there quite often just to remember her, think about her, wonder what she's doing now, what she looks like.

Also, while a student at the University, I was often asked to speak and teach in various outlying churches in the area. One church in particular in a small community about 15 miles from Vermillion even invited and "called" me to be their probationary Pastor until I was graduated, after which time they would officially ordain me as a Pastor in their denomination. My wife and I prayed much about that and finally determined that was not part of God's future plans and purposes for us.

I often have wondered through the years what might have happened to me and where I might have been today had I accepted that "call" to become a Pastor. I probably would have ended up as a Pastor in one of that denomination's large churches in either Minneapolis or Chicago where most of their Pastors ended up as they progressed through normal "promotional" opportunities. I think I might have made a good full-time Pastor, but that was not to be.

Two final matters concerning my time in Vermillion, South Dakota, at the University of South Dakota.

As mentioned earlier, immediately after I became a newly created Jesus-believer, I instinctively knew that God wanted me to begin giving him 10% of my income. I continued to do that through the years—and still do so. One Friday evening while at the university, God "spoke" to my wife and me to give away all the remaining groceries in our small apartment's kitchen.

There weren't many, but we packed them up and gave them to another student and his wife and baby who lived in the same student housing complex. That meant we couldn't purchase any more food until Monday afternoon when my wife would receive her paycheck. We knew we wouldn't starve to death that weekend, but we were sort of concerned about how hungry we might become.

We went to bed Friday night trusting God that He would either provide us with something to eat that weekend or simply help us get through the weekend without any food. Early Saturday morning while we were still in bed, there was a knock at our door. Bleary-eyed, I stumbled to the door and there stood a woman from our church with two large bags of groceries in her arms.

She informed us that God had told her to get up early and bring us some groceries. With that said, she handed the bags to me and walked off! Coincidence, or groceries from a loving, caring, concerned Father? You decide.

Incidentally, someone once told me there are no coincidences with God. That's not entirely accurate if you think of coincidences in terms of "co-incidents orchestrated by God."

The "Charismatic Renewal"

'Nuther Side Bar: A few years before we moved from Chicago to Vermillion we began to hear rumors of some sort of nationwide "charismatic revival" breaking out in various places throughout USAmerica among mainline churches and businessmen, having originated with a Father Dennis Bennett at St Luke's Episcopal Church in Seattle, Washington, and among some Catholic college students at Notre Dame University in Indiana. We had no clue what a "charismatic revival" or outbreak was, but we wanted to remain open to whatever God might have in store for us.

Somewhat simultaneously, that same type of revival had broken out among New York City gangs under the ministry of a young country preacher, David Wilkerson, from Pennsylvania, who felt God had "called" him to go to New York and work among the gangs there. We learned that David Wilkerson had even written a book recently that was just then appearing in bookstores and on newsstands.

That leads me to another matter I want to share with you about those years in Vermillion. Word reached us that there was to be a major Billy Graham Crusade in Omaha, Nebraska, about 125 miles south of Vermillion. Some of us Jesus-believers in the UCF felt God wanted us to attend the crusade as counselors. We received a few weeks of training in Vermillion and then set out in a caravan of cars for Omaha. Upon arrival there, we checked into a cheap hotel (remember, we were poor, starving students in those days!).

One night during the Billy Graham Crusade, I was restless in our hotel room and for some reason just couldn't get to sleep. I decided to get up, get dressed, and go to the bus terminal across the street and have some hot tea or a soft drink. While there, I thumbed through the books at a bookstand. There in front of my eyes was a book with the title, *The Cross and the Switchblade,* subtitled *The Thrilling True Story of a Country Preacher's fight Against Crime on the Streets of New York.* The book's author? David Wilkerson!

I purchased the book, and then stayed up the rest of the night reading it. I could scarcely believe what I was reading. David wrote matter-of-factly about events occurring in New York; they were just like those events which had occurred in the Book of Acts in the Bible: miracles, supernatural occurrences, people speaking in tongues, supernatural provision for God's workers, and the like.

The book was either full of lies or I was holding in my hands something I had never heard of before occurring in the twentieth century. I had been taught—and believed—that such miraculous, supernatural events and experiences had ceased in the worldwide church by about the year 100 A.D. and would never again occur in church history. What was I to believe now?!

Shortly thereafter, Dennis Bennett wrote a book entitled *Nine O'Clock in the Morning* about the same types of miraculous events, incidents, and experiences occurring there in Seattle and throughout the nation. I was confused because of my theological background, but was open to whatever God might have in store for me in my future service, teaching, and ministry. Little did I know what God had in store for me within the next year or so.

Chapter Eight

Ages Twenty-Seven To Thirty

Now I bring you to the fall following my January graduation with a B.A. degree and a newly issued secondary teaching certificate in my hand. We had applied for a teaching position for me with about a dozen schools scattered around the nation, trusting that God would open up for us the one He wanted us to take.

That August we found ourselves pulling a U-Haul trailer back to the Chicago area where I had been hired by a middle school in Harvey, Illinois, a suburb south of Chicago. My beginning annual salary was a humungous $4,900, good money for that era! I had been hired to teach language arts and social sciences to 6th, 7th, and 8th graders.

I didn't know at the time I was hired that it was an all-black school with me being the first "token white" teacher in the school. Don't misunderstand me; that wasn't a bad thing by any means. It just was. It proved to be a tremendous teaching experience during my four years there.

Most of my students were second-generation black children whose parents had moved from the housing projects and slum areas on the near southside of Chicago to the southern suburbs. My students were extremely well-behaved, motivated, friendly, outgoing. It was a great experience. Many of their parents sort of "adopted" Sharon and me and we were often invited to backyard barbecues, dinners, and to their churches.

We chose to attend a Baptist Church in the nearby community of Chicago Heights. While there, a "revival" broke out in our church. I still don't understand why and how revivals occur. I know that some churches actually "schedule" what they term revivals in the fall of each year. I know the dictionary definition of "revive," but I just don't understand much about revival. I'm just grateful to have been privileged to be part of various revivals through the years.

I guess about all I understand about them is that God sovereignly causes them to occur in response to prayer and a deep hunger in his children for a deeper relationship with God.

I became a licensed Deacon and licensed Lay Minister and Preacher in that little Baptist Church, as well as an adult Sunday School teacher. God even used me to start a telephone visitation program which we called "Televisitation." As far as I can determine it might have been the first program of its kind in the entire nation. I was continuing to grow and learn by reading, studying, and obeying! my Bible and attempting to cooperate with the Holy Spirit as He continued to transform me inside by applying the Bible to my life.

Robin Elizabeth Born!

A highlight of our time on the south side of Chicago was that our oldest daughter, Robin Elizabeth, was born on September 12th. Two parents couldn't have been more excited, especially after having lost Heather Lee a year or so earlier. Robin is still my little "baby girl" and I will always love her deeply and dearly even though she's no longer a baby now, but a grown, married woman. Robin lives in Wall, South Dakota, about 50 miles east of Rapid City and I get to have lunch with her next Wednesday! Yay!

Since the time I had become an authentic Jesus-believer in that shower years earlier, I had often wrestled with the question of whether or not God might someday "call" me to be in full-time ministry, whatever that really meant. During those years in the Chicago area, after years of pondering the matter and praying about it, I finally concluded that was not what God had in mind for me, and I never questioned it again, although from time to time I had opportunities to become a full-time servant of God.

I made a deliberate choice to remain bi-vocational for the remainder of my life and God has honored that decision. That is not to say He doesn't call others to full-time ministry, just not me. And I'm content with that.

I just used the term "bi-vocational": our Pastor preached a sermon recently that in light of the fact that we have one foot here on earth, so to speak, and another foot in Jesus' coming Kingdom, we are also "bi-locational" beings, too. Just a thought I felt like sharing with you who are reading these words. So, I'm both bi-vocational and bi-locational.

Once again, as already noted, I continued teaching the Bible and related subjects in various settings. I had the privilege of working—"counseling"—at another Billy Graham Crusade held in Chicago. As noted above, I knew by this time that God wasn't going to call me to full-time ministry, but I would remain a "tentmaker" to support myself (as Paul was an actual tentmaker in the New Testament, continuing to be bi-vocational). I had opportunity to speak in various churches on the far south side of Chicago and serve God in other ways, as well as by continuing to teach.

Baptism In The Holy Spirit

As mentioned previously, a mid-twentieth century phenomenon called "The Charismatic Renewal" began almost simultaneously in three locations: Seattle, Washington, New York City, and at Notre Dame University in Indiana in the late 1950's and early 1960's—and continues to this day. That event was preceded by a similar event a generation or so earlier that began in a livery barn on Azusa Street in Los Angeles in 1906, called "The Modern Day Pentecostal Outpouring of the Holy Spirit."

They both involved an encounter with God termed "the Baptism in the Holy Spirit" mentioned 4 times in the Gospels in the New Testament and experienced by many Jesus-believers in the early Church in the Book of Acts following the Gospels.

After a major, tectonic shift in my personal theology that took a number of years to change, God primed my inner being and prepared me for that Charismatic Renewal to happen in my own life;

God had plowed up the fallow ground of my inner being and the soil was ripe for planting the "seed" of my own baptism in the Holy Spirit.

After first hearing about the Charismatic Renewal, however, I dragged my heels for almost 5 years, because of some anti-charismatic teachings I had learned early in my new life as a Jesus-believer. After having worked through that negative teaching, one day, however, I decided to sort of put God to the test concerning my own potential baptism in the Holy Spirit.

Here's what I foolishly did. An Episcopal laywoman, Mrs Jean Stone, had been baptized in the Holy Spirit and was traveling around the nation teaching and assisting other people to have that experience. She also published a short-lived magazine titled *Acts 29* (Get it? The biblical book of Acts has only 28 chapters) which I had been reading for a number of months. It contained testimonials of ordinary people like me who were being baptized in the Holy Spirit all around the world.

I knew at that time Mrs Stone was holding meetings up and down the west coast of the United States and was solidly booked up in that area for the next few months. She was heavily scheduled on the west coast; I was living in the Chicago area. It was highly unlikely—next to impossible—that she would visit the Chicago area any time soon.

One cold, windy February day while praying, I "told" God: *"Here's the deal, God; if Mrs Stone were to somehow magically be in the Chicago area next week, I will let you baptize me in the Holy Spirit!"* How foolish of me to have challenged God in that manner. He takes great delight in orchestrating all sorts of miraculous encounters we feel are impossible.

This is an important point: I seldom, if ever, purchased and read the Sunday edition of *The Chicago Tribune*. But one Sunday I felt compelled to purchase a copy on the way home after church. When I sat down to glance through it Sunday afternoon (the *Tribune* is a very thick paper), I noticed a tiny, inch-square ad down in the lower right hand corner of the left page I was glancing at about halfway through the main section of the paper.

Have any idea what that little ad said? It read something like this: *"Mrs Jean Stone, noted Episcopal laywoman, will be in the Chicago area one night only while she is passing through this area enroute to the east coast. She will be speaking at 7: 30 p.m. at the _______ church. Please call_____________ for more information."*

Have any idea where the church was located where she would be speaking that very evening? It was a little "Pentecostal" church only a few blocks away from where we were then living! What can I say? I had made God a seemingly impossible challenge; He took me up on my challenge. I almost decided not to go and hear Mrs Stone that evening, but at the very last minute I decided to face the bitter cold and the blustery wind, left my home, and began walking down the street to that little church.

There were perhaps three dozen people there; Mrs Stone was sort of a dull, bland, dry speaker, not displaying much enthusiasm. As she spoke I was experiencing a wide range of feelings: I was amazed at what God had done to get both of us there that evening, but disappointed that Mrs Stone wasn't more flamboyant and more of a polished speaker; I was frightened God would baptize me in the Holy Spirit, yet I desperately wanted Him to do so; I was embarrassed to be there in that little nondescript church, yet had a sense of anticipation that something very notable was about to happen to me.

When Mrs Stone concluded her brief message, she said something like this: *"If you're interested in being baptized in the Holy Spirit tonight, I'll be walking among you where you're seated, placing my hands on you and praying for you to receive the baptism in the Holy Spirit; and then you will begin speaking in a language you have not learned as initial evidence that you have been baptized in the Holy Spirit.*

So, if you're interested in being baptized in the Holy Spirit, please raise your hand and keep it up until I get to you. The minute I remove my hands from your head and stop praying for you, open your mouth and begin speaking your new language as evidence of your baptism in the Holy Spirit."

I was thinking, *"That's it? That's what it's all about? No flashes of lightning and rolling thunder? No voices out of the clouds? No earth tremors? This can't be what this 'baptism in the Holy Spirit thing' I've been thinking and praying about for a few years is all about."*

Down the aisle came Mrs Stone heading right for me. She laid her hands on my head, prayed a brief prayer for me in English, and told me to open my mouth and begin speaking my new language. Panic! I wasn't "hearing" any new language in my mind and thoughts. What could I do? So, I just uttered one sound, "*Gluggghhh.*" She excitedly exclaimed, *"That's it! That's your first word in your new language, just as a young infant utters its first word; keep practicing your new language!"*

You can't possibly feel the disappointment I felt at that moment. I had expected bells and whistles, flashing blue and red lights, voices from the sky, angelic choirs singing around me—stuff like that—and here I had uttered one, non-sensical sound, and that woman had the audacity to say that was the first word of my new, supernatural, spiritual language. Mrs Stone made a few closing remarks and then the Pastor of the little church dismissed us for the evening.

I began to walk home completely dejected and disappointed—in Mrs Stone, in God, in everything, but as I approached my door—I was perhaps 100 yards away—all of a sudden I opened my mouth and what sounded like a sentence or two in a strange language came out of my mouth. Then a couple of more sentences, then a few more, then what sounded like a paragraph, then two paragraphs, then more. All in the space of perhaps just a minute or so. As the saying goes, the rest is history.

The least I can say is that my life began to change dramatically after I was baptized in the Holy Spirit. Life became very "supernaturally natural" instead of merely natural. Almost daily I began to experience supernatural events in my life after my baptism in the Holy Spirit that cold February evening—experiences which continue almost daily, even today, many years later.

During that era in my life, an international organization of Christian businessmen had formed as a result of the charismatic outbreak of the Holy Spirit; it was named The Full Gospel Businessmen's Fellowship, International (FGBMFI). There was a large chapter in Chicago which I joined, and we experienced and witnessed many, many supernatural miracles through the outreach of the Chicago chapter of FGBMFI during those years in the Chicago area.

As a matter of fact, I organized and incorporated a new FGBMFI chapter on the southside of Chicago and was elected its first president.

At this point in writing this book, I had to make a serious quality decision. What decision? Should I include some teaching about the Holy Spirit in this main section of the book, or should I place it in the back as Appendix One. After giving it a great deal of consideration . . . and praying about it, it seems that God wants me to make it an Appendix.

However, I really, really, really want you to read the Appendix, because it also contains a lot of my own personal experience as part of my autobiography. Some of my personal, autobiographical experiences are interspersed and woven throughout the teaching. Please don't neglect reading the Appendix; if you do, you'll miss out on a lot of personal information I want you to know about me as part of this autobiography.

In fact, what I'd like you to do is stop right here, read the Appendix, and then come right back here to this point in the book. Will you do that for me? I hope so.

Churches In Homes

One final matter concerning those years in the Chicago area. Let's jump across the Pacific Ocean to China in the 1930's and 1940's. God made a new creation-man out of a humble Chinese man and began to use him in wondrous ways to teach the Bible and preach throughout China during those decades.

His anglicized name was Watchman Nee. Among other things that God did through that humble Chinese Jesus-believer is He used Watchman Nee to give birth to the "House Church" movement in that great nation—a vast network of churches that met in homes rather than in church buildings. God used that movement to essentially save the entire Chinese Church during the Communist takeover in 1949 and in subsequent years of Communist rule.

By the time I began to hear about Watchman Nee, he had become a prolific writer and many of his books and other literature were beginning to be translated into English and other languages.

Little did I know when I began reading some of his books while I was in the Chicago area that Watchman Nee had already spent a number of years in solitary confinement in a cold, damp, dirty Chinese prison—after first having had his tongue and both hands cut off so he could no longer teach or write! He died a lonely death in that prison only a few years after my years in the Chicago area.

In China, Watchman Nee—following the pattern of Jesus—had a following of 70 close disciples or "trainees," with 12 of them being his "inner circle" of disciples just as Jesus had an inner circle of 12 disciples from among his 70 disciples. When Watchman Nee was imprisoned, those 70 disciples were scattered throughout China and other countries.

One of them, Witness Lee, came to the United States and was ministering and teaching in the Chicago area while I was there. I began to read and study some of his teachings—and listen to him speak—and read more of Watchman Nee's writings which I felt were solidly biblically based.

From way back in the early days of my new life as a Jesus-believer I had begun to develop a feel for worship, ministry, and service outside the four walls of traditional churches. I liked the warm atmosphere and closeness of meeting with other believers in homes and small groups.

Not that I disdained regular types of institutional church worship, but I simply came to like best meeting, teaching, sharing, singing, praying, celebrating communion, and the like in a home setting. Of course, I was being "fed" such teaching from Watchman Nee's and Witness Lee's writings and ministries.

Incidentally, if you're interested in knowing more about Watchman Nee: his life, his ministry, his teachings, his writings, just go to any internet search engine and type in the words, *Watchman Nee, Chinese Christian,* and you'll find a number of web sites devoted to him and his teachings and ministry in China during the 1930's and 1940's. For that matter, you can do the same to find information about and by Witness Lee who died in the 1990's while in his nineties.

Ordained To Christian Ministry

During those years I spent in the Chicago area I was ordained to the Christian ministry based upon my previous Bible School studies, my learning and being "discipled" under Witness Lee, and other reasons. I was ordained by an international missions agency which has since been subsumed by another, larger, international missions agency. I have kept my ordination current all these years and officiate at various weddings, funerals, and Jesus-believer events needing the services of an ordained minister. As mentioned earlier, however, I have never been a full-time minister or pastor, always bi-vocational.

One other important event occurred in my life some time during the 10th year of my new life that had begun in the shower that April of my 17th year. It was now ten years since I had been born[2] (born again, born from above, re-generated, converted, whatever term best suits you; they're all biblical).

I had been working hard for ten years to live a good and godly life, to live a consistent Jesus-believer life, to become a whole (holy, but not "holier than thou"), complete person in Jesus.

No one else knew this because I kept it pretty well hidden, but I was just plain old tired and worn out from trying to live a godly life. Trying so hard to live a decent, clean, godly life just warn't workin'. I was exhausted from attempting to live a whole (holy) life for ten long years. I was very close to giving up.

Little did I know that's the point in my life for which God had been waiting all along for me to come to—the point of giving up trying so hard to live a wholesome life. I don't remember the time, or place when it finally dawned on me: *No one except Jesus Himself can live a godly life!* It was one of those moments when you slap your forehead with your hand and mutter, *"Duh, why haven't I known that all along?"*

I Quit!

At a magic moment in time, I just simply gave up ever again attempting to live a Jesus-believer life—and I haven't done so all these years since! I just simply turned my life over to the control of the Holy Spirit (Jesus in his unbodied form) who was already living inside me and told Him I would no longer make any attempt to live a whole (holy) life.

I informed Him that if He wanted to live his own LIFE **IN** me, and **THROUGH** me, **AS** me, that was fine, but if He wouldn't do that I would no longer foolishly make any attempt to live His life for Him, even if my entire life fell to pieces and came to a standstill.

I have followed through with that simple commitment I made to Him that day and have never again since that time tried to live a godly life. And He has honored his side of my commitment to live his own LIFE **IN** me, **THROUGH** me, and **AS** me since that day. Sometimes when I relate that Great Transaction to people, they will ask me something like this: *"Well, Bill, how's that working for you?* I respond, *"It's not working for me; I don't do anything. It's Him who is working, not me."*

Did you notice in the previous two paragraphs I capitalized the word **LIFE**? I do that deliberately in most of my writings about God and Jesus. Why? Good question? When anyone is born[2], at that atomic second in time God places his very own LIFE inside that person. What is God's life? Again, I'm glad you asked the question. Here's why.

LIFE!

At this point in writing this book, I had to make another important decision: should I include some teaching about God's LIFE in the main portion of the book, or should I place it in the Appendix. Again, God said to place it in the Appendix.

Again, I ask you to read the Appendix, because I feel what the Bible teaches about eternal LIFE has been grossly misunderstood by millions of Jesus-believers, and I think my teaching about the subject might give you some real clarification about what eternal LIFE really is. Please read the Appendix; don't just skip over it because it's been placed at the back of the book.

Chapter Nine

Ages Thirty To Thirty-Four

Our time in the Chicago area was beginning to draw to a close. God seemed to be leading us back to Rapid City, South Dakota.

We loaded our U-Haul rental trailer in early August that year and headed for Rapid City, South Dakota, where I had been hired to teach language arts and social sciences at South Junior High School beginning in early September.

Ironically, I discovered that my principal was Mr Norman Nordby, who had been my counselor back when I had been in high school in Rapid City; during my high school years, Mr Nordby had put up with a lot of trouble from me, and now he was to be the principal of a new-creation Jesus-believer who had given him so much grief a few years earlier. He was pleased to see that I had ""made something of my life," because when he remembered the type of teenager I had been he told me that he honestly felt I would have been dead by the time I came to teach under his supervision. He was very surprised to see me!

The Derksen Church In The Home

The first thing we did after we got settled in our new little home in the Canyon Lake area of Rapid City, was to ask around town among the Jesus-believer community if anyone knew of someone who held Bible studies in their home or met as a house church.

Right away, we were informed by the owner of the downtown Bible and Book Store that a Mr and Mrs Donald and Mary Lou Derksen held such meetings in their home in the Rapid Valley area. I immediately telephoned Mr Derksen—Don—and we were warmly welcomed into their home church meeting one evening the following week. That began a very exciting time in our Christian lives that unfortunately turned very sour in only a couple of years; more about that later.

As co-incidents would have it, Don and his wife, Mary Lou, had been in the Chicago area recently and also had been discipled for a brief while by Witness Lee. Also, Don felt very strongly that God wanted him to remain bi-vocational, too. It seemed like Don and I meeting and getting to know one another was a "match made in heaven." In a couple of years, it turned out that it might have been a match made elsewhere.

And, I did believe at first that it was a match made in heaven before some strange things began happening to our relationship a year or so later. God began to develop and mold Don and me into teaching and preaching Elders of our house church and we were slowly growing in numbers and outreach to the community.

Later, another young man, Darrell Kenworthy, joined us and became an Elder. Darrell had been a Pastor of a local institutional church, but had been summarily fired when his church board found out he had begun associating with Don and me, and working a bit in our home church "on the side."

Shortly before my wife and I began meeting, worshipping, and serving God with the Derksen's house church, Don had invited a man named "Prophet Fuqua" to come to Rapid City and teach their small group in a series of meetings. After we had joined their group, on occasion Don would mention this matter or that matter that Fuqua had previously taught them before we joined their group.

I remember "knowing in my knower" at the time that some things Fuqua had earlier taught them were just "one bubble off level," but in the excitement of what God began to do in that little group I really didn't give much thought to what Fuqua had taught before we joined the Derksen house church. With hindsight, I should have heeded my "knower" and fled that group immediately! Fuqua had planted some very serious seeds of false teaching in Don Derksen and members of the group before we arrived.

About six months after we had begun to work and serve in the home church, once again revival broke out. This was now the third or fourth time that revival had broken out where I was involved; I still didn't understand "revival," but I simply welcomed its outbreak and wanted to be part of whatever the Holy Spirit chose to do among us. The revival that broke out was mostly among college age and high school age students. As more and more young people got "saved" and baptized in the Holy Spirit, we began to run out of room for our meetings in the Derksen home.

Some of the young people involved in the outbreak of revival began holding meetings in one of the meeting rooms at the local YMCA. There were about a half dozen young people involved in those meetings—sort of a "satellite" group linked to our house church. God led me to contact the Director of the Rapid City YMCA to see if we could use a large multi-purpose room in the YMCA basement to hold weekly meetings for young people. The Director graciously consented to let us use the room at no charge!

Once we began meeting there weekly, I was sort of segwayed into the ministry of an evangelist and our weekly meetings grew enormously. We met in the basement of the YMCA for about a year and a half while also continuing to meet in the home of the Derksen's. During that year and a half, hundreds—actually over a thousand young people—were born again, many of them also baptized in the Holy Spirit. I am still in contact with a number of those young people—now all grown up, of course—and, in fact, one of them telephoned me just last evening to make an appointment with me to have coffee together next week.

I've just returned from having coffee with that young man—not so young now, however; he's 58 years old! We just took a "walk down memory lane" together. He and his wife, first encountered Jesus during those meetings at the YMCA over 40 years ago. Their journeys during the intervening years have been a bit circuitous and they were away from Rapid City for many years, but moved back a few years ago.

They're doing well; they have maintained their personal relationships with Jesus through the years and they're still excited about what God has done in their lives, what He's presently doing, and what He will yet do in time to come. It's gratifying to see that they've "hung in there" and are doing well—and that God used me in some small way to get them started on their spiritual journeys. We'll get together for coffee again soon, I hope.

I could write pages and pages of miraculous stories and testimonials of all the awesome things God did during those meetings at the YMCA. But I think I'll leave those stories and testimonials up to the young people themselves to tell you when you meet them in Jesus' coming Kingdom and get to spend time with them hearing their stories. You'll learn to love those hundreds of young people (eternally young when you meet them), and you'll learn of the amazing, miraculous things God did in their lives during those months.

But it was not all good. One time when we were baptizing some of the new Jesus-believers in the YMCA swimming pool, members of a local church board arrived with two policemen in tow to have me arrested for conducting "unauthorized" baptisms. (As a matter of fact, I always obtained parental permission to baptize if the baptizees were minors—and also received permission from the Director of the YMCA.) I was handcuffed and taken to the police station.

When it was time to file charges against me, it was determined by the magistrate that I hadn't broken any laws and the police had to let me go. That further aroused the ire of the church board members and in retaliation they fired their pastor for his involvement with us; that young pastor was Darrell Kenworthy whom I mentioned earlier. Incidentally, the president of that particular church board is still active in church affairs in Rapid City and whenever he sees me, to this day he will not acknowledge my presence or speak to me these many years later.

On one other occasion, a father of a young man who was born again in our meetings became very angry that we were "stealing sheep" from local churches. (We were not; we constantly referred new converts to local churches for them to be enfolded and embraced by various congregations throughout the city.) But this father mistakenly believed we were "stealing" his son away from their church. He happened to be a Deputy Sheriff.

He angrily stomped into one of our weekly YMCA meetings one evening and shouted at me in the presence of a couple of hundred young people: *"Bill, if I thought I could get away with it, I would gun you down right here, right now!"* That kinda got my attention! That gentleman is now retired and lives only a few blocks from me.

Joel William And Rachel Lee Born!

On the home front, it was during this era of our lives in Rapid City that our son, Joel, and our daughter, Rachel, were born. I believe we were a loving, close-knit, godly family, but unknown to me at the time some bad things were beginning to occur that later resulted in my wife, Sharon, manifesting some deep-rooted problems, leading to our divorce a few years later. That's another story in and of itself which I'll tell you about later. Of course, there's never just one side to a divorce; I had my share of responsibility in our breakup, too.

Everything was not always fun-filled, exciting, and awesome. With revival and leadership come some "built-in" attacks by our enemy, Satan. He caught us on our blind side and wreaked some real havoc toward the end of that era in our lives, all having their seeds way back in Prophet Fuqua's false teachings before we ever joined the Derksens.

Another great thing that happened during this time is that a local chapter of the FGBMFI was formed in Rapid City—which Don Derksen and I immediately joined for fellowship and outreach—and God did some amazing things in and through that local FGBMFI chapter. It disbanded a few years later and there has never again been such an effective citywide men's group here in Rapid City. Through the years, various men have attempted to form similar groups but they've always been very short-lived.

During our time of association with the local FGBMFI chapter, I was asked by a representative from the international office to write my life's testimonial, and that story appeared in their international publication, *Voice Magazine*, entitled *"An Ordinary Life."* I have always considered myself to be a very, very ordinary person—who happens to serve an extra-ordinary God! At the time, I received letters from all over the world about how my article touched in a positive manner the lives of hundreds of other men.

One other thing that happened to me during those months was that I "saw" an angel. I won't go into any detail at all about that event, because to this day I'm still not certain beyond reasonable doubt that I actually saw what I think I saw. I've only told a very few people about the incident. I'm simply noting it here in my autobiography as a matter of record.

I'll know the truth of the matter only after I die and awaken in Jesus' coming Kingdom, when, I assume if I really did see an angel, I'll be able to meet him face-to-face. Incidentally, he did tell me his name when I "saw" him, and that name has been emblazoned indelibly in my mind all these years. I'll disclose it to you some day when you get to meet him/her/it.

Note: Throughout the remainder of my life story, I'll be writing about some other "bad" things that happened to me during my brief mortal journey. Naturally, I'll be telling you only my side of the story. There are always two sides to any story involving conflict and bad things. I recognize there is another side to some of the bad things that happened to me; I accept that, but I can only tell you my side of the story.

Someday, if you're interested in hearing the other side, you'll just have to ask the other parties involved and hear their side of the story. The first of those "bad" things that happened in my life appears in the next paragraph.

Now I'm going to make a very, very, very l-o-n-n-g story very short. One evening in early June after we had been involved for about a year and a half with the Derksen house church, with the local FGBMFI chapter, with the youth evangelistic meetings at the YMCA, and with various other outreaches and types of ministry and service to other people, there came a knock at the front door of my home.

"Is This A False Prophet?"

On my porch stood Don Derksen and some other men from the house church. I invited them to come in; they declined. Don thrust at me a mimeographed paper with these words in large, bold print on the first page: ***Is This A False Prophet?*** The paper was about me, listing 21 "false" things I had done. Don handed me the paper, told me I was no longer welcome in their church, and the men turned and walked away into the twilight of early evening.

I won't even begin to explain what the paper contained. I have a copy of it in my files. After "the dust settled," I came to my own conclusion that the paper had been written about me largely out of jealousy and envy because God seemed to be using me more than He was using Don. I'm sure Don would have disagreed with me about my conclusion. Don seldom ever spoke to me again except on two occasions. Don died a few years ago in a local nursing home.

In case any of you reading these words are interested, shortly after I was thrust out of the Derksen church I did come to a point where I was able to forgive Don and others involved in my ouster, but I never had an opportunity to tell them in person that I had forgiven them. Forgiveness is essentially for the "forgiver," not the "forgivee." Forgiveness is so the forgiver doesn't retain an attitude of anger and unforgiveness which can often result in what the Bible terms a "root of bitterness," a very spiritually and emotionally destructive attitude.

Looking back with "20-20" hindsight, I actually thank God that I was ousted from the Derksen group at that time. I believe my ouster was actually orchestrated by God behind the scenes to protect me from a very spiritually destructive situation that the Derksen group was getting into.

It seems that Don and Darrell Kenworthy had for a number of months been (without my knowledge as a fellow Elder) secretly investigating the life and ministry of a recently deceased, internationally renowned healing evangelist named William Branham. Branham himself had a legitimate ministry both throughout the United States and abroad during the 1940's to the mid-1960's; at the time the Derksen's and others here in Rapid City were researching

Branham's ministry in the late 1960's and early 1970's, he had died a few years earlier (1965) in an automobile accident under curious circumstances.

For inexplicable reasons, after Branham's death a cult following of him began to develop around the nation, loosely headquartered in Indiana and New Mexico. Some strange, bizarre teachings began to arise out of that following to the point where his adherents were claiming such things as that he was Elijah who was to come just before Jesus' return to earth, that he had been a "perfect prophet," having never, ever prophesied anything false, even that he would be resurrected to life (in a special resurrection) just before Jesus returned. The Derksen church became one of the leading exponents of those types of teachings and one of the leading groups among Branham's followers.

Even though Don Derksen died a few years ago, their house church has "morphed" through the years into a regular institutional church, meeting in a building here in Rapid City, now pastored by one of Derksen's sons. They still follow Branham's teachings, they still predict Branham will be resurrected before Jesus returns; they are a very small, separatist, exclusivist church which doesn't even allow people to join them without first subscribing to some very stringent rules and edicts by their leadership.

For many years, their church was named "The Church At Rapid City." That's "religiousspeak code" for "We're the only true, authentic church in Rapid City; all other churches in town are false."

Recently, they re-named their church the "Evening Light Tabernacle." In "end-time code" I think that means "This ol' world is getting darker and darker—it's almost the evening of the world—and our church has the only light that will save people from the deepening darkness."

Note: Just a couple of Sundays ago an acquaintance of ours happened to visit a Sunday morning service at the Derksen's Evening Light Tabernacle. She lived in the area of town where their church building is located and was searching for a new church home at the time, so it was natural that she would visit a church near her home.

From the minute she walked in to attend their Sunday morning service, she perceived that something was amiss, but couldn't quite "put her finger" on what might be wrong. She told us they talked more about a person named Branham than they talked about God or Jesus.

When the service ended and she got up to leave, she was intercepted by two men and one woman from the church. They proceeded to tell her that they were glad she was visiting their church, but then handed her a little leaflet containing some of their "rules for attendance"—a little leaflet they had made up to give to visitors.

They then proceeded to summarize to her what was in the leaflet, telling her verbally that if she chose to "join their church," she would have to change the way she dressed, would no longer be able to cut her hair, and must understand that women could not speak out loud or teach in their church services.

Our friend told us there was something about they way they approached her and spoke to her that really scared her. Thereafter, she went out of her way not to even drive past their church building on her way to and from her home located nearby. I'm just telling you what she told us, and, again, that's just her side of the story. I have no reason to believe she would have lied to us about her encounter with the Derksen "Branhamites." It seems to me that they might need some better training about how to "meet and greet" visitors to their church services in a more friendly and welcoming manner.

So, I was thrust out of the Derksen church just as they were getting heavily into the Branham movement. I thank God I was ousted from them at that time, even though I went through a period of chaos and depression after I had been ousted from them. I was "lost," in many respects, not knowing where to go or what to do, feeling my life of ministry and service to God was over.

Sidebar: Just a few days ago as I'm writing this autobiography, I perceived the Holy Spirit wanted me to write a friendly note to Don's widow, Mary Lou, just to ask her if she might be interested in meeting Anne and I for coffee or lunch. I don't know whether or not Mary Lou will respond to my note; I hope so—if for no other reasons than for old time's sake or to effect just a tiny bit of reconciliation after all this time.

Mary Lou did respond to my invitation, and we have been getting together to visit every few weeks for a year or so; she has visited in our home and we have visited her in her apartment. Our visits have been warm and congenial with no animosity or hard feeling about the past.

Before I end this account of our relationship with the Derksens and and our evangelistic meetings at the YMCA, I want to tell you about our relationship with the "Jesus People Movement" during those years we were with the Derksens. The Jesus People Movement was a spontaneous, international revival that broke out among hundreds of thousands of young people worldwide during the mid- to late-1960's, being sort of a subgroup of the much larger worldwide "Hippy Movement."

Interstate 90, a major east-west thoroughfare in the United States passes right through Rapid City. Part of the nature of the Jesus People Movement was that there were thousands of young Jesus People crisscrossing the country carrying the Good News about Jesus all over the nation. Thousands of them passed through and stopped in Rapid City.

The Jesus People Movement had an amazingly effective worldwide "grapevine" by which news of what God was doing around the world was passed on. Word began to get out about what God was doing among the young people of Rapid City, and many Jesus People traveled to Rapid City to be part of what God was doing among our young people. We were even featured in many of their underground "Jesus People Newspapers" which flourished by the hundreds, if not thousands.

One thing Don Derksen and I did to accommodate both the Jesus People coming to Rapid City and our own young people was to rent a building near the Fairgrounds and turn it into a Christian Coffee House. Kids could come there just to visit, to listen to music, to share Jesus with others, etc. We named the coffee house (the exterior of which we painted orange and black) The Great Pumpkin. During the brief time we operated it, hundreds of young people from all over the nation "crashed" there overnight; we usually served them coffee and a light breakfast in the mornings when we could afford the coffee and groceries.

Don and I could never understand why The Great Pumpkin was never as "successful" as we envisioned it might become. We hired a fellow Jesus-believer from our group to manage it—a young man whom we loved and trusted. Twenty years later—by sheer accident—I learned that the young manager we had hired had been seducing, raping, and having consensual sex with many of the young Jesus People females who visited the coffee house or "crashed" at it! No wonder it was never successful.

I hope that young manager has sought and received God's forgiveness for what he did. Years later, while attending some national training with the National Guard, I even befriended a fellow student, a female sergeant from the Washington State National Guard, who personally confessed to me that the young manager had raped her when she passed through Rapid City years earlier as a young Jesus People; she had forgiven him, but I often wonder how many other young womens' lives he may have ruined by his sin and immorality.

A couple of years after we closed The Great Pumpkin, it was destroyed in the Rapid City Flood of 1972.

Ku Klux Klan

Here's a sidebar about something that occurred during those years I was associated with the Derksen group. My parents began to empty out the old stone homestead house because it was becoming unlivable and unsafe. While cleaning out a storage room upstairs, we came across a large trunk that had been sort of hidden in a corner for years. Upon opening it, we discovered the trunk was full of Ku Klux Klan regalia and paraphernalia that had been stored there by Dad's parents.

Then the story came out. It seems that my grandparents had been deeply involved with the Ku Klux Klan during the 1920's. In fact, they had been very active members of the Klan in Rapid City. Years later, I even discovered a photo of them in a Klan march through downtown Rapid City during that era.

Some memories then returned to me about how during my childhood, grandmother often spoke of how she hated "Jews, N———s, and Catholics." As a child I had never understood that; in fact, with hindsight, I doubt if she had ever even seen or met a Jew or black person! I don't know much about the Klan's activities in Rapid City during those days, but it seems my grandparents had been heavily involved.

The regalia we found in that trunk suggested they were very much involved with the Klan; we found typical Klan garments, hoods, sashes, awards, medallions, and the like. We burned those items, but with hindsight I wish we had saved them and donated them to a museum in Rapid City, if for no other reason than their historical value.

Okay, back to the Derksen Group. Because of the vacuum my ouster from the Derksen group created in my life, I fell prey to some other, very false teaching not many months thereafter. That's a very long story, too, but I'll try to shorten it as much as I can. One Sunday afternoon as my wife and I were resting at home licking our wounds (the children were outside playing in the yard), there came a knock at our front door.

Standing on our porch were a distinguished looking man and woman who introduced themselves as Doctor and Mrs Jantzen from Hot Springs, a community about 40 miles south of Rapid City. We had no clue why they were at our door, but out of common courtesy we invited them to come in and sit down. That was a very bad mistake!

The "End-time Move Of God"

Dr Jantzen was a staff physician at the Veterans Administration (VA) medical center in Hot Springs, about 40 miles from Rapid City. They had heard through the local "Christian grapevine" that we had been ousted from the Derksen church and had driven up from Hot Springs to offer their sympathy and ask if there was anything they might do to help us in our time of confusion. They seemed very sympathetic, very godly, very warm and friendly, very well-intended.

During the conversation, they disclosed that they were involved with a large, worldwide group called "*The End-Time Move of God.*" As they described the group and their involvement in it, it seemed to us to be a pretty benign group simply teaching truths about events they felt would precede Jesus' return to earth to establish his Kingdom.

They asked if they could leave with us some cassette tapes of messages by the group's principal leader, Sam Fife. We thought that would be okay; after all, we weren't hearing many Bible-based messages then, and it sounded like Sam Fife was quite a good speaker and teacher. We listened to one of his messages, then another, then another, and before we knew it we were excited about Sam's messages and what God seemed to be doing around the world in and through that "end-time group."

Flashback just a year or two. While with the Derksen church, we came to hear about a man from Springfield, Missouri, named Bill Britton, who had an exciting international ministry teaching some rather unorthodox, Bible-based principles and subjects. We kind of checked Bill out, even going to Springfield on one occasion to meet him and visit his church there, *The House of Prayer For All Nations*.

Bill and his congregants were warm and friendly, welcoming our little "South Dakota delegation" with open arms. Bill's teachings proved to be sound, biblically-based, and orthodox enough that we began to read and distribute some of his literature.

On one occasion, Bill even came to South Dakota and conducted a series of meetings in our home. We trusted Bill; he was a good and godly man. Unfortunately, he died in the very prime of life while his worldwide ministry was just gaining momentum. We came to understand that Bill had previously been loosely involved with Sam Fife. What we didn't know is that Bill and Sam Fife had parted ways earlier because Bill began to sense that Sam was getting into some real false teachings and practices.

Okay, back to the Jantzens and Sam Fife's end-time movement. We kind of concluded that Sam's teachings must be okay since we mistakenly thought he had previously been involved with Bill Britton whom we had come to love and trust—not realizing that earlier Bill and Sam had come to a parting of the ways. Our trust in Bill made us mistakenly come to trust Sam and his teachings.

We even invited Sam to come to our home and conduct a series of meetings attended by some people from around the nation and Canada. As I recall, we had about 30 people in attendance with every nook and cranny in our home filled with wall-to-wall people for the 10 days Sam spoke and taught in our home.

Sam seemed to take a liking to me and appointed me an Elder in their movement—and I was hooked. For a while I traveled throughout a five-state region with Doctor and Ella Jantzen, teaching and ministering to various home groups involved in the End-Time Move of God. I was excited and pleased to be part of a movement in which I felt the fires of revival stirring once again.

One peculiar teaching of Sam's that began to be more and more prominent involved "end-time farms" that he founded in various other nations in very remote locations—and in remote locations in the United States also. They were designed for people from urban areas to re-locate there and "hide out" from the soon-coming "Antichrist."

Something inside me knew immediately that that was a pretty bizarre, anti-biblical concept, but because I had been welcomed into the group with such open arms, because Sam had appointed me an Elder, and because I was rapidly becoming prominent in the movement, I mistakenly thrust aside my doubts and misgivings and continued to be an active part of the movement.

The movement held a huge annual "holy convocation" in Miami, to which we drove that summer we had been welcomed into their group. It was an exciting convocation, especially with music that we deeply loved. We got caught up in the excitement of things and before we knew it we had agreed to move to one of their end-time farms located in Peru, South America, to be part of the leadership there. What a horrible mistake!

Peruvian "End Time Farm"

We sold everything we owned—including a new home we had just built in Piedmont—and in mid-January the next year we found ourselves on an intercontinental flight to Lima, Peru. With us were Robin and Joel and our new baby, Rachel Lee, who had been born in early December. We arrived at the "end-time farm" after a horrible bus ride from Lima over the Andes Mountains to the jungles—to the little village of Tingo Maria alongside the Inti River (Rio Inti).

From the village we took a dreadful jeep ride to the farm located about ten miles from the village. How can I best describe the farm?

What a dump! The conditions were absolutely primitive, the water unsafe to drink, everything was out in the open and very unsanitary. We immediately knew what a horrible mistake we had made, but were too timid to admit our mistake and get outta there! I fell into a deep depression and suffered an almost fatal heat stroke.

I'm still attempting to make a long story very short. We finally screwed up our courage and asked the leader there to take us into Lima so we could book a flight to return us to the United States. The leader reluctantly agreed to do so, but once we arrived at a seedy hotel in Lima, he just drove away and left us there.

During the drive to Lima, he made it very clear to us that by leaving, we were disobeying God, stepping outside his will for our lives, becoming apostate, and God would never again bless our lives.

In Lima, we didn't know where we were, we couldn't speak the language, we didn't know anyone who could help us; the U.S. Embassy had been evacuated because of unrest in the country. We were totally alone and had no clue what to do. We had our three children with us, and we were all ill and emaciated. You can't imagine our feelings of despair and hopelessness!

We finally were able to check into the seedy hotel near where the farm's leader had dropped us off in downtown Lima, and we found someone who could speak English, who—for a large fee—helped us make airline reservations.

I forgot to mention that we had all our remaining money—cash—in a money belt strapped around my waist; I think we had about $8,000.oo remaining. Our airline tickets to return to USAmerica cost well over half that amount.

Enroute to the Lima airport, our English speaking driver warned us that because of the present unrest and imminent coup in the nation, if we had any money on us, we should hide it well because it was illegal to take any money out of the country. As we arrived at the airport, there were armed soldiers everywhere.

I became frightened (and whether or not the taxi driver had been telling us the truth), just before we exited the taxi, I ripped off my money belt and threw it at the driver. To this day I chuckle when I think what that driver must have felt when he opened my money belt and found almost $4,000.00 in U.S. cash there. Over the years I've prayed that the money was a blessing to him and he used it wisely!

We arrived back in the United States on a cold March day with only $37.00 remaining and all our earthly possessions in six small suitcases. We looked like destitute, emaciated refugees from a prison camp. We were taken in by some old friends in Sioux Falls, South Dakota, whom we had known since our days at the University of South Dakota. They graciously let us stay in their basement for a few weeks while we were trying to put our lives back together. Those were very bleak, dark days in our lives.

Because I became so ill with a heat stroke in South America and also because I began to succumb to deep depression, my memories of the time we spent there are pretty foggy, but I do remember a few things.

First, I remember much of what we ate while there. Our staple items were rice and soy beans—as well as bananas; I never knew how many different ways bananas could be eaten or prepared: raw, steamed, boiled, broiled, fried, deep-fat fried, and, seemingly, a hundred other ways.

Our rice and beans were stored in big "gunny sacks" and were full of maggots and tiny pieces of rocks and "grit." After a while, we got used to just eating the maggots and grit right in with the boiled or steamed rice and beans! I guess the maggots gave us added protein in our diet.

Let me tell you why I don't each much chocolate any more. On the farm we raised cacao trees. When the cacao pods were ripe, we plucked them and then placed them on huge concrete pads to dry. I noticed hundreds of thousands of cockroaches among the cacao pods on the drying pads. Next, the pods were opened in order to retrieve the beans. Then when the beans were dry, we shoveled them into large gunny sacks—right along with the cockroaches!

Then the gunny sacks with the cacao beans and cockroaches in them were loaded on trucks to be transported to the processing plants. One day I rode along to a processing plant. When we unloaded the gunny sacks full of beans and cockroaches into big hoppers for processing, I assumed that in some way the cockroaches would be separated from the beans; they never were!

To the best of my knowledge, as the beans were being put through the processing stages to become raw chocolate and then shipped around the world, the "processed" cockroaches went right into the processed chocolate. I hope you'll continue to enjoy your chocolate candies and beverages after this disclosure of the "evils" of the worldwide chocolate industry.

One day while another "end time farmer" and I were out clearing brush with our machetes, the other man (who was about four feet away from me) shouted "*Snake!*" I glanced down and there was a huge Bushmaster headed straight for me, about 18 inches from me. Fortunately, my machete was on the downstroke or it would have struck me; instead, on the downstroke I severed its head.

The Bushmaster snake is one of the few species of snakes which will actually attack humans, with its venom from one strike being enough to kill 100 humans! I was so terrified—and angry—that the snake had dared to attack me, that we took it back to the farm's kitchen, butchered it and had it in a tasty stew for our evening meal that day! That'll teach it to have the audacity to attack me!

My mother pregnant with me
1937

Age 18 months
1939

Age 2 years
1940

Age 5, with sister "Bobbie", age 9
1943

Oak Ridge, Tennessee Age 9
Brother John Age 5
1947

High School Graduation
1955

In Air Force in Newfoundland
January 1957

With Sister Bobbie
1958

At Moody Bible Institute
1961

Bill and Anne with Chinese students in China
1986

4 generations
Joel (L), Me (C), Dad (R), Grandson Zane in front

Robin, Rachel, and Joel

Chapter Ten

Ages Thirty-Four To Forty-One

From Sioux Falls, a few months later we were able to move back to the Rapid City area where we continued to try to put our shattered lives back together. I remained seriously depressed (actually to one depth or another for 3 more years), feeling shame, humiliation, a sense of failure, loss. As far as I was concerned, for all practical purposes God had completely abandoned me. I was "dead" inside.

Ironically, a few months after we moved back to the Rapid City area, Doctor and Mrs Jantzen showed up on our doorstep just as if nothing bad had ever happened and attempted to welcome us right back into *The End-Time Move of God*. To say the least, I politely declined!

Shortly thereafter, some other followers of Branham (not from the Derksen "branch" of the movement) approached me to ask if I might be interested in becoming involved in that "great move of God." Again, I politely declined. Don't tell me God doesn't have a wry sense of humor, as from behind the scenes He continually works out his plans and purposes for our lives.

One bright spot is that shortly before he died, Bill Britton drove clear from Springfield, Missouri, to embrace us, to encourage us to go on with our lives and ministry, and to offer to help us in any way he could. He even stayed in our home for a couple of days, just hanging out and loving us. I am deeply grateful to Bill for having done that, and I look forward to embracing him and thanking him properly for that when I next see him in Jesus' Kingdom.

Interestingly, through the years since those "bad" incidents I have described, God has been very gracious in permitting me at various times and in various ways to counsel and help a number of refugees (I call them the "walking wounded" or sometimes the "living dead") from the Derksen church, from the Branham movement, from the *End-time Move of God*, and similar toxic movements.

I've been able to pray with some of them, encourage them, offer them guidance about picking up the shattered pieces of their lives and moving on, and just generally counseling them and helping them out in various ways. What an awesome, extraordinary God I serve!

On one later occasion, God even used me to help out Don Derksen after he had suffered a severe mental and nervous breakdown; that's a very interesting story in itself. Don and I will be able to talk about it when I next see him, too, in Jesus' coming Kingdom. If you're interested in hearing the story, you can sit near us and listen while Don and I talk about it.

On the practical side of things, when we arrived back in the Rapid City area, somehow I knew I didn't want to go back to teaching public school; I found great employment as a medical administrator at a nearby VA medical center, and life seemed to become somewhat normal again although I remained depressed and my wife was beginning to enter into some unwholesome situations—both of which were factors contributing to the later breakup of our marriage.

It was a quiet time in our lives, but a very "empty" time for me. Seemingly no God, no ministry, no teaching, no service to others, no nothing—except I continued to read, study, and attempt obey my Bible each day and attempt to pray. Nothing seemed to be working for me in terms of my spiritual life, but outwardly life wasn't too bad. Our children knew they were loved, we had the support of my parents, we had a place to live, food on the table, clothes to wear. Things could have been much worse after the Branham and End-Time Move of God debacles.

I Began To Write

We were now in the 34th year of my pilgrim sojourn here on planet earth. I remained seriously depressed, but was beginning to see a faint light at the end of depression's dark tunnel. I even resumed some Bible teaching to a small group that began meeting in our home and I began teaching a small group on Sunday evenings at a local Methodist church.

For the first time, I began putting many of my teachings into writing, and even had some of my writings published in a few obscure religious publications, which helped make me feel a little better about myself.

My First Two "Heresies"

It was during this time, too, that I learned (from my own study of the Bible), espoused, and began to teach two of my first heresies. I say that kind of "tongue in cheek." I simply began to examine the Bible more studiously and began to change my personal "theology" about a couple of biblical teachings. Remember, "theology" is simply one's personal understanding about God. We each have our own theology.

Changing my theology from time to time through the years of my pilgrimage has not been without controversy and without losing a few friends along the way because of my heresies. Each of us has our own little "box" we place God in, and if He dares to break out of our box, that can sometimes get us in trouble with established theology and theologians . . . and with people who have certain mindsets about God and how He works among humans.

The first heresy I began to embrace, espouse, and teach during those years was the simple belief that the Bible teaches God will ultimately save every human being from sin and death—through the completed work of Jesus of Nazareth on their behalf. Not just some humans, but all of them.

The second heresy I began to teach was there is no such future event as a so-called pre-tribulation "rapture" of the Church before Jesus returns.

Both those so-called heresies have gotten me into a lot of trouble and caused me to lose some friends along the way, but I have to be true to what I understand the Bible teaches, no matter where such understanding takes me.

You, personally, may not feel those two matters are heresies—and you may not even care whether or not they are (or maybe you've never even heard of them), but, believe me, the evangelical religious establishment cares, and takes such so-called heresies very, very seriously.

If you're interested in reading my teachings about those two matters, once again I refer you to my web site where my unorthodox beliefs are posted for all the world to read. Some of my other heresies are posted there, too; I'll let you figure out which of my teachings are "orthodox" and which are "unorthodox." Sometimes, there's a very thin line between the two.

Finally, it was during those years that I felt "led" by God to join a local unit of the Army National Guard part-time; I wasn't sure why God wanted me to do that, but I simply felt it was something I was supposed to do; that led to some great things happening in my life beginning about ten years after I enlisted.

I was able to enlist in the Army National Guard with the same rank I had held in the Air Force years before, so my National Guard service one weekend a month and 15 days of annual training each summer helped me earn a little extra income for my family and gave me great opportunities to be a witness for Jesus in that setting.

Lessons About Death And Dying

During these years, I learned some very valuable lessons about death and dying. Previously, I mentioned that I found employment as a Medical Administrator at a nearby VA hospital after we returned to Rapid City from Peru.

One of my job responsibilities was to take care of the administrative matters when any of our inpatient veterans died. Some who died had been hospitalized for many years without ever having had a visit from relatives, or even a card or letter—nothing, nada!

However, when the veteran died, various relatives came "crawling out of the walls" to apply to receive "dear old Uncle Ed's" possessions and money—"Uncle Ed" whom they had never visited or contacted in years, often for decades. And fight—oh, how the relatives would fight!—over even the smallest little item that had belonged to "dear Uncle Ed." I grew so weary of seeing that type of thing happen. It angered me, and I determined that I would always have my own death instructions, my will, my living will—everything—in order in the event of my own death.

A couple of humorous events happened during the time I was administratively in charge of death and burial details.

We had one inpatient veteran named "Buddy." Many of the staff and other patients nicknamed Buddy "the Loser" because it just seemed that not very much ever went right in Buddy's life. After Buddy died and his coffin was being carried by six fellow inpatients to his burial site in a nearby National Cemetery, the bottom fell out of Buddy's coffin! Honestly. For months the joke around the hospital was that "loser" Buddy couldn't even "die right."

To add insult to injury, the local funeral home director who handled the arrangements for Buddy's service and burial had skimped on dressing Buddy in his coffin; he failed to put underpants, trousers, shoes, and socks on Buddy's body in an effort to save a little money! After the bottom fell out of Buddy's coffin, there his half-naked body lay in the snow for all to see.

On another occasion, an Orthodox Jewish inpatient died. Years earlier, he had had one of his legs amputated and his wife kept the amputated leg in their freezer at home! When the patient died, it was my administrative responsibility to see that the frozen leg was packed properly in dry ice in an "orthodox" container and then transported to the funeral home to be placed in the deceased's coffin alongside the remainder of his body. That was a first for me.

For years, since I had those job responsibilities at the VA, I have always gone through all my death instructions once a year, made sure my wife and children know where everything is at, who gets what, what type of memorial service I want held, what songs to sing or play, who to invite, who to officiate, and the like.

And, later when we moved from Rapid City to the Gulf Coast, we gave away all our family memorabilia, antiques, furniture, and the like to our children before we moved. Everything we own now has no intrinsic sentimental value; it's just "stuff" that we don't cling to anymore. It helps us "travel light" through life now without clinging to anything that has sentimental value. And, it's nice to visit in our children's home and see all the old family heirlooms, furniture, memorabilia, and antiques on display.

Then, years later when Dad and Mom were getting older, we had them mark on all their family antiques and valuables, photos, memorabilia, etc., exactly which grandchild they wanted to have various items. When Dad died, I was in charge of emptying out his house. For those items that had not been previously marked for dispersal to specific grandchildren, I had each grandchild let me know which items they wanted.

If there was a dispute over who wanted what, I insisted they come to some compromise agreement. Then on a pre-designated day after Dad's burial, I had all of the grandchildren come to Dad's house with trucks and trailers to pick up what had been designated for them to receive or what items they had selected. I told them all that after that day—if they had not picked up their items, the next day anything left in the house would be picked up by the Salvation Army.

It seemed rather a cold, mechanical way to handle such matters, but it worked. There was no fighting, no wrangling, no hassle. Each grandchild got what he or she wanted (or that they had been designated to receive), and it was accomplished very smoothly. I just didn't want a repeat of the terrible events I had witnessed when I was in charge of death and burial details at the VA hospital.

Chapter Eleven

Ages Forty-One To Forty-Seven

Those relatively quiet, uneventful, but rather empty years now bring us to the 41st year of my earthly sojourn.

My wife and I were divorced and she married my former best friend. Sharon and I deliberately chose to remain on good terms with each other "for the sake of the children," and we have honored that commitment all through the ensuing years.

For example, right in front of me as I type these words, is a photograph of our entire family all posing and smiling happily together at our daughter, Robin's, recent wedding. We're all present there for a "family" photograph: my wife, Anne, and me, Sharon and her third husband, and all the children including Robin's new husband, Kim. Kind of an interesting, motley bunch of folks. But, all good looking . . .

Sharon and I having made that commitment to stay on good terms through the years has proved to be a good thing. I'm grateful we chose to do that. Just a few years ago, I received lengthy letters from both Sharon and her present husband asking me to forgive them for the responsibilities they had both played in our divorce. Of course, I freely forgave them even as God through Jesus has freely forgiven me! I, in turn, asked them to forgive me for my role in the breakup of our marriage.

From my own divorce experiences and from counseling many people through the years, I have learned that divorce always—

always—has two sides. There is never an occasion where one person is wholly guilty and the other person wholly non-guilty. In fact, I never counsel people in terms of guilt or blame—only in terms of degrees of responsibilities. There are always two sides.

Speaking of divorce (and remarriage), I have written a controversial teaching about the subject; It's posted to my web site if you're interested. It's entitled ***Divorce and Remarriage.***

Or, if you don't have access to the internet and wish to read it in "hard copy," it's Appendix Three in the back of this book.

Anne Woodley!

Again, it was then the 41st year of my earthly journey. I had finally been healed of my long depression. Life was getting better and brighter. I had a great job which I loved going to each day. Anne and I had met through a Christian singles group, me in South Dakota, her in Canada. I won't tell you that Anne was a "mail order bride" because she hates for me to say that.

We met by correspondence in June of that year while I was at "Summer Camp" with my National Guard unit. After a few months of correspondence, cassette tapes mailed back and forth, and numerous phone calls, we knew we had fallen in love and God wanted us to be married. Anne, too, had previously been married and had a 13-year old daughter, Sharon.

I flew to Canada to meet Anne in person for the first time, and a week later we were married by an Assembly of God Pastor in a little church in Lewiston, New York, right across the border from Anne's home in Canada. We have now been married over 31 years; it's been a good, loving marriage, but not without its rough spots as in any marriage.

We know in our knowers that God brought us together, and our love for one another keeps growing and maturing. Of course, one thing that has helped our marriage to last for 31+ years is that Anne was privileged to marry such a wonderful, near-perfect husband!

After we were married, I flew home to Rapid City to await Anne who drove here from Canada a few weeks later for us to begin married life together. We both felt God was leading us to begin worshiping and serving Him in one of the Episcopal churches in Rapid City, a far cry from each of our church backgrounds.

The Pastor was a warm, loving, charismatic man and our time among our Episcopalian brothers and sisters was great. I became a Lay Speaker and Lay Leader and served on the church board. I taught adult church school classes and was once again enjoying a close, personal relationship with God. We became part of the "charismatic" Jesus-believing community in Rapid City, which crossed all denominational bounds; we attended and participated in various charismatic events throughout the community. I continued to do some writing.

Pets

'Nuther SIDEBAR: May I write a little bit now about pets? I guess I don't even have to ask you; after all, it's my autobiography—I can write what I want. When I was growing up, we never had pets, especially house pets. Oh, there were always cats and dogs that hung around the barns and we even named some of them. But they were never real pets in the true sense of the word, "pet."

When Anne and I were "courting" by mail, by telephone, and by cassette tape I quickly learned that pets were very important to her. She had two cats, Tippy and Patches. I knew I was in trouble. First of all, I was very allergic to cats. Second, I had no clue what it was like to have cats in the house. When Anne, Sharon, and the cats arrived in Rapid City I remained very aloof and cold towards Tippy and Patches and it even bothered me to see Anne and Sharon hug and pet them—and even kiss them. Yuck!

Over time, however, I sort of warmed up to them and when they died even agreed with Anne that we should get another cat whom we named "Puter." The women who worked with Anne found him and brought him to their office. He snuggled up next to Anne's computer keyboard, hence the name. I kinda liked Puter, but after we moved to Tulsa, Oklahoma, he got out of the house by accident and ran away one evening. We never saw him again.

Meanwhile, Sharon (Anne's daughter) had talked me into letting her get a small dog, sort of a generic little female we named Muffin.

I tried to be warm and loving to her, but just couldn't seem to get the hang of it. I wasn't mean or abusive to her; we just sort of went our separate ways. When it came time to "put her to sleep," I broke down and cried—which really surprised me. Shortly thereafter, one Sunday afternoon in November, Anne came home with a tiny little puppy stuck in her coat pocket—another generic little creature we named Sadie.

For whatever reasons, I strongly reacted against Sadie, creating some serious problems between Anne and me. It wasn't Sadie's fault. She was actually kind of a cute little thing—even though she chewed a hole in our nice new carpet! My attitude toward Sadie created so many problems between Anne and me that we actually had to see a marriage counselor to help us work things out. I worked hard at learning to love Sadie. Today, she's over 13 years old and I dread the time when we might lose her. She's just part of our family. She's a sweet, loving, trusting, gentle little lady.

In the meantime, we had two other cats—Bear and Panda—which I came to love deeply. It was very difficult for both Anne and I when we had to put them to sleep. Sadie is still with us and a few years ago she was joined by a sweet little calico cat, Abby, which Anne rescued from death at the local Humane Society. I'm to a point now where I can't imagine our life without pets. God has brought me a "fur piece" (hey, it's a play on words meaning a far distance) in my relationship with pets. I'm now very grateful for the ones we have had through the years.

Speaking of pets, I want to write a few lines about Dad and dogs. During the early 1980's, a developer purchased about 40 acres of land across the road from Dad's front pasture. As more and more houses began to be built in the development and lived in, more and more dogs began to roam freely throughout the locale.

It's unfortunate, but it seems to be a "dog thing" that they will often run around in small packs. Some of those packs of dogs began to cross the road and run in Dad's front pasture, often chasing Dad's cows and calves, sometimes running the calves to death. That angered Dad, so he had some flyers printed and went around to each home in that development to give each homeowner a flyer informing them that if their dogs continued to run in Dad's pasture and chase his cows, he would shoot them.

Well, Dad did just that. Over the course of 25 to 30 years, I imagine Dad shot upwards of 100 dogs. That was bad enough, but after he shot a dog, Dad would throw it's body right in the middle of the main road leading into the housing development—so that the people living there would either have to stop and remove the dog's body or run over it. I'm sure Dad's killing of their dogs both enraged and saddened many of those homeowners through the years.

In some respects, I can't really blame Dad for killing the dogs (they shouldn't have been allowed to roam loose), but his practice of placing the dogs' dead bodies right in the middle of the road leading into the development is certainly questionable. The whole matter probably could have been handled in some other manner, but that was just how Dad did things. I don't know if my brother continues the practice; I hope not. I really don't want to know.

Life Enrichment Services, Inc.

Back to my main story. During those years, I was even involved in starting a short-lived "Community School of the Bible" which met evenings in the Episcopal church educational wing. We offered Bible classes and other classes in subjects related to the Bible. It was then, too, that we incorporated as a legal, not-for-profit, religious and educational ministry named *Life Enrichment Services, Inc,* the name taken from 1 Corinthians 1: 5 where we are admonished to "enrich" the lives of others.

Our ministry has served as a great means of reaching around the world to enrich the lives of others through one-on-one teachings, through my writings (most of them are now on our ministry web site), and through opportunities to funnel financial gifts to other ministries, missionaries, etc.

Because of a lot of graduate work I had taken in psychology and counseling, I also began to do some "lay counseling" during those years, continuing to the present. In fact, I was even a charter member of the American Association of Christian Counselors (AACC). God used my counseling to help many individuals and couples during those years and continues to do so. For the past few years I have practiced a type of counseling loosely based upon a field of thought named Theophostic ("God's Light") Counseling. I have seen a great deal of success using that type of counseling.

Bi-Vocational

As an aside, I want to mention again at this point that many years ago when I first began teaching the Bible and related subjects, and later when I began writing and counseling, I made a commitment to God that I would remain bi-vocational and never charge for any work I did in those areas. I have never charged for my teachings, counseling, writings, and pastoral services—and I never will, although I could have made much more money through the years by charging for my services.

The only thing I have ever charged for is my books—and even at that, I turn right around and give the royalties to our ministry, Life Enrichment Services, Inc. God has always provided for us; we have never lacked having any of our legitimate needs met by God, our Source for everything in our lives. Granted, some of our *wants* have not been met, but we long ago sorted out the differences between needs and wants.

It was during those years, too, that I left my employment with the VA and laterally transferred to a full-time federal service position in the Army National Guard in Rapid City. I was both a full-time National Guard federal employee during the week and a part-time "weekend warrior" one weekend a month and one 15-day annual training period each year.

That decision to transfer from the VA to the National Guard proved to have been a very good career choice over the years, giving me many opportunities for ministry and service to others through my various National Guard assignments and an excellent retirement package when I was retired several years ago due to a mandatory retirement age for my particular rank. God has been s-o-o-o faithful in meeting our needs through the years!

During my last 10 years of full-time National Guard service, I was very privileged to receive special training and then present

Increasing Human Effectiveness seminars throughout the state of South Dakota and in other out-of-state venues. These were highly successful seminars, through which many lives were touched and changed for the better.

At times, I was able to "adapt" the seminars from a purely secular seminar and present them to Jesus-believers in various religious settings—again, with much success in changed lives and relationships. I still present various segments of those seminars with a biblical "flavor." I thank God for being able to be involved in so many lives changed for the good through the years!

Chapter Twelve

Ages Forty-Seven To Fifty-One

Oral Roberts University

I first became captivated by the life and ministry of Oral Roberts some time in the mid- to late-1950's, reading his books, listening to his radio programs, watching him on television, and reading his monthly magazine, *Abundant Life*.

From the 1950's to the 1980's, in both my marriages we joyfully planted "money-seed" into Oral's ministry above and beyond our normal giving of 10% of our income. We followed the construction of the first buildings for Oral Roberts University (ORU) with great interest, even contributing specifically to the building of the Learning Resources Center. Little did I know at the time that I would later study most of my graduate courses on the fourth floor of that very building!

During the 1970's my former wife and I were even invited to the ORU campus for special "Partner's Meetings" hosted by Oral and his staff. Those were precious times of renewal, fellowship, and re-creation I will always treasure.

When Oral Roberts University opened in Tulsa, Oklahoma in 1963, I remember telling my wife that someday I would attend there; I didn't know when or how; I just knew that I would. 22 years later, it happened.

About midway through my National Guard employment years, Anne and I felt that God wanted me to quit my work and pursue some graduate work at Oral Roberts University. That was a major decision, but we chose to obey God, sold our home, and off we went to Tulsa.

My years at ORU were exciting and wonderful. Anne didn't find those years quite so exciting for various reasons, but she knew God wanted us there, so she made the best of matters. We were able to purchase a nice home not far from the campus. Anne found employment, and I began my studies.

How exciting to sit under the teaching of my professors at ORU, a couple of whom I still remain in close touch with. One of my favorite professors died just a couple of months ago and I added one more name to that list I maintain in my Bible's margin next to 1 Thessalonians 4: 13.

During those years, Oral Roberts himself and his "darling wife, Evelyn" (as Oral called her) still lived near the ORU campus. Oral would often visit our graduate classes—just popping in unexpectedly—and would share with us students whatever he felt God wanted him to. It was an amazing privilege for me to "sit at the feet" of such a man of God.

And—on one or two occasions—while I was attending Oral Roberts University, he would single me out to come sit and visit with me in the campus dining hall. In many respects, Oral was just as ordinary as anyone else, but—like me—he served an EXTRAordinary God!

As I mentioned previously, speaking of Oral, I just received word today while doing some more writing in "Him 'n me," that Oral Roberts died yesterday at the age of 91! (2010) He died while writing (in longhand on yellow legal-sized writing pads) two more books. I am feeling very sad as I write these lines. I will miss Oral although I haven't seen him in person for over 25 years. I consider him one of my major life-mentors and disciplers.

Immediately upon learning of his death, 5 major life-lessons come to mind that I learned from Oral's life and ministry:

1. God still heals people. Early on in my Jesus-believing years, I was taught (and came to wrongly believe) that physical healing was only for "Bible days" and not for our day and age. Oral taught me otherwise. He taught me that God heals through the "twin streams" of both medicine and prayer.
2. Oral had a saying that he often closed his television shows with: "*Something good is going to happen to you!*" Again, in my early years as a Jesus-believer, I came to wrongly believe that God was somewhat stern and judgmental, not that He was a good God. Oral's teachings that God is a good God began to change my theology; I came to truly believe Psalm 119: 68. (You can look that up and decide for yourself whether or not it's true).
3. Oral also had a saying, *"Expect a miracle!"* I even had a little magnetic sticker with that saying affixed to my refrigerator for years. Hmmm, wonder whatever happened to that? Again, I was wrongly taught earlier that, generally, miracles sort of ended with the closing of the early "apostolic age." That's not true! *"God is the same yesterday, today, and for all the ages of time and eternity."* (Hebrews 13: 8)

Miracles have been continuing to happen all the while; some of them just whizzed on by me because I had not been taught to expect they were coming my way. I have about a dozen books that have been very meaningful to me during my mortal journey—books I re-read every year along with my Bible. One of those books is ***"A Daily Guide to Miracles,"*** by Oral Roberts.

4. Oral taught that God is in the "now" of our lives. Early on, I had been taught that truth objectively, but had not made it a part of my subjective belief and experience. Oral helped me to come to see that God is very much a part of my day-to-day life by means of the Holy Spirit Who lives inside me.
5. ***Miracle of Seed-Faith*** is one of Oral's earliest teachings he put in print in a little paperback book he mailed to people by the hundreds of thousands of copies. I still have my original copy on my bookshelf right behind me as I'm writing these

> lines. As mentioned above, I have a number of books besides the Bible I re-read every year; ***Miracle of Seed Faith*** is one of them. My copy is very worn and ragged by now.

Yes, Oral Roberts was one of my mentors, teachers, and disciplers. I am saddened that he died yesterday. But, I will see him again in another place and another time, *"and with rapture old acquaintance renew,"* as an old southern Gospel song puts it. Meanwhile, I have added his name to that list in my Bible of believing friends who have died and gone on ahead of me to that "Better Land."

I won't go into any details, but as I started my studies at ORU, we were just barely squeezing by financially on Anne's income and we began praying for part-time employment for me, perhaps on campus as a graduate assistant or the like. I did find on-campus employment for a few weeks, but quit quickly when I became the subject of sexual harassment from a female professor for whom I was employed as a teaching assistant; I won't tell you any details about that, but it was a very humiliating brief episode in my life.

After that, in a marvelous, miraculous, unexpected manner, God arranged for me to receive a generous monthly living stipend all the while I remained at ORU, even paying for my books and tuition! We were overwhelmed and greatly humbled by his providing for our financial needs in such a miraculous manner.

China And South Korea

One January while attending ORU, I attended a meeting on campus in which some speakers presented opportunities for college students to spend part of a summer in China teaching English as a Second Language (ESL). God "spoke" very clearly to me in that meeting, and I returned home that evening to announce to Anne that God wanted me to go to China that next summer. Anne's immediate reply was: *"Not without me!"* Anne has always had a bit of gypsy in her and she was more than ready to go to China.

To make a long story short, God miraculously provided all the necessary expenses for us to go, and in mid-May of that year we were on our way to China as Team Leaders of a group of 28 others "called" to go to China with us. We spent our time in the heavily industrialized city of Lanzhou in Gansu Province.

We were involved in many miracles while we were in Lanzhou. I'll mention only a couple of them. One notable example is this. I was invited by the Communist Party Chief of the "corporation" we were teaching in to teach about American History to all the Party "Cadres" in that particular area. Since history was a love of mine, I looked forward with excitement to teaching for about a six-hour block of time they scheduled me for.

Everyone in my audience was gathered, the video camera was ready, and at the very last moment the Party Chief took me aside and asked me if I would mind—instead of teaching U.S. history—teaching the history of Christianity! I didn't mind. I ended up teaching a six-hour block which was video-taped and later broadcast on State TV throughout China! As far as I know, those videos might still be broadcast in China.

The second miracle, among numerous others. All 30 of us carried Chinese language Bibles in our luggage as we entered China; as I recall, we each had a dozen or so small Bibles in our luggage which we had acquired from Jesus-believers in Hong Kong where we stayed a few days before entering mainland China.

We prayed that the Chinese customs inspectors would not even see them when they searched our luggage; we prayed that God would literally blind their eyes so they wouldn't see the Bibles. They didn't! Not one! The opened our luggage and searched every suitcase; they didn't see even one Bible in the luggage of 30 people! I could go on and on telling you about many miracles we saw God perform all the while we were in China.

Ever since we were in China—although as of this writing we have never returned—I have prayed daily the following prayer for China:

"I pray that You, the Lord of the Chinese church, will continue to send Chinese harvesters into China's ripe harvest fields; I pray that ***non-Chinese*** *Jesus-believers outside of China will merely assist, support, and serve the Chinese church—not interfere nor impose. I pray that* ***Chinese*** *Jesus-believers outside of China will have their*

eyes opened to see how they can help their brothers and sisters in China.

I pray that one of the most momentous works of God in all of history occurring in China today will soon spill over in the power of the Holy Spirit to the rest of this planet's populace; I pray, Lord of the Harvest, that you will come quickly and establish your Kingdom over all the earth, including China."

Years later while in the 72nd year of my mortal journey, God miraculously put me in touch with a Chinese man and his wife, Freddie and Dorothy Sun, who travel throughout China establishing Bible schools. I was heartened and excited to learn that one of their most power-full Bible schools is in our city of Lanzhou! God then led us to begin providing some financial support for the school, which I hope and pray we can continue to do right up until the day we end our mortal journeys.

Oral Roberts University and Oral Roberts himself had some connections with the Pastor of the world's largest Christian church in Seoul, South Korea, *Yoido Full Gospel Church,* pastored by Dr David Yonghi Cho. The church hovered at a membership of about 700,000 at the time. While I was earning my first masters degree in theology, Oral Roberts and Pastor Cho arranged for an exchange internship program between some of Dr Cho's Pastors and some graduate theology students from ORU.

The summer after we had been in China, I was one of the first four ORU graduate theology students selected to spend a summer pastoral internship at the Yoido church! It was an amazing summer of intense activity and learning from Dr Cho and other leaders there. We four were treated like royalty while we were there.

As his "gift" to us, near the end of our internships, Dr Cho ordained each of us as an "Associate Pastor for Life." What an honor and privilege it was for me to have been selected for that first internship program! Again, God miraculously provided the necessary funds for me to spend the summer there.

I ended up studying at ORU for three years. While there, I earned two masters degrees: one in theology and one in education. While there, too, I felt God leading me to begin writing and mailing a monthly publication entitled *The Communicator.* At first, it went to a dozen or so people. When we ceased publication about ten years later, it was being read by hundreds of people all over the United States, Canada, and in many foreign nations.

It proved to have been a tremendous opportunity for me to hone my writing skills and share my teachings with a pretty extensive audience. We received many, many positive responses through the years and many lives were enhanced, enriched, and transformed as the Holy Spirit used that little monthly publication to touch their lives.

Upon leaving ORU, we felt God leading us to move to the Seattle, Washington, area to form (and pastor) a new church there. Another long story, but that proved to be a very bad mistake on my part and it resulted in dismal failure. Once again, I fell into a deep depression, feeling that God had utterly abandoned me.

If it had not been for Anne taking matters in her own hands and making arrangements for us to return to South Dakota, I might have very well ended up destitute on the streets of Seattle. Honestly. We returned to South Dakota with my "tail between my legs," feeling humiliated, shamed, abandoned, and lost. For a couple of years after we returned to Rapid City, I spent most of my time living in a dark, murky "cloud of unknowing."

Chapter Thirteen

Ages Fifty-One To Sixty

Meanwhile, I was re-hired full-time by the South Dakota Army National Guard, we purchased a small townhouse on the west side of Rapid City, and outwardly life returned to some semblance of normalcy, except for the emptiness inside me and the feeling that God had once again abandoned me. Anne found new employment, too, and we sort of resumed our life in Rapid City where we had left off four years earlier when we moved to Tulsa.

While in Tulsa, I was able to join the part-time *Air* National Guard so my military time remained unbroken (for retirement purposes). It was quite an interesting change to go from the Army National Guard to the Air National Guard, once again donning an Air Force uniform after having been discharged from the active duty Air Force many years before.

Back to Rapid City: it really wasn't life as it had been before. I felt that something (Someone?) had gone out of me never to return. I felt cold and dead spiritually—but, once again, I kept reading studying, and attempting to obey my Bible all the while. I don't remember one single event or one single thing that triggered my re-awakening to renewed spiritual life, but over the first couple of years after we returned to Rapid City, springtime began slowly to return to my heart.

Once again, we began to have small gatherings in our home—not so much for Bible study at first, but just for fellowship and association with other Jesus-believers. We attempted to return to the Episcopal church we had previously attended—and looked around for other churches where we could worship and serve God, but nothing seemed to "gel" for us. We just hung in there, associated with other Jesus-believers, studied the Bible now and again in our home, and gradually God's LIFE began to come back into my mortal life.

Meanwhile, Anne's daughter, Sharon, who had been living in Michigan with her husband who was in the Air Force, was undergoing a very messy divorce from her husband after years of mental, emotional, verbal, and physical abuse by him. By then her son, Christopher (our grandson), was about six years old. We invited Sharon and Christopher to come live with us, and we fixed up a couple of rooms in our basement for them to live in until she could get on her feet and move into a place of her own.

Sharon has had many ups and downs through the years, but just within the past couple of years she has finally begun to get her life together and recently graduated from Licensed Practical Nurse (LPN) training where she lives at the other end of our state—and has already begun training to become a Registered Nurse (RN). We're very proud of Sharon for the progress she's finally making in her life.

Christopher has had many problems through the years, too, but seems to finally be getting his life in some order recently. A few years ago, he and the young woman he has been living with, Jamie, had a beautiful little baby, Londyn. Our first great-grandchild! She is a sweetie, and just got her first pet, a cat, "Chewie," named after a character in the Star Wars movies. Just recently, our great-grandson, Jagger, Londyn's little brother, was born. The generations come and go.

Through those dark years after we had returned to Rapid City from Seattle, somehow I continued to write and mail *The Communicator* each month in sort of a "fake it 'till you make it" mode. As I began to emerge from my depression, I took more and more joy in writing it each month and once again began to receive some very positive responses to it.

For some reason undisclosed to me to this very day, just two months before my mandatory retirement from my full-time Army National Guard employment, the Holy Spirit instructed me that I was to discontinue writing *The Communicator.*

I obeyed Him, but it was very difficult for me to do. It was my "baby," and I missed writing and mailing it and replying to the various responses I received. Through the years, God used it to help many people on their mortal journey through life.

Chinese Graduate Students

Meanwhile, Anne and I both began to feel a tug at our heart strings about the following. The South Dakota School of Mines and Technology in Rapid City (where my dad had attended many years before) had a well-known undergraduate and graduate engineering department in which students came to study from all over the world, many of them from China. Anne and I contacted the international student organization on campus to see if they knew of any Chinese students we could befriend and help enculturate.

There were any number of them from whom to choose. We arranged to meet a young graduate civil engineering student from a large city in southern China. His name was Wang Zhiewei. We fell in love with him immediately and he asked us to choose an English name for him; we chose "David." We spent many hours with him—having him over for meals, teaching him about our culture, taking him out to the ranch to visit my parents, introducing him to our children and friends. We really came to love him deeply. All too soon he was graduated and was off to his first job in southern California.

We've stayed in touch with Zhiewei through the years. Several years ago he traveled back here to have us meet his Chinese wife, Rebecca, and a few years ago brought his family—including his two children, Vivian and Christopher—back here to visit us. Zhiewei is now back in China working as an engineering consultant and real estate developer for a large international firm.

One thing stands out in our memory when I think of Zhiewei. The large city he came from in China had a geographical size about the same as Rapid City. Rapid City had a population of about 50,000 at the time we met and came to know Zhiewei. The city he came from in China had a population of 6,000,000 in approximately the same sized space as Rapid City!

Ziewei was actually frightened and uncomfortable at first with the wide open spaces here in western South Dakota after having come from such a crowded area of China. Also, he was fascinated that one could actually see clearly the night sky with it's millions of twinkling stars. He first experienced snow in Rapid City, too, and really enjoyed winter sledding.

After Zhiewei left, we befriended a Chinese married couple, Tianri and Sun Zhu, and spent many happy months with them. They had a son, Adam, while still here in Rapid City. They are presently in the Houston, Texas, area, and we remain in touch from time to time by telephone. Then there were Paul and Ruby Liu and their daughter, Rita. David Zhou became a dear friend, too. And others.

Presently we have befriended a young married Chinese couple, "Bin" and Qi, who are graduate students here in Rapid City. They are a delightful young couple we are quickly coming to love. They even invited us to attend their wedding here in Rapid City last summer.

We've also been back in personal touch recently with the young man, Ma Min, who was our government liaison official while we were in China. He's married now to a lovely Canadian woman, Kim, and they recently came to visit us and share their testimonials and tell us about their work in China with a few friends we invited into our home to meet them. Ma Min was not a believer in Jesus while we were in China, but became a believer shortly after we had been there—based partly on how our group of ESL teachers treated him and displayed God's love to him while we were there.

He went on to study at a famed Bible College in Canada and at Oxford University in England. Ma Min and Kim are presently workers in China, helping to bridge the gap between Chinese and outsiders from the western world. We are privileged to help financially support their work there.

Once again, during this era in our lives we began holding Bible studies in our home, in a sense "morphing" them into a home church. A number of people passed in and out of our home during this time, and although we moved away from Rapid City for a few years, we returned about 6+ years ago and immediately began to open our home to such activities again. We are presently teaching a two-year "Bible Survey 101" course I devised—with about 10-12 people in regular attendance. We've seen some awesome miracles in just the past couple of weeks!

My First Book

During this era, too, we were privileged to present some seminars helping people to become debt-free, and we became involved with a small, but growing, Bible-based network marketing company. While we were involved with that company I wrote my first book entitled, *Network Marketing for Christians*. I never expected it to become a best seller, but it seems that it has been of value to a number of Jesus-believers involved in network marketing—to help them work in that type of business for the right reasons which God can honor.

Also during this era in our lives, I worked at home toward (and was awarded) a "LifeLong Learning" Ph.D. degree. I don't count that type of degree to be as important to me as my earned masters degrees and other graduate credit I earned, but, still, it's nice to have the Ph.D. diploma and know that I finally reached that "level" in my lifelong pursuit of educational excellence. Receiving a Ph.D. degree had been a goal of mine for many years.

Shortly before I was retired from my full-time employment with the National Guard, Anne chose to enter the field of real estate and did very well for a few years before we moved from Rapid City to the southern Gulf Coast of USAmerica—from which we returned after being there only a little over two years. That's a long story, too.

At the time I retired, I asked God to make my retirement a "re-fire-ment" and He has been very faithful to me in allowing that to happen. Unfortunately, about the time I began my retirement years and began to get re-fired, for reasons too complicated to mention here, I once again fell into a deep depression—this time lasting for six l-o-n-n-g years! God sovereignly healed me of that long bout of depression just two years ago from the time I'm writing these words. More about that later, too.

My Second Book And Ministry Web Site

In spite of the depression, however, I was able to write and have my second book published, entitled *LIFEgiving (*subtitled: *Clear Directions For You To Have a Successful and Prosperous Journey Through Life*). Like my first book, my second one hasn't been a best-seller either, but it has sold a few copies steadily and consistently since it was published. Of course, I'm presently working on this book, my third. My fourth book will be about the Holy Spirit and will tentatively be entitled *Friends Forever.* I hope to have it published within a few months after this book is published.

My Tattoos

Many years ago when I took basic training for the United States Air Force, I almost got a tattoo during one of my weekend furloughs. At the last minute, I decided against getting one, but for years wished I had done so.

For whatever strange reason, the year after Mother died I decided it was finally time to get a couple of tattoos. I was sixty-one years old at the time! I decided on getting a celtic cross tattooed on my left forearm and an eagle in flight on my right forearm.

Just for the record, here's what the two tattoos mean to me. My eagle tattoo (a soaring eagle with wings fully outstretched) is based upon a full range of symbolism about eagles found in the Bible, most specifically in Isaiah 40. I think of "eagle saints" rising above the trials and tribulations of this world, soaring to "high places" in God, lifting high above the earth, seeing the events of my life and life on this planet from God's perspective.

I think of eagles riding the updraft winds of the Spirit of God, free and unfettered in those lofty heights. I think of the clear vision of eagles, reminding me of God's (and my) vision for my life, both throughout the eons of time and in the eternal state.

I had the eagle tattooed on my right forearm because in most cultures the right arm is the symbol of strength, power, and authority. I have strength, power, and authority through my relationship with

Jesus. Moreover, it reminds me that I am seated with Jesus in heavenly realms on the right side of the Father's throne.

My celtic cross tattoo on my left forearm reminds me of many things. First, the cross itself reminds me that Jesus died on the cross in order that God might forgive me all my sin and save me from death. The cross on my forearm is empty—as Jesus' tomb is empty—because Jesus did not remain on the cross or in the tomb. He broke the dominion and power of sin and death in my life and is now fully ALIVE. I, too, am fully alive with his LIFE. I have exchanged my old life for his new LIFE in me, all because of the cross and his resurrection.

Additionally, the cross serves as a constant reminder to me that Jesus is always and ever drawing all people to Himself throughout all time and eternity. He said that if He were lifted up on the cross, He would draw all humanity to Himself. He *was* lifted up on the cross; He *is* drawing *all* humanity to Himself.

The green of my cross tattoo reminds me of the new LIFE I have in Jesus, freely given to me by God. The "marbleized" effect of the green reminds me that my new LIFE is fused and blended with God's very own LIFE He has placed within me. Our identities are inseparably one. The black borders of my cross remind me that God's new LIFE within me is encased within my human body, this earth-suit I wear.

The Celtic circle behind the cross reminds me of the great circle of life all living creatures participate in on this planet—and of the circularity of LIFE and eternity, a state of being in which God is fully present and fully resident. The four semi-circles on my cross remind me of the four elements of life: earth, wind, fire, and water. The "gold" borders remind me of the divine nature of God, his divine LIFE encompassing my life. The white blended throughout reminds me of the purity and righteousness of God which He has given me through Jesus.

The two arms of the cross joined to the top of the cross speak to me of the tri-une nature of God and that I am a trinity, too: spirit, soul, and body—three, yet one; one, yet three. The bottom of the cross reminds me that I am a created being, "below" God, yet having a vertical relationship with my Creator through Jesus. The horizontal bar reminds me of the integrative relationship I have with all other people and creatures of God's vast creation. He is the Creator; I am a created one.

Therefore, my eagle tattoo and my Celtic cross tattoo are pictorial representations of the complete story of Jesus and the full and free salvation given to all God's creation through the finished work of Jesus on the cross. If you're interested in knowing more about "Celtic Christianity," there's another teaching on our web site entitled "Druids, Celts, And Jesus." I've also included it as Appendix Four for any of you who might want to read it in hard copy.

The final matter I want to write about during this era in my life is that God led us to establish a ministry web site on which we posted most of my life's teachings. Presently, there are about 50 of my teaching essays on the site, with more being added from time to time. As of this writing, over 50,000 people have visited our web site since it was placed on the World Wide Web. We've received both positive and negative responses from all over the world. Come visit our site at www.leservices.org.

Chapter Fourteen

Age Sixty To?

The Traveler

A couple of years ago, God led me to begin writing and publishing by e-mail a free monthly teaching devotional "magazine" (e-zine) entitled ***The Traveler***. Each month's issue contains teaching about our mortal journey through life. We began by e-mailing our first issue to approximately 75 addressees.

Presently, we have thousands of worldwide readers each month . . . on six of the seven continents of planet Earth. For example, an inquiry from Norway popped up in my e-mail inbox just a couple of minutes ago. Just yesterday, we added an easy-to-subscribe notice on our web site so people can subscribe to ***The Traveler*** from the web site.

Isn't it fantastic how God has led that skinny, mixed up, modern pagan kid who was born[2] in that shower many years ago?! What a privilege it has been for me to teach and write about the Bible and related subjects all over the world. And, I'm not about to stop now!

As mentioned above, nine years ago, for any number of reasons we felt God wanted us to move to the southern Gulf Coast of USAmerica. We sold everything here, and off we went to fade away into the sunset of our retirement years. At first, our life there was almost idyllic. This could be one of those very long stories again, so I'll give you the very condensed version. From my viewpoint it turned out to have been one of the worst mistakes of my life in the natural realm. From Anne's viewpoint it was the best thing we had ever done.

As another sidebar, I want to mention something I really treasure. My son-in-law, Jeff, was working part-time as an announcer at a local Christian radio station. On August 18, 2002, shortly before we left Rapid City to move to the Gulf Coast, Jeff wrote and presented a brief tribute to me on the air—he just simply wanted to thank me for raising Rachel as a great young lady in order to later marry Jeff, and he thanked me for being a good father-in-law. He made a cassette tape of that tribute to me, and just a few days ago I took it from the shelf, dusted it off, and listened to it. Jeff, I really appreciate your doing that for me!

Depression . . . Again

Once again, I sank into a deep depression a few weeks after we arrived on the Gulf Coast—a deep, deep depression that lasted for six l-o-n-n-g years! Only someone else who has struggled with deep depression can ever know what that can be like. Hoping it might help to lift the depression, we decided to move back to Rapid City. That didn't help, and only served to create anger and frustration in Anne. In the new little home we purchased in Rapid City I spent more days than you can possibly imagine laying on a sofa in our darkened spare bedroom just vegetating and wasting away.

I sought some counseling and took more anti-depressant medication than I can even remember. Nothing seemed to help. Anne grew more and more angry and frustrated with our lives. She came almost to the point of leaving me, mostly for her self-preservation. It was a very bleak, dark era in our lives.

Finally, one Saturday morning we ran into some old friends, Barry and Donna Winter, who had been a very important part of our lives when we returned to Rapid City years earlier from Seattle, Washington. Barry and Donna invited us to their little church, a church known for being a church of "restoration." We began to attend, but I remained in a deep state of depression. We finally decided I would see one more counselor in a final attempt to deal with the depression. He was a Native American counselor completing his internship at the local VA clinic not far from our home.

I honestly can't say that the counseling itself began to help me. (I had given up taking any anti-depressant medication, going "cold turkey" against the advice of my doctor.) At first, I saw the counselor, Rusty, on my own and then Anne and I began going to him together because the depression was affecting our marriage so adversely. Nothing that he said or did particularly "clicked" with me, except that he told me to "get off my butt," get off the couch, and begin doing some volunteer work.

I took Rusty's advice and began doing some volunteer work—first for our local VA clinic and then for our public library (which I am still doing now a few hours a week). When I began doing that, something (Someone?) just slowly began to come back to life inside me and I began to feel a tiny bit of hope once again.

Then one Sunday morning while we were attending our church's morning worship service, I simply "knew in my knower" that things were going to be okay again. I knew that God was healing me once again. That was almost three years ago. I am healed! I hope to remain depression-free the remainder of my mortal journey. Please, God, don't ever let me return to that horribly dark and bleak place!

You know by now I've battled depression off and on most of my adult life—with bouts of varying lengths and intensity. I may have even had it during my late childhood and teen years, choosing to numb its effects with alcohol. In those days, depression was seldom diagnosed in adults, much more rarely in children and teenagers.

All I know is that I never, ever, ever want to have depression again, and I pray daily that it will never return.

If you've never battled depression as I have for most of my adult years, you can't possibly know the l-o-n-g days of feelings of lostness, hopelessness, deep despair, overwhelming worthlessness, total exhaustion, sadness beyond sadness, wanting to give up, and obsessive suicidal thoughts.

Anne and I are still working on her anger and frustration about our selling our beautiful new home on the Gulf Coast and leaving there. (That beautiful new home was destroyed during the infamous Hurricane Katrina a few months after we sold it!) I can't speak for

Anne as of this writing, but it seems to me she is making some progress in turning the matter over to God for his healing in her life. Our marriage seems to me to be much better and stronger, and I hope she feels the same way.

Every Jesus-believer on planet earth is in the process of being restored back into God's clear image; Anne and I are presently at different stages in the process, but we're both on the same path.

I've written previously about my relationship with the Bible ever since that day in the shower many years ago. I've read, studied—and tried to obey—the Bible for many years now. Without trying to impress you, I can honestly tell you that I have been privileged to have read and studied the Bible from the first to the last pages well over 100 times since I purchased that h-u-g-e Bible many years ago.

When God healed me from that last long bout of depression, I developed a new, ravenous, voracious hunger for the Bible once again, and since then have read it completely through 8 more times. I'm not trying to impress you—simply to inform you about the supreme importance of the Bible in my life for many years. I simply cannot live this mortal life I have been sent to live without the Bible. I value it more than food.

God Spoke to Me

Shortly after God healed me of the last (and I hope final!) long bout with depression, I was still feeling some of the effects of the illness. I was questioning whether or not God would ever use me again. Whether or not I would ever have a close relationship with him again. Whether or not I might simply be "placed on the shelf" and just sit around waiting to die. I wasn't depressed any more, but I was just feeling unused, helpless to serve God, had no direction, no goals, no sense of purpose or destiny as I once had.

One day I received a brief e-mail from a dear friend just asking me how I was doing, telling me he was praying for me, and that he loved me. He concluded his e-mail with these words: *"I sense right now that you are to be part of an awakening that is and will take place in the Body of Christ."* For whatever reason, that simple statement just ignited inside me and I began to feel a little sense of hope and destiny again.

I mention this next incident in Appendix One, but I want to share it with you here, too. Four months after my friend e-mailed me that note about *"an awakening,"* I was sitting quietly in a meeting where some Jesus-believer musicians got together once a week just to play, sing, and "jam." One of the men there got out of his seat to leave the room; as he was leaving, he paused, looked directly at me, and spoke the following words to me; he did not know me—we had only met on one or two occasions previously and visited only briefly:

"Bill, God knows your heart and your longings and deepest desires. He knows that you are a lifelong seeker after truth. He knows your zeal, your openness to the Holy Spirit, your faithfulness through the years.

I remind you that the truth you seek will always be found in Jesus. Keep seeking, keep asking, keep knocking. I remind you, too, that your entire past has been removed—all those bad experiences you have had were merely to test you and strengthen you.

I know all the pain you've been through. Your past is entirely gone and you are a brand-new man facing a new era in your life. Walk through the open door I have set before you. Through that open door is a new and fresh anointing for ministry and service to others.

I am giving you a new world to reach, to teach, to disciple, to proclaim the Good News about Jesus. I will give you new knowledge. Yes, walk through the open door I have set before you into a brand-new day, a brand-new era in your life—and I will be with you and in you all your journey."

One more month passed and God spoke to me again—this time directly from within my spirit—while I was sitting quietly in a New Years' Eve service at our church. Here's what He said:

"Bill, you grew up on a ranch. You know about working with cattle. Remember how sometimes you would open a gate to let the cattle out into fresh, lush green pastures on the other side of the fence?

The cattle would slowly, warily walk up to the open gate, sniff the air, pause, paw the ground, and then—seemingly suspicious something was amiss—would turn and not walk through the open gate? Next year is a new 'open gate' I have swung wide for you, beyond which there is a new and fresh anointing.

Don't be wary. Don't be cautious. Don't be suspicious. Don't be guarded. Don't be double-minded. Boldly stride up to the open gate without a moment's hesitation . . . and then walk right on through it!"

Needless to say those three messages from God to me gave me a new zest, a new zeal, and new desire to step out serve God once again in new and fresh ways.

Shortly after I was able to mentally process those three messages from God, I began to pray the following prayer almost daily and have been praying it ever since; I will continue to do so as long as I live in my "earth suit" and get up each day to serve God:

"God I want to be part of any awakening, anywhere on this planet—beginning right here in Rapid City. I want to be right in the middle of anywhere the Wind of God is blowing (no matter if it's hurricane force), where the River of Life is flowing (no matter how deep and wide), where the Fire of God is growing (no matter how hot), where the glory of God is glowing (no matter how bright), where the Rain of God is falling (washing away all my past, all my sin and guilt), and where the Reign of God is spreading (bringing all things under Jesus' mastery).

By acts of my will, by any quality decisions I need to make, I make deliberate choices to walk through any and all doors You open to me. Don't leave me out of any 'fresh move' of the Holy Spirit, no matter the cost!"

My life has consisted of one miracle after another since God spoke those three messages to me and since I began praying that prayer almost daily. These have been days of refreshing, of cleansing, of renewal, of restoration, of living in supernatural situations almost daily. These have, indeed, been days of open doors and fresh anointings of God's Spirit. And I fully expect to keep living this way up until the very day I die and go to sleep in Jesus!

For example, I mentioned earlier that in a miraculous manner a few months ago God put me in touch with a Chinese man who with his wife travels back and forth to China a number of times each year teaching and ministering to the underground church in China.

I have considered returning to China simply to visit and to possibly teach short-term in an underground seminary in the city we taught ESL in a number of years ago. In considering that possibility, God brought me face to face with my own mortality and asked me point-blank if I am willing to die for Jesus' sake and the sake of the Gospel.

You see, in China right now and in many other parts of the world—this very day—today, people are still being imprisoned, tortured, and even killed simply because they are Jesus-believers. If I were to return to China and be involved in any way with the underground church there, I would face those possibilities.

For a number of months now I've wrestled with the question whether or not I'm willing to die for simply being a believer in Jesus. I finally told God only a few weeks ago, *"Yes, I am willing to die for Jesus and the Gospel."* Granted that may not actually happen should I return to China, but it could. I've faced it, and I'm okay with giving up my life there should it occur.

Remember way back in my early days as a new believer in Jesus while stationed at Fairchild Air Force Base near Spokane, Washington? I mentioned viewing the Christian movie, *"Seventeen."* The main actress in the movie who was considering responding to God's call to become an overseas missionary sang the song entitled *Follow Me* in the movie.

Some of the words to that song are: *"O, Jesus, if I die upon a foreign field some day, it would be no more than love demands, no less could I repay . . ."* I'm okay with those words. I'm okay with dying for Jesus' sake should that ever occur. I've settled the issue. God through Jesus has done so much for me; how could I not be willing to give up my life for Him?

"If a person isn't willing to die for Jesus, then a person hasn't found anything worth living for!"

It would take another book just to tell you of the miraculous life I have again been living since God healed me of my final bout with depression almost three years ago. Miracles personally, miracles in relationships, miracles in our finances, miracles in new people we have met and with whom God has connected us. And miracles in teaching and counseling again.

Teaching And Counseling Again

Once again, I am teaching and memorizing parts of the Bible. As mentioned earlier, presently I am teaching a "Bible Survey 101" course one-on-one to a new Jesus-believer friend, and a couple of years ago we began teaching the same course in our home one evening a week with about 10-12 people in attendance. As noted above, I continue my volunteer work at the library a few hours each week.

I meet and counsel one-on-one throughout each week with various people in various stages of need in their lives—needs that only God can fill. Just recently, a friend was soundly liberated right in our living room from some tenacious issues plaguing her from her past.

Lately, I assisted a young man in being baptized in the Holy Spirit. God has recently "called" me to become involved with the Holy Spirit in "intercessory prayer" for others. And so it goes; my retirement has, indeed, been a re-fire-ment!

As noted previously, a short while ago I began writing and e-mailing ***The Traveler*** each month. I tell you all that simply to say that it's great to "be back" after those long years of depression. God is re-established on the throne of my life and has total and absolute control of my life once again. I hope that remains the case for the remainder of my mortal journey. He is my Master. I am his servant.

One other matter, about 6 years ago even in the midst of the deep depression God led me to begin working with various prisoners throughout the nation who are taking free correspondence courses from a Bible Institute in Michigan. I am a "Field Instructor" and work grading the prisoners' lessons and enhancing, enriching, and encouraging them to live out their new relationships with God through Jesus while they are in prison. Through me, God has miraculously touched the lives of over 300 prisoners!

A year or so ago, I had another interesting thing happen. Rapid City has it's own resident atheist/agnostic person who is very vocal, very articulate, an excellent writer, a pro-abortionist, a militant feminist, a person who is extremely critical of what she perceives as the hypocritical religious establishment, and many other issues she is very passionate about.

I'm not going to name that person. She has been writing letters to the editor of our local newspaper for many years, generating much controversy and much heated repartee as many readers of the newspaper—especially religious persons—respond to her rather vitriolically; some of them are downright mean, consigning her to the pits of hell.

A year ago, I responded to one of her letters to the editor; I'd like to think my response was a little kinder and gentler than some others. Shortly after I wrote my letter to the editor in response to her letter, the Holy Spirit told me I should contact her and just invite her for a visit over coffee—in the interests of just plain ol' social civility. I don't know but that I may be the only Jesus-believer who has ever done so. She agreed to meet with us, so Anne and I met her a few days later for coffee.

To make another long story very short, that person turned out to be a warm, loving caring person who feels very strongly and passionately about her convictions. We've met many times since then and have even exchanged some "apologetic" books about our positions on some issues. I hope we can continue to meet with her and simply get to know one another better.

Anne and I are not trying to convert that person; that's up to God in His own good timing. Meanwhile, Anne and I are simply attempting to be authentic witnesses to her of our personal relationships with Jesus—and simply be that person's friends.

Again, I tell you all that, not to impress you but to try to tell you that God is a good God and everything He does is good (Psalm 119: 68). He has never abandoned me, He has been working both directly and behind the scenes in my life for many years since that day in the shower, He loves me with an eternal love now and will continue to do so for the remainder of my mortal journey—and then beyond in Jesus' Kingdom and on into the fully restored universe and earth in the eternal state of being. My life really has been—and is—about Him, not about me!

My Journal

Now I want to write about my journal. At age 7, for whatever reason in my child's mind I began keeping a journal. People have asked me, *"What's the difference between a journal and a diary?* I don't know; I just call it my journal. From age 7 until we mistakenly sold everything and moved to South America to that "end time farm," I maintained that journal and it grew to many notebooks. Before we went to South America, I did a really, really dumb thing and burned my journal and other items in a huge bonfire! How foolish I was. I've regretted that for years.

When we returned from South America, however, I felt a compulsion to reconstruct my journal and spent countless hours for about 5 years after our return, writing and writing and writing, trying to remember everything that had been in that original journal. I'm not sure how accurately I reconstructed it. Then, I continued maintaining my journal until about seven years ago when I simply felt I no longer wanted to write in it.

As I'm sitting here right now inputting these words into my computer, I'm looking at about 15, 3-ring binders which comprise my journal from approximately age 7 to age 65 or so. Why did I keep a journal all those years? What will happen to it when I die? I have no clue. It's just there. I haven't looked in it for years. I haven't referred to it while writing this autobiography; I hope that what I've written here is consistent with all that I've written in my journal through the years.

Maybe some day a hundred years from now, some one will find the volumes of my journal in an old box in their attic, wonder who Bill Boylan was, and donate them to their local historical society. I guess at that point I won't be concerned about it any more.

I need to add the following incident to my life story just to show you that all is not a "bed of roses" when one is a teacher of the Bible, especially if one attempts to stay "true" to the Bible's teachings.

Until about two years ago, Anne and I had been very contentedly attending a local church where we felt very much at home, very much loved, very much a part of that local church family. It was discovered that the Pastor and a prominent woman in church activities had been having an "emotional" affair for some time. That means they hadn't yet had sex together, but had been engaging in verbal, "emotional sex." On a given Sunday morning, the Pastor and the woman chose to confess their sin before the congregation; meanwhile, he had resigned from his pastorate and relinquished his ordination credentials.

Before their confession that Sunday morning, I chose to make a brief presentation to the congregation by reading and commenting on John 8: 1 – 11. (You can look that up for yourself). I even had a friend bring 3 huge stones to church that morning, each weighing about 25-30 pounds, the usual weight of stones used in the Bible when someone was stoned for adultery and various other sins. I placed the 3 stones prominently on a table in front of the congregation as sort of a "visual aid." You'd have to have been there to see and hear what went on.

I honestly felt that their confession and my sharing John 8: 1 – 11 accompanied by the 3 stones as visual aids, would bring an end to the matter, and then we as a congregation could go about the business of forgiving the two "emotional adulterers," embracing them, and beginning their restoration process within the congregation as Paul taught should happen in his two biblical books to the Jesus-believers in the city of Corinth. I hope you realize I'm making a very long story very short here.

My attempts to see the Pastor and the woman forgiven, embraced, and restored blew up in my face! To say the very least, it didn't work. The District Superintendent of the denomination chose, instead, to follow human-devised principles of what they wrongly felt were proper principles of restoration—totally ignoring what the Bible—taken together as a whole—teaches about restoration. (If you're interested in learning those principles, please read another teaching on our web site entitled **Restoration**.)

I've also included that teaching as Appendix Five for those readers whom might be interested in reading it in hard copy.

After my attempts to begin the restoration process that Sunday morning, I was asked to leave the church, I've been labeled a false prophet and false teacher, the church board has told their membership they couldn't have anything to do with me, that I twist the scriptures to my own ends, that I take scriptures out of context, even that I'm a very dangerous person, *ad nauseum*.

Needless to say, that was a very rough time time for Anne and me—simply because I honestly tried to the best of my current state of awareness and level of understanding to implement biblical principles of restoration—as I understand them from the Bible. . . taken together as a whole. No, my dear reader, it's not a bed of roses when a Bible teacher does his or her best to teach the Bible. I just felt God wanted me to share that with you at this point in "Him 'n me." Maybe it'll be of help to someone reading these words.

Incidentally, God led us to another church after we were ousted from the one I just wrote about: Destiny Church; isn't that a great name for a church? It's a warm, loving, growing church here in Rapid City, teaching the Good News about Jesus, having great contemporary music, and a good mix of redeemed people from virtually every walk of life, race, and background. We're very much at home there; they seem to accept me "as is," even with all my heretical and unorthodox "baggage."

When we first began attending there, I made an appointment to visit with the Lead Pastor and was very "up front" with her about who I am. I hope we will remain at Destiny church until the end of my mortal journey and then have my "going away party" there. I'm looking forward to a great party. Well, not really because I won't be there, but, in a sense, I will be there, won't I? Hmmmm. It's confusing. Whichever the case—no matter—you're all invited to the party.

Well, whoever you are and wherever you are reading these lines, we're beginning to arrive near the end of my story . . . for now. A lot of people think I'm kind of weird—especially all the religious and

"God stuff." They're right. I admit it. I am sort of a maverick or renegade Jesus-believer. A rogue of sorts. And, it's true, I am a heretic, but I'm a happy heretic!

Speaking of heresies, one of my heresies is this: I feel I might have some reason to believe . . . possibly . . . perhaps . . . maybe . . . God has "told" me I have a minimum of 9 to 12 years remaining of life here on planet earth during this stage of my existence. Maybe I have more, maybe less; who really knows how long they'll be here? We'll just have to wait and see. There are a couple of instances in the Bible where God told people how long they had left to live.

But, however long I have remaining, I want that time to count for something. So I plan to go on teaching, to go on writing, to go on reaching out to others and sharing Jesus with them. That's just who I am ever since God implanted his "spiritual DNA" in me years ago in that shower.

I've been here as a *mortal* for 73+ years as I'm writing these lines. I've been here as an *immortal* 55+ years. After I die and go to "sleep in Jesus," He will return one day to awaken me from the sleep of death and then I will remain here on earth as an immortal in Jesus' Kingdom for many, many more years before this old, weary, time-ravaged earth is freshly restored and I enter God's eternal state of being. It's been an interesting 73+ years; even more so, it's been an interesting and exciting 55+ years. And it ain't over "until the fat lady sings." I hope I can add many more exciting "God things" to my story before it's all wrapped up.

73+ Years Of My Mortal Pilgrimage

As mentioned above, as I write these final lines, the years of my *mortal pilgrimage* have been almost 73+ years. The years of my *spiritual pilgrimage* have been almost 55+ years. In those 55+ years of reading, studying, and attempting to obey the Bible, I have learned that I was sent here to earth as a spiritual being to have a temporary, mortal, human experience, not as a human being to have a spiritual experience.

My mortal experience here on earth began with my conception in June, 1937, followed by my physical birth February 28, 1938.

My new-creation, new life experience commenced on April 26, 1956. The years of my pilgrimage have been few—with pain and joy mixed. When will my earthly pilgrimage end? I have no idea. But I'm ready for it to end—for me to die and be buried, to sleep in death until Jesus returns and awakens me into his coming Kingdom. It's been a tremendous experience full of wonder to have been here, but I long to go to my true Home beyond the sunset of this mortal experience!

Caring For Dad

Eight years ago Dad lay dying on a hospital bed we had set up for him in his living room where he could look out his picture window over his front pasture to the Black Hills a mile away. For years, it had been one of his few pleasures in life to sit and look out that front window and enjoy viewing his front pasture and the Hills in the distance.

Sort of by default, his care fell to me his last 3 months of life. My brother and his wife had been taking care of him for quite some time, and now it was my time to care for him. It was difficult for me at first because I remembered so many traumatic memories of our relationship during the first 17 years of my life.

However, as time passed during those three months when I was his principal caregiver, and Dad grew more and more feeble, we began to have some very long talks during the times he was awake and lucid. We talked about both our pasts. I was finally able to tell Dad I loved him and forgave him for everything, no strings attached. That seemed to give him great peace.

During our talks I was very open in telling him all God had done in my life through the years since I was 17. Dad seemed to take it much to heart; I believe he died having begun a new, personal relationship with God through Jesus. His countenance was serene as I held his hand when he took his last breath and let it out slowly—and was gone. I wept. I will see Dad again in better times in a better place.

As mentioned previously, in the old family burial plot near the Boylan ancestral home just a little east of Piedmont, where so many of my ancestors are buried, on the tombstone of a great-great uncle is inscribed these words: "*Another link is broken in our family band, but a golden chain is forming in a better land.*" I believe that with all my being.

Speaking of the family burial plot, for about two years, I've been mentoring and teaching (discipling) a fairly new Jesus-believer (although he's 60 years old chronologically), my dear friend, Jon Trimble—just sharing with him, spending time together, just "hanging out." Yesterday, he and I went on a "trip down memory lane" for me.

In bits and pieces over the past couple of years or so I've disclosed to him much of my personal history you've been reading about in this autobiography. Recently, he asked me if we could spend a day together just having me show him around the old Boylan family homestead, visit the little cemetery where my family is buried, visit the National Cemetery where my sister, Bobbie, is buried—again, just hang out together for a day.

The Rock Wall

We did that yesterday and it was a g-r-e-a-t time. A couple of things emerged from my memory banks that I shared with my friend, Jon, that I want to write about. First, in front of where the old stone homestead house used to be, there is a huge rock wall about 75 feet long, about 3-4 feet thick and about six feet high. I shared with Jon the history of that rock wall.

When my family and I returned from South America, I fell into a deep depression for three years. That rock wall was God's "work therapy" for me during that time. I wrestled with huge rocks, digging them out on the nearby hillsides, loading them in my pickup, lifting and placing them in the wall.

I remember days being so very depressed I could hardly stand it, but somehow I made myself go out and work on that rock wall. I would yell at God, cry, scratch and bruise my hands, wear myself out physically, and cry some more. Somehow, without my really knowing what was taking place at the time, building that rock wall was God's "work therapy" for me during those dark times.

The wall is still there, still standing firm. My brother who lives there now has improved on it a great deal, but I expect that wall will be there long after I depart this stage of my mortal journey.

When I showed my friend the house my dad had built when I was a teenager living on my own in Rapid City, another memory flashed into my mind about Dad. He was the original water conservationist. After he had built his house and he, Mother, and my brother, John, began to live in it, every night at 9 pm, Dad would step out onto the side porch, sort of get his bearings, and then pick a spot of lawn about a foot square where he would proceed to urinate.

Yes, a different spot every night for over 50 years! It was his way of conserving water. That particular area of his lawn still looks a little greener than the rest of the lawn even though Dad has been dead over eight years. Remember, their house was out in the country about a half mile away from their nearest neighbor; no one could see him as he urinated on a different spot each night at 9 p.m.

Final Teachings

Okay, I have several final thoughts—very brief teachings—I want to share with you before I conclude this brief story about "Him 'n me."

I have learned a few very basic truths that I have staked both my mortal life and my immortal life upon. First, I am compelled to share with you what I believe with all my heart to be this simple, unalterable, eternal fact: Calvary covers it all! The blood of Jesus shed on Calvary's cruel cross cleanses away the sin of every human ever born and has overcome humanity's dreaded last enemy, Death. Jesus' shed blood will never lose its power to cleanse and to set all humanity free from its fearful bondage to sin and death.

That cleansing fountain flowing from Calvary's mountain will continue to flow from eternity into the mortal state of humans until the very last person has been cleansed from sin and set free to be all God created and designed him or her to be! That glorious reality is so very clear to me. It's considered rank heresy by some, but I believe it, embrace it, and espouse it with all my being.

Next, I truly, honestly believe Psalm 119: 68 that teaches God is an altogether good God and absolutely everything He does is good. As indicated earlier, I believe He is always and ever working out everything that happens in the life of every human for their highest, ultimate good. I also believe 1 John 4: 8 that states simply, "*God is love*."

I believe everything that happens in the life of every human being is always filtered through God's eternal love for each of us—not a maudlin, insipid type of love, but a "tough love" whereby God sent his only begotten Son, Jesus of Nazareth, to willingly die a cruel, tortuous death by crucifixion on a Roman cross . . . for us, for me, for YOU!

Finally, I strongly believe John 6: 44 and 12: 32. I believe that through Jesus, God is relentlessly, inexorably, unrelentingly, irresistibly drawing every human being to Himself just as iron filings are drawn irresistibly to a magnet. He is drawing us with a threefold cord of love, grace, and truth, an eternally strong cord which cannot be broken by anything or anyone in all creation. Every human being will ultimately be drawn to Jesus and become inseparably united with Him for all time and eternity. Ultimately, God will be All in all; it's a complete salvation for every human ever born, which cannot be thwarted by heaven or hell.

The Blockbuster Movie

I'm not certain now how to begin summarizing this brief, condensed autobiography. Maybe I'll begin by talking about the movie. What movie? Why, the blockbuster movie about my life which I'm certain they'll begin filming any day now. I've already asked the producers to use the following people to portray my life.

My dear young 7-year old twin friends, Miles and Baker Mitchell, will portray me in my childhood. I want my grandson, Zane, to portray me in my teen years. I want Matthew Perry to play my part in my young adult years and George Clooney to play my part in my later adult years. And who else but Angelina Jolie and Meg Ryan could play my former and present wives, Sharon and Anne?!

And, of course, I'll expect some notable personality to interview me for the film's "trailer." I'm assuming the movie will be filmed "on location" here in Rapid City and nearby Piedmont; after all, some other notable Hollywood movies such as "North By Northwest," "Dancing With Wolves," and "National Treasure II" have been partially filmed in this locale.

As a result of all the publicity the movie will generate, I expect that someone will finally erect those two statues of me—one in front of the building where I was conceived and one in front of the remaining portion that still stands of the hospital where I was born. I can't wait to see the statues; I hope they're very lifelike of me in my younger years when I was still a young "hunk."

10 Words, 10 Events

You've probably already gathered that I like to write—a lot—and I like to speak and teach even more. A number of years ago a friend remarked about my writing and speaking a lot, and presented me with this challenge: *"Bill, I challenge you to take all the wonderfull things you've learned about God through the years and condense them into ten words or less!"*

His challenge "bugged me" and "stuck in my craw." I thought about it and thought about it for a few months and then finally came up with the following; here it is in ten words: ***"God saves everyone. Those who know, tell those who don't!"*** Did I meet his challenge? Did I sum it up? I think so. That's my entire belief system in 10 words.

Another time, someone challenged me to write "in a nutshell" the 10 most important events in my life. Here they are:

1. My conception in 1937 combined with my birth on February 28, 1938. If that hadn't happened, I wouldn't be here to write these 10 points.
2. The two "shower events" in 1956.
3. My first marriage in 1961 to Sharon Lee Smith of Oak Forest, Illinois.
4. Being baptized in the Holy Spirit in February 1966.

5. A "collective event": The births of my four children, Heather Lee in 1965, Robin Elizabeth in 1966, Joel William in 1969, and Rachel Lee in 1971.
6. God's faithfulness in healing me from various bouts of clinical depression, the first healing being in 1975, the last about 3 years ago.
7. Being divorced from Sharon in 1979.
8. Being married to Elizabeth Anne Woodley in 1979.
9. Another "collective" event: Attending Oral Roberts University from 1985 to 1989—including going to China in 1986 and South Korea in 1987.
10. My death . . . whenever, followed by my being awakened from the sleep of death by Jesus when He returns to earth.

Honors, Awards, Achievements

Speaking of lists, recently I told a friend I was working on this condensed version of my autobiography. He responded, *"Bill, be sure to list all your accomplishments, honors, achievements, and awards—stuff like that."* I replied, *"Nah, that's the sort of thing people put on their office walls to impress other people. I'm not trying to impress anyone."* He responded again, *"Bill, an autobiography should honestly list both one's successes and one's failures; just do it."* So following is a listing of some of my accomplishments, achievements, awards, and honors through the years:

- Studied "General Bible Studies" and Christian Education Courses at Moody Bible Institute, "The West Point of Christian Service," Chicago, Illinois, 1959-1961.
- Founder and principal teacher since 1982 of Life Enrichment Services, Inc. (LES), a not-for-profit, international religious and educational organization.
- Past writer and publisher of *The Communicator*, a monthly teaching publication of Life Enrichment Services, from 1985 to 1997.

- Ordained to the Christian Ministry in 1968. Appointed Associate Pastor for Life, Yoido Full Gospel Church, the world's largest Church, Seoul, South Korea, 1987.
- Life Member, *Disabled American Veterans,* 1959.
- Taught and ministered in mainland China, 1986.
- Taught and ministered in South Korea, 1987.
- Listed in *Who's Who In American Colleges and Universities,* 1988.
- Outstanding Academic Student, Oral Roberts University Graduate School of Theology, 1988.
- Chosen by the faculty, Oral Roberts University Graduate School of Theology, for inclusion on *The National Dean's List*, 1988.
- Three-time recipient of the *Army Commendation Medal.*
- Recipient of the *Army Achievement Medal* and *Meritorious Achievement Medal.*
- Thirty-five years combined military service in the United States Air Force, Air Force Reserve, Air National Guard, and Army National Guard.
- Taught and ministered at various locations in Central and South America during the 1990's.
- Certified National Facilitator for *Edge Learning Institute,* 1990.
- Presented *Increasing Human Effectiveness* seminars nationwide to the military, business, and industry throughout 1990's.
- Certified National Facilitator, *Training In Group Effectiveness and Relations (TIGER),* 1980.
- B.A. in Secondary Education, Psychology, Language Arts, and Social Sciences, State University of South Dakota, 1965. M.A. in Theology, Oral Roberts University, 1987. M.A. in Education, Oral Roberts University, 1988. PhD. In Adult Learning Processes, 1995.
- Completed numerous graduate courses in Counseling and Psychology from: University of South Dakota, Northern Illinois University, State University of South Dakota, and Liberty University.

- Published author of articles in *Voice* magazine, *Spirit of the Word* magazine, and *National Guard Magazine*.
- Certified Financial Independence Consultant (CFIC), Financial Independence Network, Ltd., (FINL).
- Charter member, American Association of Christian Counselors (AACC).
- Principal writer and publisher of the *Bulletin of Leading Edge Associates*, 1990's.
- Writer and publisher of *My Success Journey*, 1990's.
- Team CEO of *Scriptures*™, a Christian network marketing company, 1990's.
- Author of the book, *Network Marketing for Christians*, 1999.
- Co-Founder with wife, Anne, of the *Scottish and Irish Society of the Black Hills*, 1998.
- Author of the book, *LIFEgiving*, 2003.
- Writer and publisher of *The Traveler*, a monthly Bible teaching and devotional e-mail publication with an international readership, September 2009, to present.
- Teach and minister worldwide through Life Enrichment Services' web site with a "student body" of over 50,000 students since mid-1990's.
- Field Instructor with Crossroad Bible Institute, working with free Bible-based correspondence courses being studied by prisoners throughout the United States.

I tell you honestly that such accomplishments, awards, and honors are absolutely nothing compared to hoping that some day Jesus will say to me: *"Well done, Bill, you've been my good and faithful friend and servant."*

As I've mentioned many times during this story of "Him 'n me," I live on the eastern edge of the beautiful Black Hills of South Dakota, well-known since the 1930's for the world famous Mount Rushmore National Memorial. There is something about hills and mountains; they seem to emanate stability, strength, grandeur, security, and timelessness.

These well-loved Black Hills have done that for me through the brief years of my mortal pilgrimage. Living among them brings me peace, solace, healing, and restoration. With their lofty granite spires thrust upward to the skies, they are fingers pointing me toward the God of their creation.

The Everlasting Hills

The Bible mentions hills and mountains many times. To me, it is almost as if mountains have personalities and are Creator-conscious. Notice, for example, Genesis 49: 26 where our spiritual forefather, Jacob, speaks of blessings of God reaching to the utmost bounds of the age-lasting hills. Read Deuteronomy 33: 15 where Moses proclaimed that God's blessings include rich crops growing on the age-lasting hills.

The Psalms, too, are replete with references to hills and mountains. For example, Psalm 3: 4 tells us that when David cried out, God heard him from his holy mountain. Psalm 95: 4 proclaims that God formed the earth from the vast ocean depths to the mightiest mountains—and He owns them all.

As noted at the beginning of "Him 'n me," I was born in the foothills of these grand mountains of western South Dakota, only about a mile from where I sit inputting these words into my computer. I was born in the very shadows of these age-lasting hills.

Many days I imagine I can faintly hear the soft prairie winds whispering through the needles of pine trees blanketing the hillsides not far from our home. Sometimes, families of deer come right down the hillsides into town to feed in various yards in our neighborhood. Yes, these ancient hills have deep meaning to me and have woven themselves into the fabric of who I am.

Generations of my ancestors are buried in a small cemetery on the eastern slopes of these hills, awaiting their call to awaken from sleep and rise to the higher hills of glory—a place of sun-kissed hills of dazzling beauty no mortal eye has ever seen. A few miles farther away, other relatives, including my beloved sister, two of my grandparents, and my uncle, are buried in a beautiful National Cemetery.

I, too, will be buried there someday among the pines whispering joyful sounds, the fragrant lilacs, and the sweet-smelling honeysuckle—there on the eastern slopes of the Black Hills to await my final summons to walk among higher, heavenly hills, a place of life where death will no longer claim any victories.

During my brief span of life—only an atomic second compared to the age of my nearby mountains—from time to time I have left my Black Hills—sometimes for years at a time—but they have always called me back to their sheltering canyons and peaks. I believe I am now here to stay until a loud trumpet awakens me from my sleep of death where I will have been buried in my beloved Black Hills.

Obviously, as of this writing I'm still alive. If I'm not, however, when you have occasion to read this, feel free to stop by and visit me any time at the Black Hills National Cemetery near Sturgis, a few miles north of Rapid City. I'll be sleeping there, awaiting a trumpet call and Jesus' summons for me to wake up from the sleep of death when He returns.

You are coming close to finishing reading the life story of a very, very ordinary man. There is absolutely nothing out of the ordinary about me. I live an ordinary life. I live in an ordinary house in an ordinary neighborhood with ordinary neighbors. I wear ordinary clothes. I drive an ordinary old pickup. I have an ordinary family and friends. I would not stand out in any crowd. I am very ordinary looking, almost nondescript—with eyeglasses, hearing aids, and a slightly bulging midriff.

BUT, this very, very ordinary man named William Edward Boylan knows, loves, and serves an EXTRA-ordinary God! And that has made all the difference in my life story.

In Conclusion . . . Sort Of

To begin my conclusion, here are the paraphrased words from one of my favorite old hymns, *"Thanks To God":*

"Thanks to God for my Redeemer,
Thanks for all that You provide!
Thanks for times now but a mem'ry,
Thanks for Jesus by my side!

Thanks for pleasant, balmy springtime,
Thanks for dark and dreary fall!
Thanks for tears by now forgotten,
Thanks for peace within my soul!
Thanks for prayers that You have answered,
Thanks for those You have denied!

Thanks for storms that I have weathered,
Thanks for all that You supply!
Thanks for pain, and thanks for pleasure,
Thanks for comfort in despair!
Thanks for grace that none can measure,
Thanks for love beyond compare!

Thanks for roses by the wayside,
Thanks for thorns their stems contain!
Thanks for home and thanks for fireside,
Thanks for hope, that sweet refrain!
Thanks for joy and thanks for sorrow,
Thanks for heavenly peace with Thee!
Thanks for hope in the tomorrow,
Thanks for all eternity!

I continue my conclusion by paraphrasing some very meaningful references from the Bible:

"O Lord, you alone are my hope.
I have trusted You since my late teen years.
You have been with me since
the moment of my conception.
You called me forth from my mother's
uterus.
No wonder I am always praising you!
Many people are in awe of all you have
done in my life.
You have been my strong refuge.
Let my mouth be filled with your praise

and with your glory all my life.
Don't set me aside in my old age;
Don't abandon me when my strength fails.
Oh God, you have taught me since April 26, 1956;
And I have constantly told others
about the wonderful things you do!
Now that I am old and gray,
O God, do not forsake me
until I declare your power to this
generation,
your mighty miracles to all who come after me."

Psalm 71: 5 – 9; 17 – 19, personalized

"O Lord, You have examined my inner being
and know everything about me.
You understand all my thoughts,
and know all about me.
You chart my paths ahead of me,
and tell me where to stop and rest.
You go ahead of me and are behind me.
You bless me immeasurably!
Where could I possibly escape your Spirit?
Or where could I possibly flee from You?
No matter where I could go in the
entire universe,
you would be there, night or day.
You wove me together in my mother's
uterus.
I will praise you, for I was fearfully and
wonderfully put together in my mother's uterus.
You fashioned my days and years for me
before time was ever created and before I
was born."

Psalm 139: 1 – 16, personalized

Parting Words

To put things into perspective, recently my youngest daughter, Rachel, told me: *"Dad, you know we love you, but sometimes you're a strange little man!"* My wife concurred. I took that as a compliment. I am a strange little man; I've been "strange" ever since that day in the shower years ago when God became very real to me and I invited Jesus to come live in my life.

And, I'm planning on continuing to be a little strange for the remainder of my mortal life, through all the coming ages of time, and afterwards in the eternal state of being. That says to me I'm unique; I'm just the way God created me to be. I'm just "me." And He is Him. Yes . . . Him 'n me. I hope it always remains that type of relationship.

Here's a final secret I want to leave with you. For many years, I have secretly prayed for whoever it might be who will become my successor for my teaching and for the ministry of Life Enrichment Services.

As I've prayed again and again for my successor, I've prayed based on a principle loosely exemplified in the lives and ministries of the Old Testament prophets, Elijah and Elisha, as found in 2 Kings 2.

Elisha was the successor God chose for Elijah. God placed upon Elisha a "double portion" of the Spirit and power that had characterized the life of Elijah. (see 2 Kings 2: 9) I want that double portion—and more—for my successor, whoever he or she might be. That is assuming, of course, God wants a successor for me. I'm just simple enough to think He does have someone in mind, but maybe not. He's in charge. It's his decision. He knows best . . . always has, always will.

My secret is this: I've long hoped that my son, Joel, my youngest daughter, Rachel, or my grandson, Zane, might become the successor of my life's teachings and ministry. Joel, Rachel, Zane . . . now you know. I hope my telling you this motivates you to at least pray about it. Ask God if He may have that in mind for you. Who knows? I haven't excluded you, Robin; I just have never felt that would be anything you might want to do, although you're a good and godly young woman, my dearly loved oldest child.

I've thought long and hard about what final, parting words I want to leave with you as you finish reading my autobiography. Here they are:

Dear reader, wherever you are, whoever you are, whenever you are . . . ***when you near the end of your own mortal journey and it comes time to die, make sure all you have left to do is die!***

Of course, you do know, don't you, that you will die? In fact, the United Nations Council on the Statistics of Statistics recently came out with a startling statistical statistic; I quote their report: *"Statistically, the human death rate throughout the world has remained exactly the same for thousands of years: one death per person!"*

Okay, okay. You do know there's no such Council in the United Nations, don't you?

I encourage all who read this book to receive Jesus into your life—in this mortal life—and then live well with God and die well with God.

In preparation for both living best and dying well, a young Pastor, a good and godly young man named Eric Bonness whom I love very dearly taught me this daily prayer a few years ago:

"God, intensify my hunger for You. Get me to the point where the deepest passion of my being is for You. There is no safety anywhere else. There is nothing of value anywhere else."

That's it. That's my story so far. It's not over. There's more to come in this mortal life and, later, in my immortal life in Jesus' coming Kingdom. And then even more to come when time shall end and be swallowed up into the eternal state of being. My story is not about me; it never has been. **It's about Him** and me!

Here is information about where I'll probably continue to reside as long as I'm still living this mortal life—and about how to contact me; after I leave here, obviously the information will no longer be valid . . . but maybe they'll erect a third statue of me in front of my home and turn it into the world's only Bill Boylan Museum, visited by thousands of tourists who will stop by enroute to visit Mount Rushmore; I'm sure it'll be much more popular than the Spam Museum in Minnesota.

Bill Boylan
330 St Anne Street, Rapid City, South Dakota, USA, 57701
605-721-8879
leservices38@yahoo.com
www.leservices.org

Appendix One

Pneumatology 101

I want to teach you now about the Holy Spirit and give you a little more background about such charismatic phenomena in our modern era beginning at the dawn of the 20th century. After all, I'm a teacher and it's hard for me not to seize this teaching opportunity.

Most—if not all—of this teaching will also appear in my next book I'm working on even as I'm attempting to finish this one and get it to my publisher.

I'm actually going to focus in on the matter of speaking in tongues and what are called the "gifts of the Holy Spirit" as they relate to the experience of the baptism in the Holy Spirit. Let's just say I want to teach you a little *pneumatology,* which is a theological word meaning what the Bible teaches about the Holy Spirit; see, I can use some of those big words now and then.

So here's a little background information about this matter, helping to explain at the same time some of what happened to me that cold February night during the last few days of my 27th year of my mortal sojourn on planet earth.

Historical Background

The supernatural intervention by God into the lives of people by baptizing them in the Holy Spirit and manifesting the "gift of tongues" through them is certainly a part of New Testament teaching, and has been experienced and practiced by various churches and groups of Jesus-believers here and there throughout all 2,000 years of Church history.

The phenomena of that baptism and speaking in tongues died down somewhat toward the latter part of the 19th century, perhaps due to the rational and logical, humanistic worldview created by the so-called "Age of Enlightenment," or "Age of Reason," characterized by rational, intellectual skepticism and cynicism about all things religious and supernatural.

The experience of the baptism of the Holy Spirit and the gift of speaking in tongues burst forth anew on the world scene in the early years of the 20th century at a small Bible School in Kansas (1900) and in Los Angeles (1906) during what has come to be known as the Asuza Street Revival, which gave birth to the modern Pentecostal Movement (named from the events which occurred on the Day of Pentecost in Acts chapters 1 and 2 in the New Testament), birthing such modern Pentecostal denominations as the Assemblies of God, Church of the Open Bible, Church of God, and the like.

The gift of speaking in tongues and other manifestations of the Holy Spirit (the "gifts of the Holy Spirit") have since been practiced by millions of Pentecostal believers worldwide since 1906, but the usage of those gifts did not become evident in most mainstream Christian churches until the late 1950's and early 1960's when an Episcopal Pastor in Seattle, Dennis Bennett, was baptized in the Holy Spirit and began to speak in tongues and exhibit other supernatural gifts of the Holy Spirit, launching the modern "Charismatic Movement." (comes from the Greek word *charisma* in the New Testament, meaning *gift)*

Similar events began to occur almost simultaneously in New York City and Notre Dame University in Indiana—as I mentioned previously.

Since then, the phenomenon has spread worldwide through almost all major Christian denominations and churches with the exception of the eastern Orthodox churches, Holiness Churches, and most churches in the Reformed and Calvinistic theological tradition. Why this movement has not spread to those specific churches is an interesting question, but I will not attempt to answer that in this book.

Oh, there have been little "pockets" of outbreaks of the baptism in the Holy Spirit here and there in those "holdout" churches, but not many such outbreaks—and generally they have not lasted for any length of time because most people in those churches and denominations who claim to have been baptized in the Holy Spirit are often made to feel very unwelcome in such groups—if not downright asked to leave.

Five Prominent People

For the most part, 5 people figured prominently in the "spread" of the Charismatic Movement (including the gifts of the Holy Spirit and speaking in tongues) beyond the confines of Pentecostalism in the mid-20th century.

First, there was the Episcopal Priest, David Bennett, previously mentioned. Next, there was a man from South Africa named David DuPlessis who was nicknamed "Mr Pentecost." He traveled the world bringing the news of the restoration of the baptism in the Holy Spirit and the supernatural gifts of the Holy Spirit to both Protestantism and Catholicism, even having private sessions with various Popes. God also used Oral Roberts, a Pentecostal holiness evangelist, to build bridges between Pentecostals and mainline denominational believers.

Pope John XXIII was used by God to open up the Roman Catholic Church to the supernatural gifts of the Holy Spirit when he issued a papal Encyclical in 1962 urging the Roman Catholic Church worldwide to *"open up to the fresh wind of the Holy Spirit."* Finally, Dr Derek Prince, a highly educated British intellectual like the famed evangelical Christian, C.S. Lewis, gave intellectual underpinnings and credibility to the supernatural work of the Holy Spirit; no longer was the baptism of the Holy Spirit and the gifts of the Holy Spirit found to be limited to poor, uneducated Pentecostals.

Incidentally, I had the privilege of hearing in person four of those five persons noted in the paragraph above; in fact, Dr Derek Prince was my Pastor for a few months in the Chicago area, but that's a long story in and of itself.

And a number of years after these events occurred in my life in Chicago, I had the privilege of attending the famed Oral Roberts University for some graduate work and being taught by Oral Roberts himself in a number of my classes and seminars. As of this writing, Oral Roberts is 91 years old and still going strong, still spreading the biblical message of the baptism in the Holy Spirit!

Late-breaking news: Oral Roberts died just a few days ago!

As noted above, the only churches which have remained largely closed to the supernatural manifestations of the Holy Spirit since the mid-20th century are the eastern Orthodox churches, Holiness churches, and churches holding and espousing Reformed views and the theological traditions of John Calvin, the great Protestant Reformer.

Please get your Bible and read Acts 2: 2 – 11; Acts 10: 44 – 48; and Acts 19: 1 – 12 in your own Bible. Yep, go ahead and do that right now before you read any further in this book. Have you done that? Be honest. If you haven't, this book has been programmed to self-destruct and burn up right in your hands. It's in your best interests to read those references right now. These are the biblical occurrences of the gift of speaking of tongues among early believers in the infant New Testament Church.

Supernatural Gifts

Let me now simply enumerate the listings of the various supernatural gifts of the Holy Spirit—including tongues—found in Romans 12 and 1 Corinthians 12 and 14 which—generally speaking—begin to be operated in the lives of people baptized in the Holy Spirit. In brief, it can be said that these supernatural gifts are **bestowed** by God the Father, **administered** by God the Son, and **operated** by God the Holy Spirit. They are all operated by the Holy Spirit in and through people either to spread the Gospel to pre-Jesus-believers or to build up, advise, warn, strengthen, and comfort Jesus-believers.

Actually, there are four broad categories of such gifts found in various places in the Bible; let me list them simply in those four categories before I begin to enumerate them in the listing below:

1. Supernatural gifts generally called "motivational gifts"; these are found generally in Romans, chapter 12, but also in various other references throughout the New Testament.
2. So called "People Gifts" found generally in Ephesians 4: 11, but also found other places throughout the New Testament. These are gifts of people God gives to his Church—gifts such as apostles, evangelists, prophets, pastors, teachers, deacons, elders, and other similar people-gifts.
3. So-called "spiritual gifts" generally listed in 1 Corinthians 12 and 14.
4. Gifts of "artistic workmanship and craftsmanship" generally summarized in Exodus 35: 30 – 35. I get the sense while reading this passage that the gifts enumerated therein are more than simply heightened natural abilities, gifts, or talents. I'm not attempting to force my opinion on you; you decide for yourself.

All such supernatural gifts of the Holy Spirit are operated **in**, **through**, and **as** ordinary human beings by the Extra-Ordinary Holy Spirit! They are decidedly ***not*** merely heightened natural abilities. Human do not "possess" any of the gifts of the Holy Spirit.

They belong to the Holy Spirit, and He sovereignly **operates** them, **manifests** them, and **delivers** them through ordinary human beings such as you and me. They are his to operate, ours to deliver. He uses people to deliver his gifts to other people—because He loves people and cares for us. He sovereignly delivers "the best gift for the occasion" needed in the lives of the recipients of his gifts.

In general, there are 4 primary ways in which the Holy Spirit "speaks" to the person He chooses to deliver one or more of his gifts to other people on specific occasions: 1. He speaks through his Written Word, the Bible. 2. Through words He transmits into our thoughts. 3. Through mental images or pictures, dreams, and visions. 4. Through strong inner impressions and urgings. Of course, the Holy Spirit, being God, is not limited in "speaking" to humans in only those 4 ways.

The following is not an exhaustive list of such supernatural gifts; I'm personally convinced there are many more, some found elsewhere in the Bible, some never mentioned in the Bible; the Holy Spirit cannot be limited or restricted to someone's listing of his gifts; we can't "box in" the Holy Spirit and limit Him to someone's list. Here's a listing of some of those gifts found in the New Testament:

- The supernatural gift of **prophecy**. This is a divine disclosure by the Holy Spirit, a vocal revelation uttered by God through someone in order to build up, encourage, develop, and strengthen those to whom the prophetic utterance is voiced in a known language; it is a sudden supernatural insight into a given situation, generally for advice, warning, or comfort.

It is decidedly not merely "inspired" preaching; it is not something that improves by practice; there is no such thing as a "polished" prophet. In its simplest form, it's something very much like Mary, the mother of Jesus, uttered in Luke 1: 46 and 47 when she exclaimed, *"My soul magnifies God and my spirit rejoices in God my Savior!"*

- The supernatural gift of **ministry**. This gift is a special gift given by the Holy Spirit for a person to most effectively serve the Body of Christ in material and tangible ways; the rendering of any type of creative spiritual service. It includes, but is not limited to, those persons who are "called to the ministry."
- The supernatural gift of **teaching**. Teaching refers to those who are supernaturally gifted to instruct the revealed truth of God's Word and related biblical subjects, or to those in the public "Office of Teacher" in and to the Body of Christ (Ephesians 4: 11).

The New Testament concept for "teacher" is mind-engraver." If you're interested in a much fuller explanation of this supernatural gift, please read another teaching on our web site entitled **The**

Christian Teacher. It's too lengthy to include as an appendix to this book, but it really is a great teaching . . . even if I do say so myself. If you don't have internet access, perhaps you can ask a friend who does have access to download it and print it for you. It's worth reading . . . honestly.

- The supernatural gift of **exhortation**. This is a supernatural gift given in order to render advice, warning, or comfort, generally to God's people, but sometimes to those who are pre-Jesus-believers. It means to earnestly urge someone to do what is proper or required in given situations. It is similar to the gift of prophecy, with some subtle differences.
- The supernatural gift of **giving**. This refers either to those gifted to contribute to the emotional or physical support of others, or to those gifted to give financially abundantly to support the work of proclaiming the Gospel. It is a specific supernatural gift of giving, going beyond the basic biblical teachings that every Jesus-believer should give a portion of their income to God.

More about this gift can be found in my book, **LIFEgiving**, which can be ordered from the publisher, Xulonpress.com, from Amazon.com, or from any major bookstore.

- The supernatural gift of **leadership/supervision**. This refers to people who are supernaturally gifted to be facilitators, or to those with the public function of administration and supervision in the Church. It is being able to lead other people by serving them, by being a servant-leader as Jesus was while He was here in person.
- The supernatural gift of **mercy.** This defines persons with a special gift of strong, compassionate, perceptive emotions, or those called to perform special functions of Christian relief or acts of charity. The late Mother Theresa best exemplifies the function of this gift in our era.
- The supernatural gift of **hospitality**. This is a supernatural gift in order to provide friendly, kind, and solicitous attention to

guests. It is an outgoing, warm, friendly attention to the physical and material needs of others.

- The supernatural gift of the **word of wisdom**. This is a spoken, spiritual utterance in one's known language at a given moment, supernaturally disclosing the mind, thoughts, plans, purposes, and ways of God as applied to a specific situation. It is almost always directive, giving people clear guidance about what to do in given situations and comprehensive insight into God's plans and purposes.

It is not merely having a vivid imagination or good insight into certain matters; it is not intuition or a so-called "sixth sense." It is knowing and speaking something that only God could know about a given situation—which He reveals as He speaks through someone. It is when God supernaturally tells someone what to do in a given situation—something that person would not have known to do otherwise.

- The supernatural gift of the **word of knowledge.** This is a supernatural revelation (in one's known language) of information pertaining to a person or an event, given for a specific purpose, usually having to do with an immediate need. It is not mere human knowledge based on learning and study.

It is not heightened intellectualism. It's when God takes a little fragment of his all-knowing knowledge and speaks that out through someone to address another person. It is not a critical faculty of insight into other peoples' lives or situations. It is not a sort of heightened intuitional insight of knowledge. No, it is a clear "chunk" of God's knowledge that one could not know in any other way.

- The supernatural gift of **faith.** This gift is a unique form of faith, going beyond "generalized faith" God dispenses to every human (see Romans 12: 3). It supernaturally trusts and does not doubt with reference to specific matters involved. It is a supernatural gift enabling one to fully trust in advance what will only make sense in reverse.

If you're interested in a much fuller explanation of this gift in operation, please read another one of our teachings posted on our web site entitled **Faith.** As with a few other teachings, I've included it as an Appendix to this book (Appendix Six) since the matter of faith is very crucial to the life of a Jesus-believer.

- The supernatural gifts of **healings**. Note this is plural. It is a composite gift. Just as there are numerous human sicknesses, illnesses, disabilities, and diseases, there are as many gifts of healings.

I don't know the truth of it, but **it has been said by someone that all sicknesses and illnesses can be grouped into 39 broad, separate categories; it's interesting that Jesus was beaten 39 times the morning of his death, and Isaiah 53 states that by his beatings we were healed.** God's supernatural gifts of healings are not intended in any way to denigrate or demean the ways God often heals through modern medicine, too. God heals "miraculously" through both prayer and medicine.

- The supernatural gifts of the **working of miracles**. This is a manifestation of God's power beyond the ordinary course of natural law. It is a divine enablement to do something that could not be done naturally. It is when the power of God somehow supernaturally alters, suspends, or in some other way controls or even overrides natural laws. It is when God demonstrates his supernatural power over the natural realm. Often, miracles are "signs and wonders" God uses to capture the attention of people.
- The supernatural gift of **tongues.** This is the ability to speak supernaturally in a language not known or learned by the speaker. It is often a language used in heaven. It can also be unlearned human languages as in Acts 2. It is a transrational (not irrational) utterance of speech using human vocal apparatus, but originating in the human spirit rather than in the human mind. (see additional explanations below) As noted

above, some believe tongues to be the various angelic languages spoken in the Kingdom of Heaven.

- The supernatural gift of **discerning of spirits**. This is a supernatural ability to see into the invisible spirit world, especially to detect the true source of circumstances or motives of people in a given situation. In brief, it enables one to see into the invisible world of Satan and his demons, a realm that cannot be perceived with our natural eyes. It is to see the unseeable. Sometimes, God will operate this gift so that leaders can see into the human spirits of other people in selecting "workers" for building God's Body.

NOTE: Some well-meaning but untaught persons use the term *the gift of discernment*. There is no such gift as the gift of discernment. It is the *gift of discerning of spirits*.

There are four types of spirit-beings on earth and in heaven (at least that we know about): 1. The Holy Spirit. 2. The human spirit. 3. Angels and other similar spirits such as seraphim and cherubim. 4. Satan and demonic spirits.

- The supernatural gift of **interpretation of tongues**. This gift "translates" and "interprets" when the gift of speaking in tongues has been exercised and uttered. It interprets the transrational message of the Holy Spirit, making such a message meaningful to others when exercised either in public or in private.

Gift Of Tongues

As to the gift of speaking in tongues, see the explanation above as well as this additional explanation. Generally, tongues can best be described as unlearned, angelic languages (languages of heaven)—pure clean languages which have been untainted, uncorrupted, and unfouled as all human languages have been. Someone once wrote that tongues are languages wholly "pleasant to the ears of God."

There are 3 categories of the supernatural manifestation of the gift of tongues, based on usage:

1. Spoken, unlearned human languages generally proclaimed among pre-believers to get their attention focused on God. (Acts 2)
2. The gift spoken in a Jesus-believer's meeting, but only when someone is present who can demonstrate the gift of interpretation of tongues. (sometimes being one and the same person) (1 Corinthians 14).
3. Private devotional use of tongues in prayer, praise, and song. (1 Corinthians 14)

At this point, **please stop reading this book!** To continue on, it's very important that you first understand the concept of how God created humans as tri-unified beings, composed of bodies, souls, and spirits, in order for the remainder of this portion of this book to make any sense. Please stop and read another teaching on our web site entitled **Whole In One** before you read any further in this book.

As mentioned previously about another teaching on our web site, this is a very lengthy teaching—too lengthy to include as an appendix to this book; if you don't have internet access, perhaps you could have a computer user you know download it and print it for you.

The biblical, spiritual phenomenon called the "Baptism in the Holy Spirit—when experienced—unleashes, "uncorks," or releases the Holy Spirit from within the human spirit where He is already resident if we have been born[2] (meaning born again, born anew, born from above, born the second time, converted, etc.)

All four Gospels and the Book of Acts teach that Jesus baptizes people in the Holy Spirit. (Matthew 3, Mark 1, Luke 3, John 1, and Acts 11: 16) There are no valid textual, exegetical, or historical reasons to believe that the phenomenon of the baptism of the Holy Spirit ceased with the waning of the so-called "Apostolic Age" by the end of the first century—as I had been mistakenly taught in my early years as a Jesus-believer.

The baptism of the Holy Spirit is not when a Jesus-believer first receives the Holy Spirit. No, the Holy Spirit first comes into a believer's life in an atomic second when that person is born[2]. At that moment, the Holy Spirit and the believer's spirit are inseparably fused together and they become one spirit (1 Corinthians 6: 17).

The baptism of the Holy Spirit is a so-called "second work" of God's grace wherein the Holy Spirit (Who already lives within the believer) is deliberately unloosed by an act of our will in order to "flood" into all areas of our lives to add new dimensions of holiness (wholeness) to our lives, and usher us into a decidedly new—more supernatural—relationship with Jesus.

There's another aspect of the baptism in the Holy Spirit I will simply mention in passing, but will not teach about it in this book. John the Baptizer said of Jesus that He would baptize people in the Holy Spirit and fire. Being "baptized in fire" is another matter altogether, not within the scope of this book.

Suffice it to say that being baptized in fire opens the door for the Holy Spirit to begin anew a lifelong cleansing and purifying process in the life of the Jesus-believer. For additional teaching about God's use of fire for cleansing and purging, see another teaching on our web site entitled **Fire!**

Once again, my teaching about fire is too lengthy to include as an appendix; perhaps you could have a friend who uses a computer download and print a hard copy of this teaching for you.

A note of admonishment. Some people who have been baptized in the Holy Spirit and who subsequently exhibit some of the supernatural gifts of the Holy Spirit have, for whatever reasons, taken some sort of perverse pride that God has "chosen" them above other, "lesser," non-baptized-in-the-Holy Spirit Jesus-believers to be gifted in such wonderful matters. They feel some sort of "spiritual elitism" that they are somehow "holier" than their non-baptized-in-the-Spirit fellow believers.

Please don't ever let such foolish pride cause you to have such spiritual elitism, and holier-than-thou attitudes! The reality is that one ought to be extremely, deeply humbled that the Most High God, the Creator of the Universe, has condescended to allow humans to participate in such wonderful and blessed matters.

There is absolutely no room for pride that one has been baptized in the Holy Spirit and is able to manifest some of the supernatural gifts of the Holy Spirit. The baptism in the Holy Spirit and the supernatural gifts of the Holy Spirit are for **ALL** God's children and are given to build up, strengthen, comfort, and encourage all of Jesus' son and daughters in his worldwide Church.

Filled With The Holy Spirit

What are the differences, if any, in being baptized in the Holy Spirit and being "filled" with the Holy Spirit, the latter as taught, for example, in Ephesians 5: 18? The differences are simple. Being baptized in the Holy Spirit is a one-time event whereby the Holy Spirit is first "unleashed" from where He dwells within our spirits—having first come to live there when we were born[2].

By contrast, being filled with the Holy Spirit is a daily, almost moment by moment, process whereby we continually let the Holy Spirit fill us up with his presence and power and then "flow out" from within us . . . in the sense of overflowing. It is what Jesus was referring to in John 7: 38 and 39 when He said that "rivers of living water" would flow out from our inner beings to the dry, parched, and thirsty people around us; Jesus was speaking of the Holy Spirit when He said that. Being filled with the Holy Spirit is simply to make a conscious choice on a daily basis to yield control of our lives to the Holy Spirit, letting Him "re-fill" us each day and then flow out of us.

For example, each morning of my life, I consciously say aloud to the Holy Spirit that I am turning complete and total control of my life over to Him for the next 24-hour period—for Him to do **with** me, **in** me, **through** me, and **as** me whatever He chooses to do. I consciously "place" Him in charge of my life for that day.

The imagery of being "filled" with the Holy Spirit in Ephesians 5: 18 contrasts and compares someone being intoxicated (controlled) by wine, or being filled (controlled) by the Holy Spirit. The expanded definition of being filled with the Holy Spirit means to regularly and consistently, day-by-day, make conscious choices to be controlled by the Holy Spirit.

Ideally, God would love to have each of his Spirit-born sons and daughters be both baptized in the Holy Spirit and filled with the Holy Spirit. However, we do not live in an ideal world. Some who choose to be filled with the Holy Spirit choose not to be baptized in the Holy Spirit. Conversely, some who choose to be baptized in the Holy Spirit choose not to be filled with the Holy Spirit.

And, unfortunately, there are some who choose to do neither. It has been aptly said that the Holy Spirit is a "perfect gentleman" and does not force Himself upon anyone. Being persons of somewhat limited free will, it is our choice to be baptized in the Holy Spirit . . . or not. It is our choice to be filled with the Holy Spirit . . . or not. Such wonderful gifts from God are available to all his sons and daughters, but it is the free-will choice of each Jesus-believer whether or not to reach out and "receive" such wondrous gifts.

The differences between being baptized in the Holy Spirit and being filled with the Holy Spirit are difficult to teach, and I won't go into those differences in this book. I'll summarize the matter in this manner. Can one be baptized in the Holy Spirit, but not filled with the Holy Spirit? Yes. Can one be filled with the Holy Spirit, but not baptized in the Holy Spirit? Yes.

Ground Rules For Speaking In Tongues

Having said that, let's now move on to examine most of chapter 14 of First Corinthians in a little detail, wherein Paul lays out some ground rules for the gift of speaking in tongues. I will attempt to expound and clarify the teachings of this chapter because it is somewhat convoluted and difficult to read in most English Bibles. I will try to summarize most of the chapter in plain, simple English, but I will not address every matter Paul teaches about in the chapter.

First, this chapter opens by telling us to desire love first and foremost, but also to desire the supernatural spiritual gifts of the Holy Spirit. It's okay to equally desire to be loving and to exhibit the supernatural gifts of the Holy Spirit. Then the chapter proceeds to deal primarily (but not exclusively) with two supernatural gifts of the Holy Spirit: prophecy and tongues, and the proper use of the latter in public and in private.

The chapter proceeds to teach that Jesus-believers should desire to prophesy. As noted above, the gift of prophecy is *a divine disclosure by the Holy Spirit, an edifying revelation, or a sudden supernatural insight into a given situation, generally for advice, warning, or comfort. It is to proclaim the Word of God suited for a specific occasion or situation to build up, comfort, and strengthen the believers present during the prophecy,* as contrasted to speaking in tongues publicly.

Sidebar: I already noted the following incident in the main portion of this book, but it bears repeating here as a very timely and wonder-full illustration of the gift of prophecy. One evening I was in attendance at a local Jesus-believer jam session where local musicians get together every two weeks on a Saturday night and just "jam" to their heart's content. Present at the jam session was a man who does not know me personally; the only connection we have is that both of us know a mutual friend. This man stood up to pray during the jam session just before leaving the building.

In the midst of his prayer, what he was saying seemed to abruptly change. He looked straight at me, pointed his finger at me and begin to say directly to me something like this; I'm not quoting him word-for-word, but this is the gist of what he said to me (rather, what God said to me through him):

"Bill, God knows your heart and your longings and deepest desires. He knows that you are a lifelong seeker after truth. I remind you that the truth you seek will always be found in Jesus. Keep seeking, keep asking, keep knocking. I remind you, too, that your entire past has been removed—all those bad experiences you have had were merely to test you and strengthen you. Your past is entirely gone and you are a brand-new man facing a new era in your life.

Walk through the open door I have set before you. Through that open door is a new and fresh anointing for ministry and service to others. I am giving you a new world to reach, to teach, to disciple, to proclaim the Gospel about Jesus. Yes, walk through the open door I have set before you into a brand new day, a brand-new era in your life—and I will be with you and in you all your journey!"

That prophecy one evening was not only wonder-fully encouraging and strengthening to me, but also a marvelous illustration about how that particular gift of the Holy Spirit "works."

Again, generally speaking, the gift of prophecy is to build up, strengthen, and edify the Church as a whole, whereas tongues is generally used to build up, edify, and strengthen the individual believer (or the Church as a whole, if an interpreter is present). Note that Paul says he wishes everyone would speak in tongues, but especially that they would prophesy.

Tongues is most often used for private worship, prayer, and singing. The gift of speaking in tongues is a supernatural gift of the Holy Spirit for nonconceptual communication with God, originating in the human spirit, rather than in the mind. The difference in speaking my native language and my speaking in tongues is in the origin or source of the language, although both tongues and our native human languages use the same vocal apparatus.

Our native language originates in our *minds* and is spoken through our vocal apparatus. Speaking in tongues originates in our *spirits* and is spoken through our same vocal apparatus. Note it is the same vocal apparatus, but each has a different point of origin of the language being spoken.

Remember, I'm sort of taking you on a brief safari through 1 Corinthians 14.

It should be noted that one can also legitimately "speak" in tongues silently in the sense that it is subliminal speech not spoken aloud. It is to "think in tongues" and pray in tongues subliminally—silently.

Note that in verse 12, Paul admonishes the Corinthian Jesus-believers that since they desire to exhibit the gifts of the Holy Spirit, they should desire to excel in their use. At no point does Paul ever denigrate the supernatural gifts of the Holy Spirit or their proper use. He simply says Jesus-believers should attempt to excel in their use.

As in Acts chapter 2, Paul re-affirms that sometimes the public use of speaking in tongues is to supernaturally speak in other, known human languages so that unbelievers hearing the tongues spoken in their native language might come to believe the Good News about Jesus.

The chapter goes on to teach that those who prophesy and (by implication), those who speak in tongues are in complete control while exercising the gifts of the Holy Spirit. They are not operated by the Holy Spirit (beyond human control) in some wild, ecstatic, "holy roller" manner. Again, the Holy Spirit is a perfect gentleman and does not force His gifts upon humans who exercise such gifts. Paul's admonition is to let all things [regarding the use of spiritual gifts] be done decently and in order.

In a couple of other biblical references (1 Timothy 4: 14 and 2 Timothy 1: 6) Paul encouraged his young disciple, Timothy, to stir up or exercise the gifts of the Holy Spirit within him and not to neglect them or use them carelessly or improperly. Much more could be said about those two references, but I'll let you study them on your own.

1 Corinthians 14 continues by teaching that public tongues is generally "equal" to prophecy—as long as there is someone in the congregation who has the gift of interpretation of tongues. The gift of tongues should never be spoken in a public meeting of believers unless someone is present who has the gift of interpretation of tongues; in such cases, as a general rule of thumb there should not be more than two or three messages in tongues in any given believer's meeting.

Hearers in the congregation have the option of deciding for themselves if what has been spoken (and interpreted) in tongues is true or not. It is God's system of "checks and balances" in the public use of the gift of speaking in tongues.

In this chapter, Paul writes about the place of tongues in his personal life. It is a language that originates in the human spirit as contrasted with his native language that originates in the mind. Both are equally important. Prayer, praise, and singing, both in tongues and in his native language, were normal components of Paul's private devotional times and helped strengthen him, build him up, comfort, and edify him.

The word "edify" (build up) is not to build oneself up in the sense of making oneself better than others. No, the private use of tongues is so one can grow and mature in one's relationship with God.

Paul wrote he could make a conscious choice to pray and sing with his known, human language, and he could make the same conscious choice to pray and sing in unknown tongues—whichever usage seems appropriate at the time, shifting back and forth between the two languages as seems appropriate.

Paul never depreciates or minimizes the importance of the manifestation and use of the gift of tongues. Rather, he thanked God for its availability for use in his own private devotional life and its limited public use, the latter always accompanied by the gift of interpretation of tongues.

In summary, Paul concludes the chapter by stating again that, yes, it's proper to speak in tongues—it should not be forbidden. It is proper to speak in tongues both in public and private. Use the gift wisely, decently, and in proper order. The supernatural gift of speaking in tongues is—and should be—a natural part of the life of a Christian congregation and of the individual Jesus-believer.

Okay, that's it for today's brief lesson in "Pneumatology 101"; there'll be a test on the subject during Friday's class . . .

The least I can say is that my life began to change dramatically after I was baptized in the Holy Spirit. Life became very "supernaturally natural" instead of merely natural. And that supernaturally natural lifestyle has continued to this very day. Oh, there have been times when I have "quenched" the Holy Spirit (as Paul admonishes Jesus-believers not to do), but overall his supernatural Presence and works through my life have been consistent for a little over 45 years.

Just knowing what little I know of human nature concerning this intriguing, yet controversial, biblical subject, I have a feeling you might be asking, *"Bill, do you regularly speak in tongues? Do you regularly pray in tongues?* The answer is *Yes*. I pray, praise, and sing privately in tongues almost daily and, upon a few occasions, I have spoken in tongues in public (with an interpreter present).

That's it. That's the baptism in the Holy Spirit and the gifts of the Holy Spirit . . . in a nutshell. If you haven't yet been baptized in the Holy Spirit and begun to exhibit the gifts of the Holy Spirit, I encourage you to get baptized today . . . now. And then allow Him to begin to manifest his gifts through you as they are needed in the lives of other people in your day-to-day world.

And, if you haven't yet been filled with the Holy Spirit, ask Him to begin filling you today . . . now. Both experiences will launch you out into a whole new world—a supernatural world—of loving, supernatural service and ministry to God and other people.

Appendix Two

Real LIFE

I'm going to make a short explanation about God's LIFE very l-o-n-n-g. Here we go.

What does the Bible mean when it uses the term "eternal life" (sometimes also termed "everlasting life")?

For many years, I have asked lots of people that question; some of those people have been Bible-believing Jesus-believers, some have been anything but that. Overall, I have discovered that many people have no clear idea what the term "eternal life" really means. The most common answer I receive to that question goes something like this: *"When people die, they go to heaven; that's when eternal life begins."* Or, the second most common answer is similar: *"When I die, I will go to heaven and live there forever and ever; that's eternal life."*

Eternal LIFE

According to the Bible, here's what eternal life really is: Eternal LIFE is God's very own uncreated, self-existent **LIFE** that He alone possesses because He's God. "In a nutshell," that's what eternal LIFE is. God is the only Being possessing that type of LIFE because He is . . . well, He is God. I'll expand on that basic definition throughout the remainder of this teaching.

What does God's own self-existent, uncreated LIFE have to do with us if He is the only Being Who possesses that type of LIFE — because He is God? When human beings are born[2] (meaning born from above, re-born, born again, born anew, twice-born, converted, and similar terms) as Jesus teaches, in an atomic second a Great Transaction occurs between God and them, and they become newly created beings because God implants and infuses his very own LIFE inside them. He takes a "portion" of his own LIFE and places it within twice-born, newly created people.

So . . . eternal LIFE for humans is when God implants his own

self-existent . . .
uncreated . . .
incorruptible . . .
indestructible . . .
undiminishable . . .
imperishable . . .
measureless . . .
boundless . . .
limitless . . .
abundant . . .
wonder-full . . .

. . . LIFE within us when we are are born[2] through Jesus Christ!

In short, God displaces and replaces our old, non-eternal, mortal life that will die, with his own non-dying, immortal, eternal LIFE in all its fullness. It is the quality, inherent nature, "substance," or character of that LIFE—not its duration or length—that is paramount. (As mentioned previously, in most of my writings, I almost always capitalize God's LIFE in us to emphasize it's exceedingly wonderful quality, not merely its duration.) Eternal LIFE is a brand-new kind of life given to humans by God, brand-new both in "length" and in quality.

I hasten to point out an extremely serious flaw in the thinking of multitudes of people who feel that because God is so loving—

so "lovey-dovey"—He just naturally gives his eternal LIFE to everyone, no strings attached. They portray his love as very insipid, maudlin, and sentimental. That is categorically not true! Yes, God's love for humankind is eternal, but it is also very "tough love"—so tough it sent his only begotten Son to die on a cross, the Roman instrument of a tortuous, extremely painful death.

God gives a "portion" of his eternal LIFE only to those who place their faith and trust in Jesus—who are born[2] by the power of God the Holy Spirit! Only through the completed "salvific" work of Jesus—God The Son—on behalf of humanity is God "legally" justified in implanting his eternal LIFE inside people. There is absolutely no way for a human being to receive God's eternal LIFE except through Jesus Christ!

LIFE In The Now

Eternal LIFE is God's very own LIFE He places within us when we are born again; as noted above, however, many people tend to think of it in terms of existence that goes on and on and on forever and ever, never coming to an end. And the existence it seems to imply is a sort of religious experience in the sky "in the sweet bye and bye" which leaves many people wondering if they would even want that kind of life to go on forever—like a dead, boring, eternal church service.

But Jesus is quite clear that when he speaks of eternal LIFE, what he means is LIFE that is absolutely wonder-full and can never be diminished or stolen from you. He says, I have come that you may have LIFE, and have it in abundant fullness. (John 10: 10).

The eternal LIFE God gives us is a life far exceeding that of the highest mortal life any human being possesses, just as the highest life a human being has far exceeds that of the lowliest one-celled protoplasm or amoeba. Eternal LIFE is not the mere continuity of this mortal life in an immortal, endless life in some far-off forever. **Eternal LIFE begins now**, and will never end—in a state of being called eternity in which God dwells in all his fulness.

In a manner of speaking, all growth of a born[2] person is simply to receive increasing "dosages" of eternal LIFE from God. For many reasons, sometimes when God first implants his LIFE within us, it may lay dormant for a time. Then when we are ready, it begins to come awake in us, blossoming into its full, vibrant expressiveness in ways that only God can "grow" it in us.

There comes what I call a "magic moment" in time when God's embryonic LIFE—whether in root, in seed, or in tiny acorn form—that moment in time comes when it begins to blossom and bear fruit. That LIFE in our innermost being begins to fulfill its destiny within the Father's newly born, newly created son or daughter. (2 Corinthians 5: 17) That LIFE begins to shoot upward from where it has taken root in our spirit. It sprouts within us, sending forth new leaves and branches and fruit, flowering and blossoming until that LIFE in us is all in all.

We don't need to experience more and more of this finite, perishable, mortal life we have on planet earth in order to have a fuller life. No, we need more and more of the infinite eternal LIFE of God in us—more of his LIFE-making Presence in us in order to have lives that are truly full and abundant during our mortal journeys here in time and space.

If we will simply let God "pour" more and more of his LIFE into us by means of the work of the Holy Spirit Who dwells within us in our spirits, there will never be a limit—throughout time or in eternity—to the enlargement of our existence, to the flood of LIFE that will flow into us, through us, and out of us. Most of us simply have no conception of how full and "complete" and vast real LIFE is.

The condition of most men and women without God's LIFE in them is actually a sort of "life in death," an unreal dream existence, a "twilight zone" type of emptiness. A mistaken belief or awareness that the life they now live will one day come to an end and they will perish. It's a view that often leads to futility and hopelessness, to bleakness and despair.

LIFE eternal is not merely an endless elongation of consciousness. No, LIFE eternal is freely given to us by God's grace—a LIFE which is his own, beyond the attack of decay or death. **Eternal LIFE is an existence in which Jesus-believers partake of the very nature of God in the every day "now" of their existence!** It consists in absolute oneness with God through Jesus by means of the indwelling Holy Spirit (Jesus in his "unbodied" Spirit form).

Eternal LIFE is not some sort of endless life we're going to get (future tense) when we die. No, it's God's very own LIFE He gives to us now (present tense) when Jesus comes to live in us in his unbodied form of the Holy Spirit. It's the very LIFE of the Eternal God flowing into our mortal lives in time and space before we arrive at our eternal state of being after time has ended.

If the Son of God lives in us by virtue of our having been born^2, we now have (present tense) the Son, we have God's very own eternal LIFE within us now! (1 John 5: 11- 13) At the atomic second we are born^2, a tectonic shift occurs in our personal life and universe, and by faith we begin to get a "feel" for the LIFE of God infusing us and spreading throughout our innermost being.

As simply as I can put it in summary fashion, **here's how humans "get" God's eternal LIFE:** when we are born^2 (see John 3: 5 – 8), God takes a portion of his . . .

self-existent . . .
uncreated . . .
incorruptible . . .
indestructible . . .
undiminishable . . .
imperishable . . .
measureless . . .
boundless . . .
limitless . . .
abundant . . .
wonder-full . . .

. . . LIFE and permanently implants it within our human spirits, and we come ALIVE with that LIFE within our human spirits, inseparably and permanently fused with God's LIFE-giving Spirit within us for all time and eternity! (1 Corinthians 6: 17)

John 5: 24 in the Bible teaches us that people who hear Jesus' words and put their trust in the Father Who sent Jesus have eternal LIFE (present tense) and will not come into judgment (future tense).

They pass from a state of mortal death to immortal, eternal LIFE when they put their trust in God through Jesus.

When they put their trust in God—when they are born² —an instant, tectonic shift in their personal world and universe occurs and they become new creations in Christ. Their old, non-eternal life begins to diminish, and they become new, eternal beings with the very LIFE of God implanted within them for all the ages of time—and thereafter in the state of being called eternity.

As noted above, in John 10: 10, Jesus exclaimed that He came to give people (present tense) God's very own eternal, self-existent, uncreated, abundant LIFE. Such life is rich, full, ample, plentiful, and more than sufficient because it is God's own LIFE flowing out of eternity into our mortal, human lives, making us eternal creations rather than mere flesh and blood, mortal creations.

We Can Know That We Know That We Know

As already mentioned, 1 John 5: 11 – 13 teaches us very clearly that God has given us eternal LIFE (present tense) and this LIFE is (present tense) in his Son, Jesus, the God-Man. If we possess the Son (present tense), we possess (present tense) the LIFE of God in us; if we do not possess the Son, we do not have Gods' LIFE within us. That reference informs us that God caused such truths to be written for us so that we may KNOW (not merely wish or hope) that we have his very own eternal LIFE in us now.

Do you **know** that you have God's very own LIFE within you? If not, you can know simply by placing your faith and trust in God through Jesus and being born². It is not that *perhaps* you have God's LIFE in you, or *maybe* you have God's LIFE in you, or you can only *hope* you have his LIFE in you. You can ***know*** beyond any doubt!

Beyond The Far Shores of Time

To gain a better understanding of what I'm attempting to teach about eternal LIFE, **it would help to understand a little about the differences between time and eternity.**

So, let's examine for a few moments the concepts of time and eternity. They are both integral parts of the broader truth of God's very own LIFE within his twice-born sons and daughters. I'll attempt to teach these two concepts as somewhat separate from one another, but, of necessity, there is much overlapping of the two. When we look at the subject of time, we will also look at other concepts that are finite, temporal, non-absolute, and relative.

Only the Holy Spirit, the true Author of the Bible, can teach us in depth about time and eternity. And I encourage you to ask Him for assistance and enlightenment as you continue to read this section of my book. He can fill in the many gaps I've left out of this section because of my own limited understanding. I freely admit there is much I still don't comprehend.

There is much yet to be learned as the Holy Spirit gives us illumination and enlightenment. In a sense, there is much about time and eternity that only time to come and—later—the eternal state of being can clarify for us. In considering time, we will also touch on such concepts as infinity, space, the universe, and that part of Albert Einstein's Theory of Relativity pertinent to this teaching.

A concept we must grasp immediately at the outset is **time is an integral part of the entirety of all created phenomena** (Hebrews 1:2) consisting of past, present, and future—just as humans are created phenomena having youth, middle age, and old age. No, we cannot touch, smell, or hear time, but it is there, ever-present, always flowing out of the past through the present and marching into the future.

Yes, time was created; it had a beginning, it shall have an end. It is a created entity among countless other entities which are part of the entire created universe.

Time is as much a "class" or "phylum" of God's creation as, for example, rocks, elephants, trees, and water are classes of creation. Before the creation of the universe, time did not exist; at the end of the eons of time it shall cease to be. It will be swallowed up into eternity just as all death (the first death and the second death, which is the lake of fire (Revelation 20: 14), will be swallowed up into God and cease to be.

Time—composed of milliseconds, seconds, minutes, hours, days, weeks, months, years, decades, centuries, millenniums, ages, and eons—was created in the beginning and will be dissolved and cease to exist at some point in the future.

This phenomena we call time was created by God for humanity. Why? I'm greatly oversimplifying, but it was created to aid fallen, sinful humans to accommodate ourselves to this material, mortal, and temporal plane of existence and to aid us in living out our days and years in preparation for a new, totally spiritual, non-material, glorified existence beyond time in a state of existence called eternity.

We will all pass from a physical, material existence into a glorious spiritual existence; **time serves only to aid us—to give us time, so to speak—to prepare for that new spiritual state of being**. And each of us has been allotted a certain amount of time to make such preparations. Let us use our time wisely and responsibly in ministry and service to God and others!

We are spiritual beings sent here to earth to have a temporary, finite, mortal human experience—not human beings sent here to have a spiritual experience!

A proper understanding of time as a created phenomena having beginning and ending is an absolute prerequisite to a proper understanding of eternity. Because it is a created phenomena, time can be studied to some extent just as any other part of the creation of God can be studied. For example, we know by definition what time is: *"A system for measuring duration."* Or, it can be defined as: *"A continuum in which events succeed one another from past through present to future."*

We know how to measure time: with chronometers ranging from incredibly precise atomic clocks to Mickey Mouse watches. We know how it functions by its effects in passing: maturity, decay, corrosion, erosion, deterioration, and the like. Someone has humorously quipped that, *"Time is the thing that keeps stuff from happening all at once!"* Someone else said it's *"the stuff that happens between paychecks."* Finally, someone wisely has said of time: *"It can only be spent, not saved."*

It's All Relative

As previously mentioned, an entire body of learning discipline for the study of time has been established by Einstein's Theory of Relativity. For purposes of this book, we understand from Einstein's theory that time and space are interdependent, inseparably related, and form a four-dimensional continuum (length, height, depth, and duration). That is to say, there is no space without time, no time without space. Space cannot be traversed without the passage of time; without the passage of time, there can be no traversing of space.

To furnish only one quick example, that is why in his post-resurrection, spiritual body, Jesus was immediately able to transcend and traverse the space-time continuum with "speed" surpassing time. By Jesus' power, space and time cohere, adhere, and consist (Colossians 1: 17). Without his binding power, space and time would become non-existent. He is not limited nor restricted in any manner by time and space. Jesus is over and above all space and time because He is The Creator of all!

We also understand from the Bible that both time and space (as we presently know them) will be swallowed up and subsumed into eternity—subsumed and changed into a higher and different state of being altogether. All that is physical and material will be swallowed up into that which is wholly spiritual, because God—toward whom we are all bound on our life-journeys—is non-corporeal (unbodied)—pure Spirit (John 4: 24). He is Wholly Other from we material, physical, corporeal beings who are presently limited by time and space.

In this regard, too, we must briefly consider whether or not time and space are finite or infinite. If they are infinite, are they necessarily eternal? By definition, space is "*the expanse in which all material things are contained.*" Infinity is to say "*that something lacks known or measurable limits and bounds*"—not that something has no limits or boundaries.

With my present understanding, I believe that space and time do have limits and boundaries, but they cannot be measured by presently known scientific and astronomical instruments. However, I am open to changing my mind as additional information becomes known. I believe space, time, and the material universe are created entities and are infinite, but only in the sense they cannot be measured by finite humans. They are not infinite in the sense of being eternal as only God is.

Now let's consider the concept of eternity. Please understand that the simplest definition of eternity is *"a state of being in which the Eternal God dwells."* We shall see that it is much more than that, but it is a state of being, first and foremost. In other words, eternity is not a created phenomena as time is. In all candor, I believe the Bible teaches very little by way of defining or describing eternity.

Why? Because the Bible is essentially a book of time and for time, not for eternity. It was written for us who are still time-limited beings, not yet totally eternal beings. It was written **to** humans, **for** humans, and does not contain exhaustive information about the state of being called eternity—simply because—until we reach eternity—our limited, finite minds could not even begin to grasp even the most elemental truths about infinity and eternity.

Where is that state of being we call eternity to be found? If we were to consider it an actual "place" (it is not!), **we will find eternity beginning beyond the farthest shores of time!**

We are presently creatures of time—journeying through time. Only when we arrive at and fully enter that state of being called eternity . . . only when He who is Eternal becomes All in All in us . . . only when time ends and is swallowed up into eternity . . . only when eternity becomes an absolute reality to us . . . only when we are spiritually metamorphosized into our eternal milieu . . . only then will we who were formerly temporal and physical beings begin to comprehend eternity and matters of an eternal nature.

Everything written in time about eternity (including this Appendix) is at best merely enlightened speculation based upon limited information.

I wrote that the Bible is relatively silent about the state of being called eternity. That is not to say that human teachings and theology haven't taught us a a few things about eternity, but, sadly, some of it over the past 1,700 years or so has come from human minds not necessarily sensitive to the mind of the Eternal One via the Holy Spirit. Praise God for the true teaching ministry of the Eternal Spirit!

God Is Eternal

We read in the Bible that God is Eternal, or, more literally, the Father of Eternity (Deuteronomy 33: 27, Isaiah 9: 6). He is called so in the sense that he is the originator and sustainer of eternity. In short, eternity is part of God. He is eternity. Eternity is in God. In continuing to consider the eternal state of being, we must completely jettison any thinking that time has anything to do with eternity or is part of eternity. Time and eternity are two separate entities. They are mutually exclusive of one another in an absolute sense.

Eternity is a state of absolute timelessness, NOT a state of unending time. Eternity is a state of being, resident in the very nature and person of God in which such concepts as past, present, future, before, after, minutes, hours, and years do not exist. **There are no endless ages of time in eternity.**

There is no "forever" in eternity. Eternity is a state of absolute simultaneousness, not a state that goes on and on and on "forever" with the passage of "unending" time.

The ages of time will end; they are alien concepts in eternity. Time and eternity have no relationship with one another just as up or down, for example, have no relationship with light or dark. The terms are mutually exclusive. Time is not part of eternity just as up is not part of light.

Eternity is NOT composed of endless segments of time or of unending ages that go on and on and on forever and forever without end.

It may seem like I'm greatly overemphasizing this point (almost to the point of boring you!), but it is absolutely essential that you understand such differences between eternity and time before you can begin to comprehend what the Bible teaches, for example, about eternal LIFE or eternal punishment. Time is not part of eternity. Eternity is not composed of unending segments of time. Eternity is not time standing still. It simply is not time in any sense that we understand time. Eternity doesn't go on and on, *ad infinitum*.

Eternity doesn't go anywhere or anywhen, nor does it do anything. Eternity simply is. It is as foolish to say that eternity goes on and on and on as to say, for example, that Texas goes on and on and on. Texas simply is a state in which people exist. So it is with eternity.

Time is created. It is extra-eternal in the sense we say something is extra-biblical. Time is a measurable, fixed, limited, created phenomena. Eternity, in contrast, is part of the very unmeasurable, non-fixed, limitless nature and person of God. Eternity transcends beyond our comprehension anything having to do with time. Eternity simply is, just as God simply is. The expression, *"It is that it is,"* has unique reference to eternity just as *"I am that I am"* has unique reference to God. Just as Jesus said, *"Before Abraham was, I am,"* (John 8: 58) it can be said of eternity, *"Before time was, I am."*

You've Got God's Full Attention

For example, if you get a good grasp of these definitions of eternity, you will be able to readily understand a matter which people have struggled with every since God first revealed himself to humanity. That matter goes something like this: *"God must be so busy with running the universe and answering more 'important' prayers than mine from billions of people, that He can't possibly find time for little old unimportant me and my prayers."* C'mon now, admit that you've had thoughts like that from time to time.

The answer to that is that God exists in a state of absolute simultaneousness, and He is able at any given time to give **his full attention at all times** to everyone and everything—**including you!** Yes, **at any given time, He can devote his full attention to you**, while at the same time, devoting his full attention to everything else . . . and everyone else . . . everywhere else . . . and everywhen else.

Basic Definitions

For my next point let's consider only briefly the definitions of such biblical English words and terms as *"forever," "forever and ever," "eternal," everlasting,"* and related expressions. In over 500 places in many modern translations of the Bible where we find such terms in the English language as the four just mentioned, they have with very few exceptions been incorrectly translated from the original Hebrew, Greek, and Aramaic languages in which the Bible was written.

There are many excellent, scholarly books and treatises written about this matter of the differences between time and eternity. For example, see www.tentmakers.org. On that website, you'll find more teaching about this subject (and related concepts) than you can read in your lifetime.

However, for an excellent non-big-words summary teaching about this matter, I highly recommend a book by a friend of mine, Gerry Beauchemin, entitled **Hope Beyond Hell**. It can be ordered from www.hopebeyondhell.net, or from the author at gerrydenise@yahoo.com, or telephone him at 1-956-831-9011 or 1-979-540-9900. It's the best summary statement of this teaching I have read in over 40 years.

"Forever" can most often be translated as *"age-lasting"* or *"continuing for the ages of time."* *"Forever and ever"* and *"everlasting"* should be translated as *"for the age(s) of the ages"* or *"enduring for the ages of time."* None such biblical words or expressions are about segments of time that go on and on and on without end.

I am simply saying that these words are all temporal words expressed in temporal languages—fallen languages of a fallen race of beings, languages that are inadequate to wholly express and define that which is eternal. They are not words having to do with eternity; they are only about time.

In the original languages, the biblical emphasis on such words seems to be upon the quality, purpose, and "character" of such words rather than upon an unending duration. In other words, eternal LIFE or eternal fire means the nature, quality, or purpose of the LIFE or fire rather than their length or duration.

Again, eternal LIFE is the . . .

self-existent . . .
uncreated . . .

incorruptible . . .
indestructible . . .
undiminishable . . .
imperishable . . .
measureless . . .
boundless . . .
limitless . . .
abundant . . .
wonder-full . . .

. . . LIFE God has permanently implanted in his twice-born sons and daughters.

It is a LIFE, the seed of which we now possess within our human spirits and which will fully blossom in eternity after the farthest ages of time have ceased to exist.

Fire!

Eternal fire, or fire which burns forever and ever—for ages and ages of time—((Revelation 20: 10 ff) is fire which has the quality of purging, disciplining, correcting, and cleansing, but which will burn itself out for lack of "fuel" at the end of the ages of time.

True, the Bible says such fire is unquenchable, meaning that it cannot be put out nor extinguished by external forces, but such fires will simply burn out at the end of the ages of time (or some "time" in the eternal state) when they have burned up all their "fuel" and served their intended purposes of purging, disciplining, cleansing, and correcting all humanity.

The emphasis in the Bible is upon fire's purposes, not its duration. I've given only a few examples of such words and expressions. An exhaustive—and startlingly convincing—personal study can be made of every such word in the Bible with the use of a good Bible concordance. Also, you may want to take a few moments and read a teaching on our web site mentioned earlier: **Fire!**

In summary, it can readily be seen that both time and eternity are concepts beyond total comprehension by fallen and limited human beings. Even under the pure teaching ministry of the Holy Spirit, our "darkened" minds and understanding are too limited to fully grasp their meanings.

Nevertheless, even a dim understanding of such concepts will help change our imaginings and preconceived notions of space, time, the universe, God's nature and personality, God's "size," God's inherent eternality, and our own "future" eternality.

An 11th century Jesus-believer named Hildebert of Lavardin wrote these words about God's "size": *"God, You are within all things, but not enclosed; outside all things, but not excluded. You are above all things, sustaining them; wholly beneath, the Foundation of all things. You are wholly outside, embracing all things, wholly within, filling all things."*

Upon thinking about the matter recently, I wrote these thoughts: *"God, You are the absolute All at the precise center of all the multi-dimensions of time, space, and eternity . . . but there is no circumference."*

God is cultivating within his people an eternal nature, a nature no longer rigidly bound to and regulated by time, by clocks, by seasons, by cycles. The thoughts of God's people are becoming boundless and eternal, no longer limited, controlled, and motivated entirely by memories of the past, by present events, or by dim hopes for an endless future in the "sweet bye and bye."

God's people are becoming age-less and time-less, are being "caught up" to God and his throne, are becoming truly and genuinely eternal beings in many ways. The fledgling eternal spirits of God's people are growing up into the limitless expanses of God's own eternal, spiritual nature. His people are becoming new eternal creations, no longer limited by the restrictions of the space-time continuum and by our physicality and materiality.

We have come to understand the reality—as I stated earlier—that **we are not temporal human beings having a brief spiritual experience; no, we are eternal spiritual beings having a tempororary human experience!** We are seeing with our "eyes of faith" the reality of a state of being called eternity—resident in the very nature and person of God—and our hearts strain and leap upward toward that "place" in God that awaits us beyond the eons of time.

I hope that brief Appendix about the concepts of time and eternity help you more fully appreciate the wonder-full, rich, abundant, eternal LIFE God has implanted within you through the eternal sacrifice and total and complete salvation God has given you through God the Son, Jesus! He implanted that LIFE in you at the time of your new-creation, second birth, and it will continue to grow within you throughout all the eons of time—and then beyond time into the eternal state! Thank God for such eternal LIFE and salvation!

Appendix Three

Divorce And Remarriage

Down through the corridors of almost 24 centuries of time echoes this exclamation by God: ***I hate divorce!"***

That statement (found in Malachi 2: 16) troubled me for many years. Why would God make such a statement? Did He arbitrarily and capriciously wake up one morning and decide He would hate a few things—including divorce? What might have been his reasons for making such a strong statement?

First, you need to read the statement in its context; God made the statement remonstrating Israelite men who had divorced their Israelite wives in order to marry foreign—pagan—wives, something God had forbidden them to do, knowing that such marriage alliances detract from a pure (unmixed) relationship with the one true and living God.

That principle has been carried over into the New Covenant wherein God forbids Jesus-believers to marry pre-believers (2 Corinthians 6: 14).

But the statement *"I hate divorce!"* goes deeper than that. The reason God hates divorce is that He was divorced . . . and He knows the pain of divorce; He knows the terrible hurt of divorce. He knows the agony and suffering involved in most divorces. God divorced Israel and Judah for commiting spiritual adultery (idolatry). You can read about that in Jeremiah 3: 8 and related references in the Old Testament. God hates divorce because He knows how much it hurts the parties involved in divorce. Understand this very clearly: God hates divorce . . . ***not*** divorced persons! He loves people who are divorced . . . no less, no more than He loves everyone.

God knows—humanly speaking—that some marital situations are just plain unbearable and unrepairable, and He doesn't expect a mere fallible mortal to endure such a failed relationship forever. Even God didn't endure Israel's unbelief forever! He divorced her. You might want to think about that for a while.

What Jesus Said

Having given you that brief background, let's now examine what both Jesus and one of his spokespersons, Paul, have to say about the matter of divorce. Both Jesus and Paul deal very constructively and positively with divorce. Let's explore in detail what they have to say.

Let's listen in on a conversation between Jesus, his disciples, and a few Pharisees (religious leaders of Jesus' time) as recorded in Matthew 19: 3 – 11. (There are quotes in this passage from Genesis 1: 27 and 2: 24, and Deuteronomy 24: 1 – 4 in the Old Testament.) In the conversation beginning in Matthew 19: 3, Jesus reaches back in time before He gave the Law to Moses, and shows how God really intends things to be. By doing this, Jesus demonstrates there are weak points in Moses' law—because it's a law that applies to sinful and weak humans.

Please understand that Jesus actually came along and "expanded" Moses' law; that is, He amplified, clarified, and explained the "spirit" of the law contrasted with the "letter" of the law. Centuries earlier, King David and King Solomon had done the same with Moses' law, amplifying, clarifying, and giving the spirit of the law Moses had proclaimed centuries before their time. After Jesus, God used Paul and other New Testament writers to make the same type of clarifications under the New Covenant.

This sometimes causes confusion among Bible-believers because they don't understand the "progression" of the law since Moses. This is particularly true about some things Jesus said because He often talked with Jews who were trying to find favor with God by keeping the law of Moses. He told them time and time again what the "spirit" of Moses' law was—with the idea that it is impossible to please God through keeping the law of Moses. He said the law of Moses could not be kept in its entirety by anyone (Himself excluded).

Looking again at Matthew 19, in this reference Jesus is attempting to explain the depth and the narrowness of Moses' law about divorce and remarriage. Jesus is saying that not all humans are able to accept and live with what He said about Moses' commandment concerning divorce. Even his own disciples didn't want to hear it; they were actually saying that, in their opinion, if divorce and remarriage are not possible under the law of Moses, they don't want anything to do with marriage—even Peter whom we know was already married!

Jesus is saying, *"If you can keep the rules God handed down to Moses, that's good; if you can't keep them, leave them alone!"* He is saying it's a commandment that is best kept, while realizing fully that not all people can keep it. Confusing?

Maybe this will help. While reading the four Gospels (the entire New Testament, for that matter) keep three things in mind: 1. *What Jesus said.* 2. *What Moses said.* 3. *What Jesus said Moses said.* Simply keep in mind who is speaking, to whom they are speaking, and exactly what the speaker is saying.

Often, when Jesus explains in more detail what Moses said, people mistakenly think this is what Jesus says and teaches. That's the case in Matthew 5: 31 and 32, for example. Jesus' comments about divorcing someone, about fornication, and about adultery are his amplification and clarification of what Moses wrote.

Often, Jesus' explanations are to show that no one can keep the law of Moses . . . so they need a new covenant; the old law (covenant) was given by God to Moses so that people would have a "tutor"—some general guidelines to live by—until Jesus came to fulfill that law and give it a new and higher meaning. For example, Galatians 3: 23 – 25 states: *"The law of Moses served as our tutor, trainer, and guide to Jesus, who is now a ' higher Law.'"* God's laws are now written in the hearts of people rather than upon tablets of stone.

Another example. Jesus speaks about "looking on a woman" with lust being the same as committing adultery. (Matthew 5: 28) All He is doing is explaining the true spirit of Moses' law. Jesus is not instituting a new law; He is simply explaining the fact that no one can find favor with God by keeping Moses' laws. Then in Matthew 7 Jesus summed up the subject by explaining that anyone who builds his "house" on Moses' law builds on shifting, unstable sand. Anyone who builds on Jesus' new law (New Covenant) builds on a firm, solid Rock.

What Paul Said

Now let's examine what God has to say through Paul about divorce and remarriage. His main teaching on this subject is in 1 Corinthians 7. He wrote that in view of a situation he calls "the impending distress" (verse 26), his readers in the city of Corinth shouldn't even get married in the first place.

Historically, we know "the impending distress" was a terrible time of persecution soon to be unleashed against Jesus-believers throughout the Roman Empire. We know Paul's recommendation against marriage in "the impending distress" was not a permanent recommendation by God because it does not fit the flow of the Bible's overall teachings about marriage; God highly regards marriage. Paul's restrictions were only because of "the impending distress," there being no need to heed such restrictions in normal times and circumstances.

In 1 Corinthians 7, verse 1, Paul admonishes people to remain unmarried. But . . . if they do marry, here are the rules (verse 2 and following). In verse 8, he says to the unmarried and the widowed it would be best if they stay single. But . . . if they choose to marry, here are the rules. In both instances, he teaches if people get married, work at it; commit to it; give it every chance they can.

Verse 10 says don't get separated. Verse 11 says if you do separate, here are the rules. Verse 15 says don't get divorced. But . . . if you do, here are the rules (verse 16). Verse 27 says don't get remarried. Verse 28 says if you do remarry, here are the rules. God says if people happen to get divorced, it's okay. It's not what God intended from the very beginning, but it happens. If you're divorced, don't go looking for another spouse unless you feel you really need to; if you do remarry, it's okay . . . it's not sin.

Real Sin: Hardness of Heart

What actually causes divorce? Is there one single cause that is instrumental in all divorces? I believe there is. Jesus put his finger on that basic cause in Matthew 19: 8: **Hardness of Heart!** Divorce is only a symptom of the real problem—hardness of heart—which creates intolerable situations that can be resolved sometimes only by divorce. Hardness of heart is the real problem, not divorce. Hardness of heart occurs when people stubbornly resist the loving activities of God in their lives, wanting to do their "own thing" in spite of what God says or does.

Sin in its very essence is living a self-filled, self-consumed, self-seeking, self-focused, self-centered life instead of a God-filled life. That type of emphasis on "self" rather than upon God all too often leads to hardness of heart in a marriage.

For example, one spouse may have a "soft heart" and want to remain married, whereas the other spouse has a "hard heart" and wants to get divorced. If the spouse having the hard heart is unwilling to change, then the hardness of heart could very well lead to divorce, even if the soft-hearted spouse does not want to be divorced. In such cases, it's not the divorce that is sin; it is the hardness of heart—the emphasis on self rather than upon God and what He wants for one's life.

Please understand this very clearly: I am not encouraging divorce, nor making light of it! I am merely attempting to shed some light on a very difficult matter. I do not have the final word on the matter; I am merely sharing what little biblical insight I presently have about this matter. But I do want to help divorced people. Far too many separated and divorced people cry themselves to sleep every night (and do many regrettable—even crazy—things) in reaction to condemnation heaped upon them by misinformed people . . . and by themselves.

Some spend the remainder of their lives after divorce and/or remarriage in misery and self-condemnation—or condemnation by others. We must not condemn those who have experienced divorce and remarriage. Usually, some situations caused by hardness of heart "kill" the marriage long before the actual date stamped on the divorce papers. One or both spouses—having hard hearts—created the situations that became intolerable. That hardness of heart is sin; divorce is merely a response to that sin.

When He is asked to do so, God can—and does—forgive any and all sin . . . including hardness of heart! There is no condemnation to those who are in Jesus . . . single, married, widowed, divorced, or remarried!

No Position To Judge

What should be my response—my position—toward someone who is separated or divorced? Each situation is unique, but I can say this: we are never in a position to judge, condemn, or criticize someone for being divorced.

There are four reasons why this is so:

1. We do not know how hard a person worked to save his or her marriage; we do not know who was "at fault." In fact, it is never true that only one person is at fault. Don't think of fault; think of responsibility. Each party to a separation or divorce is at least partly responsible—never just one person. There are degrees of responsibility for both spouses, more than simply which spouse is at fault.
2. We do not know the power of the "forces" that assailed the marriage and each of the parties in the marriage. We do not know the emotional, mental, and character strengths and weaknesses of the divorced persons; we never know another human intimately enough to know the depths of their strengths and weaknesses. We don't know how hard they may have fought to keep the marriage intact; or, how weak they might have been in those areas of their lives that might have served to strengthen the marriage had they been stronger.
3. We never know the ***exact, precise*** details of the circumstances or events (as experienced and perceived by the parties involved) which led to their actions.

4. There is no way we can ever know exactly and precisely what **we** would have done in the exact, same circumstances or events.

For these reasons—and more—we are never in a position to judge, condemn or criticize a person who is separated or divorced . . . or subsequently remarried. It is particularly true that a person who has previously been a party to a divorce is never in a position to judge someone who is presently undergoing a separation or divorce. Of all people, such persons ought to be a source of strength and support; they need to just "be there" in a positive manner for the person presently suffering the pain and anguish of separation or divorce.

Most of us don't understand even a small fraction of our inner selves and why we sometimes do what we do; our insight into our own motives and behavior is at best very clouded and murky. God alone knows us perfectly. God alone executes perfect judgment arising from his full and perfect knowledge. And, *"Shall not the Judge of all the earth judge in a perfectly righteous manner [because He alone has all the facts; He alone knows the truth, the entire truth, and nothing but the truth about all our deepest motives and actions]?!"* (Genesis 18: 25)

In many respects, the Bible is a teaching textbook. For most teaching subjects covered by the Bible, there are usually one or two major references about that subject. Along with one or two major references, there are usually many other "minor" texts and references about that subject. For the subject of this teaching, I have selected the two major texts (Matthew 19 and 1 Corinthians 7), but since this teaching is not exhaustive I won't cover many of the minor texts—although there are many of them.

I simply don't want to make this teaching too lengthy. Keep in mind, then, that I am covering only a couple of major texts about divorce and remarriage; I am not covering many, many, minor references—although for the most part, all the minor texts (when properly understood) teach the same as the major texts.

I'm not trying to "pull the wool over your eyes" by using "proof texts"; as I always tell all my students, *"Check me out. Don't simply take my word about what I teach. I'm human; I make mistakes. I'm not the final authority about what the Bible teaches."* On the subjects I'm teaching herein, if you, the reader, check me out with an open mind I think you'll come to see my conclusions are correct. If not, well, I've been wrong before and probably will be again . . .

And . . . just so you'll know where I'm at in my own understanding and comprehension, I'll say it as plainly as I can: The Bible does not teach that divorce and remarriage are unforgivable sins. Divorce is forgivable and remarriage is not a sin. Jesus and Paul deal constructively with both matters and show us how to deal with them, too. But in order to understand both subjects, we must separate what many Bible-believers mistakenly teach from what the Bible actually teaches about divorce and remarriage.

A More Detailed Examination

Let's look at in more depth what God teaches through Paul in 1 Corinthians 7, one of our two major texts. In the first part of the chapter, Paul teaches that in view of impending, distressful events happening in their first century world it would be best not to get married in the first place; we won't address that issue in this teaching. In verse 10 Paul tells married women not to leave their husbands. The verse goes on to teach, however, that if she departs, let her remain unmarried or be reconciled to her husband; and let not the husband divorce his wife in such a situation.

Thus, in verse 10 Paul closed the door on separation by telling wives not to depart. But in verse 11 he opens the door by stating if she departs—recognizing that some could not follow the instructions and would choose to depart. In the 15th verse, Paul goes on to teach, *"But if the unbelieving depart, let him depart."* This does not mean a non-Jesus-believer who departs, but an "unbelieving" Jesus-believer—a believer with a "hardened heart"—(whether male or female) who is not under bondage in such cases but is called to peace. The false commandments and religious traditions of most Jesus-believers keep such people under bondage; God calls them to peace.

Here's one of Jesus' comment on such a case: Look at John 4: 18. Jesus did not tell the woman at the well to go find her first husband.

No! Jesus told her to worship God. Some well-intended (but misguided) Jesus-believers even tell a divorced and remarried person to divorce their present spouse and go remarry their first spouse. They say the first spouse is the proper one and if they marry anyone else they are living in adultery. Such bondage! No. Jesus calls us to peace and tells us to worship God.

Now back to 1 Corinthians 7. Verse 16 says, *"There is no assurance to a spouse if they stay that the other spouse will cease their unbelieving."* This is another verse many Jesus-believers use to heap guilt upon a spouse to keep them from leaving an unbelieving spouse. But God says let them go. Yes, life would be better for both spouses if they tried to work out their problems together, but that doesn't always happen. That's just the way life is sometimes among mortal, sinful humans—some can't resolve their marriage problems, and they have to depart.

Why does God permit separation? Why does He permit divorce? Because he went through his own divorce as we read earlier, and he knows how tough it can be trying to stick it out with a spouse who's causing intolerable pain to the other. Look at Jeremiah 3: 6-8. God got so upset with Israel (his spouse) that he divorced her. The book of Hosea refers to the same situation.

Let's summarize 1 Corinthians 7 in this manner:

Verse 1 says don't get married.
Verse 2 says if you do, here are the new rules.

Verse 8 says don't get married.
Verse 9 says if you do, here are the new rules.

Verse 10 says don't divorce.
Verse 11 says if you do, here are the new rules.

Verse 15a says don't divorce.
Verse 15b says if you do, here are the new rules.

Verse 27 says don't get remarried.
Verse 28 says if you do, here are the new rules.

Those, then are the Bible's main teachings about divorce and remarriage. There should be no condemnation from others. There should be no self-condemnation or self-recrimination. Jesus does not condemn you. God does not condemn you. You are free to live life to the fullest with the joy and peace the Holy Spirit (who lives inside you) gives everyone who is "softhearted" (not hardhearted), pliable, humble, and open to God's living his own life in them, through them, and as them.

[This teaching is loosely based upon an article published in September 1979 by David Ebaugh, who has since that time exited this mortal stage and continued on to the next stage of Life's Great Journey through time and in eternity. David was a dear Jesus-believer brother and a great teacher of the Bible. I miss both him and his teachings.]

Appendix Four

Druids, Celts, And Jesus

Here's a story about God and the Celts that's been passed down by word-of-mouth for centuries.

"Clouds boiled up to cover the sky and the sound of a mighty wind filled all the world. And though it was bright midday, the heavens grew dark as twilight after the sun has set. Not the slightest breath of wind could be felt, yet the roaring of the unseen wind grew louder. There was thunder, but no lightning, and the hair stood up on the necks of people and beasts alike. Jagged chunks of hail fell out of the sky and lay in the grass smoldering as on fire.

All at once a voice was heard crying out to them. They turned and saw approaching out of the west in the direction of the setting sun, a mighty champion fair and tall—taller than any three of the tallest among them and more wonderful to look upon than the most handsome person they had ever seen. His eyes were the color of the windswept sky, and his teeth were straight and white. His chin was smooth-shaven, and his brow was high and fine.

For a cloak. the magnificent stranger wore a shining garb as radiant and rainbow-hued as crystal, and for sandals, hammered bands of purest gold. His hair was pale as flax and uncut, falling in curls to the middle of his back. This mighty champion carried two stone tablets in his left hand and a silver branch with three fruits in his right, and these were the fruits which were on the branch:

apples, hazelnuts, and acorns. Around his waist he wore a girdle of bronze plates, and each plate could have served as a platter for four kings. In his girdle he carried a knife with a blade made of glass that was sharper than the sharpest steel.

Around the stranger's neck was an open golden band as thick as a baby's arm, and on the ends were jewels: a ruby on the right and a sapphire on the left. His hands were broad and strong, and when he spoke, his voice sounded like the waves upon the shore 0r like the rushing of many waters.

He came to stand before the assembled kings of Eire [Ireland], and he said, Greetings, friends—if friends you be.

The princes and princelings quailed before him, but the High King drove his chariot to where the stranger stood. He raised his hand in kingly greeting and said, I am king here, and this is my realm. I welcome you, champion—if champion you be. What has brought you here?

I have come from the setting of the sun, and I am going to the rising. My name is Treluilngid Treochair, answered the stranger.

A strange name, replied the king. And why has that name been given you?

Easy to say, replied Trefuilngid, because it is myself, and no one else who upholds the sun, causing it to rise in the east and set in the west.

The high king regarded the towering stranger with curiousity. Forgive me, friend, for asking, he said, but why are you here at the setting of the sun when it is at the rising you must be?

Easy to say, answered the marvelous stranger, but not so easy to hear, I think. For, in a land far away from here, a man was tortured today—and for that reason I am on my way to the east.

This tortured man, inquired the king, of what account was he that one such as yourself should take notice?

You cut to the heart of the matter, to be sure, replied the stranger, for the man of whom I speak was born to be the ruler of the world. He was called the Prince of Peace, Righteous Lord, and King of Kings.

At these words the king and his noblemen groaned. Certainly this is a grave injustice, and deeply to be lamented, observed the king, yet such things are known to happen from time to time. Even so, it does not explain why you have come among us like this.

The man I speak of was crucified and killed by the men who tortured him, Trefuilngid explained. His name was Esu, and he was the rightful High King of Heaven, Son of the Strong Upholder, Lord of Life and Light. When he died, the sun stepped aside, and darkness has covered the face of the earth. I came forth to find out what ailed the sun, learned of this outrage, and now I am telling you.

The king drew himself up and said, I thank you for telling us, friend. But tell us one thing more: Where can we find the vile cowards who perpetrated this injustice? Only say the word, and rest assured we will not cease until we have punished them with the death they undoubtedly deserve.

Your wrath is noble and worthy, friend, replied the magnificent stranger, but it is misplaced. For in three days time the same man who was crucified will break the bonds of death and rise again to walk the world of the living. Through him death itself will be conquered forever.

When they heard this good news, the king and all the noblemen and bards of Eire wept for joy. They demanded to know how this had come about, and the glittering stranger told them, It has been ordained from before the foundation of the world. But it has been revealed to you now so that you may prepare your people for the age to come.

Now you know how knowledge of the Truth came to Eire."

Whether or not that is a true story remains to be seen. But if you are a Celt, such a story in Irish history has a ring of truth to it, for we Celts believe in such magnificent stories about our history in this world.

Alternative History

Now I will continue this teaching by sharing with you just a very little of "alternative history"; there is much more than I could possibly write in this brief teaching. Alternative history is history not generally taught or accepted by traditional, mainstream historians, but it is not necessarily history that is untrue.

Mainstream secular history informs us that the people known as the Celts first arrived in the southern British Isles (biblical Tarshish?) around 600 BC. Those historians inform us that the Celts "probably" came from Spain or Portugal, but they cannot be certain of their origins. There is some indication that a "branch" of the Celts were living in Galatia (in modern Turkey) at the time Paul wrote to them the New Testament Book (letter) of Galatians, and that the Celts originally came from what we now call the steppes of Russia.

Most of the traditional Celtic history we have today came from the writings of the Romans when they invaded the British Isles. After the Romans invaded the southern British Isles, many of the Celts fled to Ireland and survived there until about the 7th century AD. It wasn't until the late 18th century that the world saw a revived interest in the Celts and in all things Celtic; from approximately 400 AD until then, not much was known or remembered about the Celts.

The Celts living in the British Isles—including Ireland—were described as tall and clean-shaven, dressed in very brightly colored clothes of many colors (think Joseph's coat of many bright colors in that saga in the biblical book of Genesis). They were described as very formidable, fierce warriors—including their women.

586 B.C.: Israelite Refugees

Interestingly—coincidentally?—some Israeli refugees from the final Babylonian invasion (586 BC) of the biblical southern Kingdom of Judah are said by some non-mainstream historians to have fled Israel—through Egypt—at that same time—by sea around the Rock of Gibralter, past Portugal, Spain, and Gaul (France), and then on to the British Isles. Hmmm. Interesting. 586 BC (alternative history) and 600 BC (mainstream history) are pretty close in historical time . . .

Some "alternative historians" inform us that among that small band of Israeli refugees were the aged prophet Jeremiah and one of the daughters of the last king of Judah, Zedekiah—as well as some Old Testament priests of God, and some "lay persons."

Tradition has it that one item the refugees brought with them to the British Isles (for reasons unknown) was a sizable stone pillar, the "pillow of Jacob" mentioned in the 28th chapter of Genesis. When the Romans later defeated them, the Celts carried the stone to Scotland, where it was known as the famous Stone of Scone. It was later moved to southern Britain and became the coronation stone of British kings and queens at Westminster Cathedral where it remains to this day.

Since they were fleeing refugees, they did not have opportunity to take much with them—only a few personal belongings, and, unfortunately, not any of the written Old Testament Scriptures. As mentioned above, there were a few priests among the refugees, having with them only their oral tradition and personal memories of how to "conduct" worship of the One True and living God when they arrived in the British Isles.

In Ireland, the Celts came to be known as the "Tuatha de Danaan," possibly from the Israeli Tribe of Dan, one of the original 12 tribes of Israel; In the time of Joshua, the Danites originally settled in the west-central region of Canaan bordering the Mediterranean. Note the interesting similarities of word construction between Dan**aan** and Can**aan.** Upon reaching Ireland, they established a "sacred" hill named Tara, the seat of their kings and a center of worship just as the Hill of Zion in Jerusalem had once had been the capitol city of Israel (before the kingdom was divided in two), a center of worship, and "sacred" hill to the Israelites.

However, neither in Britain nor in Ireland did the Celts build temples, believing that God "did not dwell in temples made with hands" (1 Kings 8: 27; Acts 7: 48 and 17: 24). They believed that, collectively, humans were the Temple of the Living God (1 Corinthians 3 and 6).

Another stone, the Stone of Destiny, was later carried to Ireland and became part of the coronation ceremonies of various Irish kings at the sacred hill of Tara.

The Druids

Those Old Testament Israelite priests noted above later came to be known as "Ceile De": Druid priests who later became Jesus-believers to preserve the True Path and guard the Holy Light. The Druids have received a lot of bad—false—press through the centuries. Most traditional, mainstream historians claim they were a wild, bloodthirsty lot who practiced human sacrifices, black magic, sorcery, and the like.

That is not true! They were simply Old Testament priests who—without the written Old Testament—simply conducted worship as well as they could remember from when they had been in Israel before fleeing to the British Isles. Their worship practices were passed down orally from approximately 600 B.C. until Jesus-believers came to their lands. The Druidic priesthood simply attempted to lead God's people—the Celts—in the worship of the one True and Living God as best they could remember, no longer having the written Old Testament scriptures to rely upon and guide them in their worship practices.

Also upon arriving in the British Isles, the early Celts began to divide their society and culture into four classes: **Druids** (priests), **Filides** (judges and lawyers [think "judges" as in the Old Testament Book of Judges]), **Bards** (who maintained their oral history), and **Seers** (somewhat like the Old Testament Prophets). They had a very "high" culture for that time in history, especially in the arts and crafts. Sometimes, the Druids were also judges, philosophers, scholars, and teachers. The priests were both men and women: Druids and Druidesses. Male and female were equal in all aspects of Celtic life.

The Celts (including the Druids and Druidesses) were very literate, but for the most part they chose to rely on oral remembrances rather than upon writing. They believed that to write down things was to "weaken" the power of the mind. Much of their oral traditions consisted of very lengthy poetry, very similar in content and form to the biblical Book of Psalms.

They did not perceive nature as God or Mother Nature as God; The One True and Living God was simply in everything and was to be worshipped as being in everything. Yes, they always believed in the one True and Living God, but as the years passed they began to perceive God as being in everything: in the howling winds, in the rushing waters, in groves of trees, in the abundance of crops, in roaring fires, in all the fecundate earth. They never worshipped Mother Earth or Nature, but simply worshipped God as being entirely pervasive in everything—in all his creation.

Religious Beliefs of the Early Druids and Celts Before Jesus

Here is a very brief synopsis of Celtic and Druidic religious beliefs . . . First, they kept holy days they called Sabbats (think biblical Sabbaths). They believed that everything—everything!—was sacred, that God was in everything and somehow sustained everything by his almighty power.

Colossians 1: 17 informs us that in some mysterious way, all created entities cohere and consist by the power of Jesus Christ. We know from modern science, for example, that nothing in the entire universe is actually "solid," that the entirety of everything is always in motion; think of the whirling electrons and neutrons of the atom, for example—how each atom is constantly in motion, all its component parts revolving and whirling around each other (without flying all apart!), although to the naked eye those atoms making up a stone, for example, may appear to be solid.

The Celts believed that the One True and Living God was the Power or Sustaining Source by which all things cohere and consist—that God was truly and personally present in everything.

Everything was sacred to the Celts and Druids, but some things were "more" sacred than others. For example, they worshipped in sacred groves of trees and on sacred hills, often conducting animal sacrifices as they remembered them from their history in the land of Israel.

The sacred groves of trees were viewed as "bridges" between this "DarkWorld" ("OtherWorld" or "Shadow World") and "RealWorld" ("RealRealm"). But, they really saw no true separation between this world and RealWorld where God was "headquartered." They "connected" spiritually to all of nature wherein everything was sacred, but—as mentioned earlier—did not worship nature or "Mother Nature." They worshipped God who created Nature.

They saw God in the cycles of nature, probably dimly reminiscent of Genesis 8: 22 and related biblical references.

They perceived the sacredness of the four "elemental forces" of nature: Earth, Air, Fire, and Water. They held a "creation theory" very similar to the biblical record of creation in Genesis chapters 1 and 2.

Interestingly, before they ever learned of Jesus, one of their ancient worship symbols was a cross!

The Druids studied and taught not only "theology," but also the natural sciences and astronomy. They studied and practiced all types of herbal medicine. Their principal religious belief was life after death and resurrection into RealWorld or RealRealm.

The old Gospel hymn, "This is My Father's World" (written in 1901) contains within its words distant echoes of the old Druidic and Celtic beliefs; here are the words to that song:

"This is my Father's world.
And to my list'ning ears
All nature sings, and round me rings
The music of the spheres.

CHORUS
This is my Father's world
I rest me in the thought
Of rocks and trees, of skies and seas
His hand the wonders wrought.

This is my Father's world,
The birds their carols raise.
The morning light, the lily white
Declare the Maker's praise.

CHORUS
This is my Father's world.
He shines in all that's fair.
In the rustling grass
I hear Him pass;
He speaks to me everywhere.

This is my Father's world.
O let me ne'er forget
That though the wrong
Seems oft so strong,
God is the Ruler yet.

CHORUS
This is my Father's world.
The battle is not done.
Jesus, Who died, shall be satisfied,
And earth and heav'n be one."

The Druids established amazing schools among the Celts, teaching and leading in the worship of God as best they could remember from their life in Israel, and reading, writing, and fine arts. **To become a Druid Priest, one spent 20 years in study and preparation!**

Their diluted worship of Jehovah God persisted right up until the time of Jesus of Nazareth.

Jesus In Britain

Again, alternative history informs us that shortly after the resurrection and ascension of Jesus, Joseph of Arimathea (Jesus' great-uncle and Mary's uncle) was instructed by God to flee with Mary and some other Jesus-believers to the British Isles where Joseph had extensive land holdings and tin mines.

Alternative history informs us that the very first worship building for Jesus-believers was built by those refugees near the southern shores of the British Isles. There is some historical evidence that

Jesus, as a boy and teenager, often spent time with his great-uncle Joseph in Britain while Joseph conducted business there. In the absence of Jesus' stepfather, Joseph of Nazareth, his great-uncle, Joseph of Arimathea, became sort of a "father figure" to the young Jesus. Some alternative history also informs us that Jesus' mother, Mary, was buried in an unmarked grave in southern Britain.

When Joseph, Mary, and other early Jesus-believers met up with the Celts and Druids already living in Britain and proclaimed the Gospel of Jesus Christ to them, the Celts and Druids readily received Jesus as their Lord and Savior because they were "prepared" by their oral history and tradition which taught about a coming Messiah or Savior. Remember the Celtic story with which we introduced this teaching . . .

Yes, they readily received Jesus and incorporated their new faith into their worship of the one true and Living God. It was a very easy transition for them to receive the Good News about Jesus; after all, they had been "waiting" for 600 years to welcome and receive their Messiah!

Celtic Jesus-believers continued to perceive God in everything as the pre-Jesus Celts and Druids had for centuries. They saw God as being All in all (see 1 Corinthians 15: 28). They believed and practiced a very pure, pristine form of "biblical universalism" (**not** the type of liberalized universalism found in some circles today such as in Unity or Unitarianism which denies the deity and totality of redemption provided by the all-encompassing life and work of Jesus Christ). See John 6: 44; 12:32, 1 Corinthians 15: 24 – 28, and related biblical references.

The Celts were generally defeated by invading Roman armies around 300 AD, were assimilated into other cultures, and essentially disappeared as a distinct people from the world's stage by about 400 AD. As noted above, some of them fled to Ireland where their culture persisted for another 300 years or so. But as noted earlier, in the past 100 years or so much about their history, culture, and beliefs has been revived by historians, archaeologists, and the like.

Early Celts In Scotland

There is some other "alternative history" I want to enter into my teaching at this point simply because it touches upon Celtic history.

As noted in the Bible, after the death of King Solomon in the Old Testament narrative, the 12-tribed Kingdom of Israel was divided into two kingdoms: 1. The northern kingdom consisting of 10 tribes, known as the Kingdom of Israel. 2. The southern kingdom consisting of 2 tribes, known as the Kingdom of Judah. At times the two kingdoms co-existed peacefully, at times they warred with one another.

In 722 BC, the northern Kingdom of 10-tribed Israel was invaded and taken away captive by the Assyrian Empire. Some of the people of the Kingdom of Israel were assimilated into various people-groups within the far-flung Assyrian Empire. But, a remnant of them migrated into what is now northern Europe, Scandinavia, and Scotland (the latter area because they wanted to get as far away as possible from the rest of the known world).

Those remnant peoples from the northern 10-tribed Kingdom of Israel carried with them some remnants of Old Testament worship of Jehovah God and practiced it for quite some time.

100 years or so later, when the remnant peoples of the southern Kingdom of Judah arrived in the southern British Isles, the two remnant peoples sort of co-existed—the Israelites in the northern British Isles and the "Judah-ites" in the southern British Isles.

Warning: The alternative history about the migration of the remnant peoples of the northern 10 tribes falls under the broad "umbrella-heading" of a modern teaching labeled "Anglo-Israelism." Anglo-Israelism is taught today in some fringe, counterfeit Christian groups; a great deal of it falls under much cult-like teaching which is very deceptive; one must be very selective in studying about Anglo-Israelism.

Also, the Mormon Church (The Church of Jesus Christ Of Latter-Day Saints) has some teaching akin to Anglo-Israelism, but involving an alternative history of North America, not the British Isles; that teaching, too, is very deceptive, having no basis in any historical fact.

Having said that, **Yes, I am a Celtic Jesus-believer!** I believe God pervades all that is—the entirety of his creation: the universe, the earth, the air, fire, water, trees, all animals, etc. I believe the salvation provided by Jesus Christ—by his virgin birth, by his sinless life, by his crucifixion, by his resurrection, by his ascension, by his present ministry, by his coming again—is total and complete for all humankind—that there will come a time when God will be All in all. (1 Corinthians 15: 28) I believe the Scriptures (**taken as a whole and properly understood**) teach that very clearly.

Here are the words to a modern Celtic song which convey, in part, the concept of God's universal, saving, redeeming, restoring love for all humankind; it is sung to the Irish Celtic tune of "O Danny Boy":

"I cannot tell why He whom angels worship,
Should set his love upon the sons of men,
Or why, as Shepherd, He should seek the wanderers,
To bring them back, they know not how or when.
But this I know, that He was born of Mary
When Bethlehem's manger was His only home,
And that He lived at Nazareth and labored,
And so the Savior, Savior of the world is come.

I cannot tell how silently He suffered,
As with His peace He graced this place of tears,
Or how His heart upon the cross was broken,
The crown of pain to three and thirty years.
But this I know, He heals the brokenhearted,
And stays our sin, and calms our lurking fears,
And lifts the burden from the heavy laden,
For yet the Savior, Savior of the world is here.

I cannot tell how He will win the nations,
How He will claim His earthly heritage,
How satisfy the needs and aspirations
Of East and West, of sinner and of sage.
But this I know, all flesh shall see His glory,

And He shall reap the harvest He has sown,
And some glad day His sun shall shine in splendor
When He the Savior, Savior of the world is known.
I cannot tell how all the lands shall worship,
When, at His bidding, every storm is stilled,
Or who can say how great the jubilation
When all the hearts of men with love are filled.

But this I know, the skies will thrill with rapture,
And myriad, myriad human voices sing,
And earth to Heaven, and Heaven to earth, will answer:
At last the Savior, Savior of the world is King!"

A Celtic Jesus-believer is no better (or worse, for that matter) than other "types" of Jesus-believers—all authentic believers are one organic body in and through Jesus Christ; we are one now and we will all be one at the end of the ages of time when God consummates his plans and purposes for the entirety of his creation—and we will continue to be one with the All in eternity. There will come a time—at the end of the ages of time—when every human knee shall bow and every tongue confess Jesus as Lord to the glory of God the Father. No one can confess Jesus as Lord except by means of the indwelling Holy Spirit. (Romans 14: 11; Philippians 2: 11; 1 Corinthians 12: 3)

We Celtic Jesus-believers believe and teach that all creation will be redeemed and restored to a condition far better than the original, fallen creation which groans in travail until the children of God will be unveiled and revealed to the entire waiting universe. (Romans 8)

Appendix Five

Restoration

In Romans 8: 18 in the New Testament portion of the Bible, the writer of the letter to the Romans, Paul, made an outrageous statement: *He says that* ***all human sufferings*** *are "not worth comparing with the glory that will be revealed in us." (Romans 8: 18)* The human race has experienced unspeakable amounts of suffering throughout history.

What can possibly make that seem like nothing? **The Great Restoration of all things**. Paul then went on to write, *"The entire created universe waits in eager expectation for Jesus-believers to be unveiled [when Jesus returns]." (verse 19)* The Great Restoration of all things is being more or less held back, waiting upon the restoration of all humanity.

Two Basic Principles

Two very basic principles must be understood at the very beginning of this teaching. The first is that when **humans** restore something (such as restoring an antique car), they always attempt to restore the object to its **original** condition. In reality, humans often restore something to less than its original condition, but even in a lesser condition they consider it restored, nevertheless.

The second principle is this: **when God restores something, He always restores it to FAR GREATER than its original condi-**

tion—often up to seven times greater than its original condition! Furthermore, the Bible implies in a few places that God's restoration may sometimes reach even a hundred times greater than the original.

This teaching is about God's restoration of everything He created—including human beings. His universal restoration began in the Garden of Eden immediately after our first ancestors fell into sin, and will end when He freshly restores the entire universe and the earth.

See Isaiah 65: 17; 66: 22; 2 Peter 3: 13; and Revelation 21: 1 for references about the "new" heaven (universe) and the "new" earth; those are the only four such references in the entire Bible. In the two references in Isaiah, the word "new" is the Hebrew word, *"chadash,"* meaning *"something begun again, as in the beginning of a new cycle."* In the two references in Revelation, the word "new" is the Greek word *"kainos,"* meaning *"freshly restored."*

If you put those meanings together, the words "new heavens" and "new earth" mean **a freshly restored universe and earth begun anew by God.**

Again, this teaching will be about how God is in the process of restoring his entire creation, until in the end the entire universe and earth will be "freshly restored" and "begun again." In a manner of speaking, God will simply hit the cosmic "reset button" and all things will be freshly renovated and restored.

Let's begin with our first parents, Adam and Eve—how God is in the process of restoring them as well as all humanity "in Adam," as the Bible puts it. I have already covered that particular process of restoration in two other teachings on our ministry web site, so I will not write any more about it in this teaching; those other two teachings are: **Let There Be Light** and **Whole In One.**

If you're interested in reading those two teachings, but don't have access to the internet, ask a friend with a computer to download the teachings and print them for you.

We'll look at some Bible references about restoration in general in a few moments, but for now, I want to simply generalize with the following thoughts adapted from the writings of a Jesus-believing brother named John Eldredge:

What It'll Be Like

"In Jesus' Kingdom and, later, in the freshly restored universe and earth, things are not stained or broken; everything is as it was meant to be in the beginning—and greater. Think about this for a moment. Aren't every one of our sorrows on earth the result of things not being as they were meant to be? And so when Jesus returns and establishes his Kingdom, wonderful things will begin to unfold. 'When He spoke to people about the Kingdom of God, He healed those who needed healing.' (Luke 9: 11)

What will happen when we find ourselves in the Kingdom of God? The disabled will jump to their feet and begin dancing. The deaf will go out and purchase stereo equipment. The blind will head to the movies. The dead will not be dead anymore, but very much alive. They'll show up for dinner. In other words, human brokenness in all its forms will be healed.

The Kingdom of God will bring ***restoration****. Life will be* ***restored*** *to what it was meant to be. 'In the beginning,' back in Eden, all of creation was pronounced good because all of creation was exactly as God meant for it to be. For it to be 'good' again is not for it to be destroyed, but healed, renewed, brought back to its goodness, fully* ***restored.***

The few glimpses we see in the miracles of Jesus were the 'first-fruits' of God's restoration of all things. When He announced the full coming of his Kingdom, Jesus said, 'Look, I am ***freshly restoring*** *all things.'* (Revelations 21: 5) *He means that* ***everything in the entire created universe that has been so badly broken will be restored—and then some."***

Restoration In Job, The Oldest Book In The Bible

Back to some of the Bible's teaching about God's principles of restoration. I've already mentioned how God will restore Adam and Eve. God also taught some principles of restoration during the time of the Patriarchs (Abraham, Isaac, and Jacob) and Moses. But I want to look at just a few examples of God's restoration during the times of the kings of Israel and Judah.

Of course, many of the prophets who lived during the times of the kings proclaimed God's restoration; we'll get to some of them later. But I actually want to begin with some of God's principles of restoration as found in the oldest book of the Bible, the Book of Job.

I hope you remember the story of Job. How God essentially allowed him to be stripped of everything to test and purify his faith and humble him before Almighty God. I won't go into details, but the first 41 chapters of Job address that in full and lengthy detail. Instead, I want to focus on the 42nd chapter of Job where God restores Job.

Chapter 42, verse 10 says this: *"and the Lord turned [around] the captivity of Job and* ***restored*** *his fortunes, when he [Job] prayed for his friends; also the Lord gave* ***Job twice as much*** *as he had before."* Verse 12 goes on to say: *"And the Lord blessed the end of Job's life much* ***more*** *than his early life."*

Earlier, Job 33: 26b also conveys some very powerful inherent concepts about God restoring righteousness to unrighteous human beings. We read in Isaiah 64: 6 that all human righteousness is just filthy rags; we humans are totally unrighteous. Here in Job we read that God restores all of humanity's righteousness to them. How does He do that? God himself is the only inherently righteous Being (Jeremiah 23: 6); God the Son—Jesus—is also totally righteous (1 Corinthians 1: 30).

God—through Jesus—implants his own righteousness in humans, displacing and replacing their unrighteousness. Just those few sentences are a summary of an entire large body of teaching in the Bible.

In the time of Moses, Deuteronomy 30, verses 1 – 3 intimate and allude to the same type of restoration if in their future God's people might depart from Him and then return to Him for his restoration. Yes, such principles of God's restoration are taught here and there throughout both the Old and New Testaments.

Restoration In Elisha's Time

But now let's turn to one example during the times of Israel's kings.

In 2 Kings chapter 8, Elisha, one of God's prophets, predicted that a seven-year famine would come upon the land. In light of the upcoming famine, God—speaking through Elisha—told a widow, whose son Elisha had raised from the dead by God's power, to go to another land and stay there until the famine ended. She obeyed the prophet and did as he told her to do.

At the end of the seven-year famine, the woman returned to her homeland and went to the king to appeal to have her original land restored to her. The king had the woman's claims checked out in the court records and, sure enough, she did have a prior legal claim to the land which had previously been hers. The king decreed not only to restore her land, but for her to receive the income from the land from the previous seven years.

In Job, we saw that God restored to Job **double** what he had previously owned. Now in 2 Kings we find that God restored to the woman **seven times** what she previously possessed. Those are timeless principles of God's restoration. **He often restores from two to seven times what a person had previously lost!** He did that in those days, and He is still practicing those principles of restoration in our time. **His restoration is always more and greater than the original condition or situation.**

Other Restoration In The Bible

Here's another example from the time of Israel's kings along with a parallel example from the New Testament in the life of Jesus.

Turn to 2 Samuel 12: 6. It's about an incident in the life of King David after he had committed adultery with Bathsheba; Nathan the prophet was confronting David about his adultery by telling the fictitious story of a sin committed by another man. David responded to Nathan's story by exclaiming that that the man Nathan spoke of should **restore fourfold** what the man had stolen from another person in the story. David then understood that Nathan's story had actually been about David.

Let's look at a similar incident in the New Testament during the life of Jesus. See Luke 19: 1 – 9. Jesus confronted a chief tax collector in the IRS of his day about his need to repent and turn to

God. Zaccheus responded positively to Jesus, was redeemed from his sinful condition, and then exclaimed, *"I will **restore fourfold** what I have taken dishonestly!"*

Okay, what do we have—in principle—now? Two fold restoration. Fourfold restoration. And sevenfold restoration. (see Psalm 79: 12 for an intimation of seven-fold restoration.) Does it get any better in this life? Look at Mark 10: 29 – 31. In some few instances, some people will receive in this life **one-hundredfold restoration!** In this reference, there are some other details that are part of that degree of restoration, but I'll let you ponder those for yourself.

Revival = Restoration

I want to insert at this point in our teaching this thought which you might want to pursue with some study on your own. In the Old Testament, the words "revive" and "restore" are often used synonymously. I guarantee if you look up both those Old Testament words in an exhaustive Bible concordance, you could find yourself studying an entire body of thought about the Bible's principles of revival and restoration.

In the Old Testament, the Hebrew word for "revive" is *"chayah,"* meaning to live again. In the New Testament, the Greek word for "revive" is *"anazao,"* meaning the same as the Hebrew word. Thus, "revive" means that something was dead and has been brought back to life. The English word "revive" means the same as the Hebrew and Greek words—with the added concept of bringing something back to a healthy, vigorous, flourishing condition after a decline.

Yes, I encourage you to put all those definitions, thoughts, and concepts together for a fascinating study of your own about restoration and revival.

As already indicated, the Bible is replete with references to restoration; please take a look, for example, at Proverbs 6: 31. There is not one, single reference that teaches the entire principle of restoration found in the Bible; you must take references such as this one in Proverbs and put it together with numerous other references on the subject before arriving at the "big picture," before arriving at an honest conclusion about the Bible's overall teaching about this subject.

Now to just a few examples from the prophetic books of the Old Testament. First, turn to Joel chapter 2. There had been a horrible plague of locusts in the land, stripping away every green and growing plant. The land was completely denuded and devastated. God then prophesied through the prophet Joel (verses 25 and 26):

"And I will **restore** *or replace for you the years that the locust has eaten . . . And you shall eat in plenty and be satisfied and praise the Name of the Lord your God, Who has dealt wondrously with you."*

Look at Isaiah 58: 12 for another example. It speaks of rebuilding waste places, rebuilding foundations, repairing breaches, and restoring homes that people dwell in. It's a "word picture" of the principle of God's restoration of our broken, ruined, abandoned lives.

"Flow Chart" For Restoration

Finally, I encourage you to read the entire short book of Lamentations. It's about the prophet Jeremiah lamenting the destruction and fall of Jerusalem and pleading with God to rebuild and restore that great city. If you read through the book carefully, you will find a "flow chart" that goes something like this: **Human, self-willed sin leads to ⇒ suffering. Suffering leads to ⇒ sorrow. Sorrow leads to ⇒ repentance. Repentance leads to ⇒ prayer. Prayer leads to ⇒ hope. Hope leads to ⇒ faith. And faith leads to ⇒ restoration**.

In a general way, you can follow that flow chart throughout the Bible in terms of God's principles of complete and total restoration of fallen humanity, the earth, and the entire universe.

Before we proceed, I want to clarify and expand a basic "rule" or principle of Bible study I hinted at above. When studying any one topic or subject in the Bible, it is simply sound, honest scholarship to **study all the references** on a given subject before arriving at a conclusion about that subject. In other words, be wary of simply taking isolated "proof texts" in order to "prove" something from the Bible. Check out everything the entire Bible has to teach about a subject or topic and then draw your conclusions. That just makes plain good sense.

For example, if you choose to study for yourself the subject of restoration in the Bible, there are over 60 references to "restore" or "restoration" (and more references to "revive" and "revival") which you should look up and study—in their context—before you arrive at any conclusion about the subject. That's what I did when studying this subject before writing about it and sort of summarizing the subject in this teaching.

In following the rule or principle of Bible study I mentioned above, however, there is often one more factor to take into consideration. Generally (not always) most Bible subjects or topics will have one specific reference—a verse or two, a chapter, etc.—that sort of encapsulates or summarizes that particular subject or topic in the Bible.

For example, the subject of **resurrection** in the Bible is pretty well summarized in 1 Corinthians 15; the subject of **love** is encapsulated in 1 Corinthians 13. And so on . . .

Summary Of The Restoration Process

Following that principle, for the subject of **restoration** in the Bible, it is summarized or encapsulated in Acts 3: 18 – 21; Peter was speaking to some of the Jewish people of his day:

"God has fulfilled what He foretold and predicted through all the [Old Testament] prophets, that Jesus should suffer, undergo ill treatment, and be afflicted.

So change your mind [repent] and your life's purposes; turn around and return to God, that your sins may be wiped clean [erased, blotted out, removed]; then wonderful times of ***restoration*** *[revival and refreshing] will come from the Lord.*

And [repent so] that God may send to you Jesus, who was designated and appointed for you long before; yes, I'm speaking about

Jesus. He must remain in heaven until the time for the ***complete and final restoration of all*** *[everything in all of creation] that God spoke about by all his prophets from the most ancient times in the memory of humankind."*

As mentioned at the beginning of this teaching, the final restoration of all things God has ever created—the entire universe, including the earth and every human who has ever lived—will be fully restored to far more and greater than its original condition. Put it this way: whatever we can possibly think or imagine that the restored universe and earth will be like, it will actually be far more than we can ever think or imagine—in our wildest imaginings!

The earth and universe will be a virginal re-creation, fresh and unspoiled; a universe without blemish, whole and clean and undamaged. It will be ever new, ever changing, ever fresh as it was in it's first beginning, but this time preserved in innocence for in eternity.

The End Of The Bible

If I were to ask you to turn to the end of the Bible, you would most likely turn to the 22nd chapter of Revelation. Revelation 22 is the last chapter in the **format** of the Bible, but it is not the actual end of the Bible in terms of last **events**. The actual end of the Bible's teachings about events is in the 15th chapter of First Corinthians. Let's examine what I mean by that being the true end of the Bible.

I'm going to paraphrase and "modernize" for you verses 23 – 28:

"Jesus was the very first Person to be resurrected from the dead. When He returns, then we will be resurrected into his Kingdom. Some time after that event, there will occur the final consummation when Jesus delivers his Kingdom to God the Father after He has rendered inoperative and abolished every other opposing power in the entire universe.

Jesus will reign in his Kingdom until He puts every enemy—even our worst enemy, death—under his feet and completely abolishes them.

Having done that, then Jesus will turn his Kingdom over to God the Father and completely submit Himself to the Father.

When that takes place, then God will be All in all, everything to everyone, once and for all indwelling everyone and every thing in all creation!"

Dear reader, that's the **final restoration**, when God has completely restored every human ever born and the entire universe and earth, and He becomes All in all! Everything God is doing in your life and mine, both now, and in our resurrected state in his Kingdom is always working toward that end. Our final destiny is to be fully and completely restored through Jesus' total and finished work of complete and full salvation on our behalf.

Restored Into God's Image

Let me be just a little more specific now and think together for a few minutes about God's restoration of us: you and me.

God's vision for us . . . God's dream for us . . . God's destiny for us . . . God's plans and purposes for us are to fully restore us into his clear, unblemished image. God created us in his image. We marred his image in us. God is restoring his image in us.

The fullest—the perfect—image of God is Jesus Christ (Hebrews 1: 3; 1 Corinthians 3: 18; 4: 4; Colossians 1: 15). Jesus is the unmarred, unblemished, completely focused, and **perfect** image of God. I am an **imperfect**, marred, blemished, fuzzy, unfocused, and blurred image of God.

What does it mean to be in the image of God? **It means that I am a visible representation of the invisible God.** Let me emphasize again: Jesus is God's **perfect** visible representation; I am God's **imperfect** visible representation.

How is God restoring his image in me? **I cooperate with the Holy Spirit as He empowers me (from within where He lives in my spirit) to change my mind daily from choosing to live a self-filled life to choosing to live a Jesus-filled life.**

Changing my mind (what the Bible terms "repentance") day after day, year after year, and on into Jesus' Kingdom, then afterwards in the eternal state of the freshly restored universe and earth—changes me more and more into the fully restored image of God . . . into a less blurred image of God . . . into a more clearly focused image of God. (Romans 12: 1 and 2; Ephesians 4: 23, etc.)

Thus, God's vision and destiny for my life—and for yours—is to fully restore us into his image!

He is taking whatever steps are necessary (many known only to Him) in order to accomplish that vision for us. He is eternally farsighted. I am very often shortsighted, not seeing beyond the finite limitations of my mortal life. Tapping into God's vision for my life draws me toward my future. It helps me stay focused on my future. My life's vision—in tandem with God's—continually helps me shape my future. What my past has been does not necessarily equal what my future is to be—fully restored into the image of God.

God is love, and unconditionally and eternally loves his entire creation. Everything He does flows out of his eternal love for his entire creation and is filtered through his love. (1 John 4: 8; Jeremiah 31: 3) He is an altogether good God, and everything He does is good. (Psalm 119: 68) Everything—everything!—that happens in our lives is working toward our ultimate, final good. (Genesis 50: 20; Romans 8: 28, and similar references **taken together as a whole!**)

Like a magnet irresistibly draws iron filings to itself, God is always and ever . . . inexorably . . . inescapably . . . unerringly . . . drawing every human being and everything else everywhere and everywhen in the entire created universe to Himself through the once-for-all sacrifice of Jesus on the cross of Calvary—restoring them to a far, far, greater condition than they were in the beginning! (John 6: 44 and 12: 32; Genesis 1: 1)

The Bible begins with *"In the beginning God . . . "*

The Bible wraps it all up with *"In the end God . . . "*

(Genesis 1: 1; 1 Corinthians 15: 28)

Appendix Six

Faith

Beyond our five senses, beyond our mind, beyond our own thoughts, beyond our consciousness or subconsciousness . . . lies an inner, limitless expanse of **faith** "residing" in our spirits. What is faith? How many definitions of faith have you read or heard in your life? Confusing, isn't it? I'm not going to spring anything new on you. The best definition I've found anywhere is right where some people least expect to find it. Where might that be? Surprise! Surprise! Right in your Bible.

Follow me carefully here. I want you to turn to a reference in your Bible, but **not in the old King James version**; that version was written almost 400 years ago. English is a "living" language, which means the language is constantly changing and growing. In some respects, 20th century English is much different from what it was 400 years ago. Having said that, please turn to your own Bible's definition of faith. It is **Hebrews 11: 1**. Most modern versions of the Bible will define faith there somewhat different than the King James Version defines it.

Definition Of Faith

Here's that definition of Hebrews 11: 1 in modern English: **Faith is being confident of what we hope for—perceiving as evidence phenomena not taken in by our five senses.** Let's analyze that definition. Before we do, though, please turn to Romans 4: 18 – 21 and read that reference, too; it's about ancient Abraham's faith being a "model" or "prototype" for our faith. It's one of the Bible's own interpretations of the definition of faith in Hebrews 11: 1.

Notice that Abraham had given up hope by reason of his five senses, but he hoped by faith; he was confident—his faith did not weaken. He didn't waver by unbelief or distrust, but was strong and empowered by faith to trust that God would keep his word and do what He had promised. That is why his faith was credited to his account as right standing with God. That's just a little bit about what this reference teaches us about faith. There's more, much more.

From the instant you were conceived, everything you have ever learned or experienced has come to you through your five senses; think about that: besides your genetic, biological being, your entire self-ness—that which makes you "you"—has all occurred as a result of data entering you from outside you through your five senses. Your five senses are how you perceive all the data coming into you from your external world.

Everything you've ever tasted, touched, smelled, heard, or seen has come into you by those five senses . . . processed through your conscious mind, and then sent to be stored in the subconscious part of your mind.

Yes, everything **outside your skin** comes to you through your five senses. In other words, by means of your five senses you have "constructed" the person living inside your skin whom you call "me" (and whom others call "you") out of the quadrillions and mega-quadrillions of bits of data you have received from outside your skin since the instant you were conceived.

Wait a minute, though, doesn't the Bible's definition say faith perceives as real fact what is **not** taken in by the five senses? Yes, it does say that. **So where does faith come from? It comes from inside of us. Faith comes to us from God who lives inside of us in his unbodied Spirit form**. For purposes of illustration at this point, let's say that in manner of speaking faith is another "sense" (not the traditional sixth sense, however) that receives phenomena and data **from inside our skin** rather than from outside our skin.

Your Portion Of Faith

The Bible says in Romans 12: 3 that God has given every human being a certain "measure" of faith as an unmerited, free gift. Ephesians 2: 8 and 9 addresses the same matter. You have a certain measure or portion of faith. I have a certain measure or portion of faith. Another way of putting it is that God has given each of us an **appropriate amount** of faith. None of us can say we don't have faith. We all have faith. The important point is in how we "use" our faith.

Some people place their faith in money . . . or cars . . . or in other people . . . or in dead, manmade religious activities . . . or in houses . . . or in Hollywood . . . or in their intellect or knowledge . . . or in reason and logic . . . or in the theory of evolution . . . or in nothing at all. And, some people place their faith in God. The differences in how people use their faith lie in the **object** of their faith, not in the faith itself. Faith is faith. Your faith—and the faith of everybody else—is the same as my faith. Yes, God has given each of us an appropriate amount of faith. How are **you** using yours? What's the primary object of **your** faith?

Yes, the Holy Spirit who lives inside each of us "transmits" reality (by means of faith) to our "inner person" from the inside where he lives in our spirits; this is in addition to the reality which comes to us from the outside by means of our five senses.

The Other Source Of Faith

There's another way in which faith is transmitted to us, too. Yet, it originates from the same Holy Spirit who lives inside each of us. Faith also comes from the Bible. Look at Romans 10: 17. Who caused the Bible to be written? The Holy Spirit. So . . . faith comes from the Bible, too. As we read and study it—and attempt to obey it!—the Holy Spirit makes it real to us. That's how we know the Bible is the "Word of God," not by means of our five senses, but by means of our greater, inner "sense"—faith!

The Bible is unlike any other book ever written; it is actually full of dynamic power and is LIFE-giving as the Holy Spirit uses it to "grow" and strengthen our faith. (see Hebrews 4: 12, especially in The Amplified Bible) The Bible is not merely printed words on paper like other books. It is a "living" Book given to humanity by God, unlike all other books.

Yes, from inside of us the Holy Spirit makes the Bible come alive as we read, study, and attempt to obey it. He's the one who causes the Bible to actually become "food" for our inner persons. See Matthew 4: 4. He's the one who causes the Bible to be more than mere paper and ink. By faith the Bible is a power-full, LIFE-giving book the Holy Spirit uses to help transform and "grow" our lives. By means of our faith-sense, the Bible actually imparts God's own eternal, self-existent, uncreated, abundant LIFE to us. By faith, it is a book unlike any other book ever written. It is **THE totally reliable, totally mistake-free Word of the Living God!**

Two Realms Of Life

Why do we need faith in addition to our five senses? We need faith because it is the only "sense" with which we can perceive God and the invisible realm of the Spirit. For example, Hebrews 11: 6 says that whoever comes to God must believe God is. Faith is the means by which we believe God exists and by which we can "see" into the invisible realm in which He lives.

I call that invisible world **RealRealm,** as contrasted with this world in which we live and move and have our mortal beings: **ShadowLand or DarkWorld**. ShadowLand is—well—just a dim, murky, shadowy world compared to the vast, limitless, bright, invisible realm of RealWorld in which God lives in his eternal state of being.

Education, science, logic, reason, philosophy—each of these has to do with the five senses, and they all have their places in God's grand scheme of things. But our five senses cannot "find" God or "prove" He exists. Only by using our "faith-sense" can we believe God exists and believe the Bible to be God's Word. How do we have faith in God? God who lives inside of us in the unbodied form of the Holy Spirit gives us faith to believe He is. That's the only way we can really know and experience a vital, living relationship with God.

You see, God is Spirit (John 4: 23), meaning He is "composed" of invisible "spirit-substance." Anyone or anything which is spirit cannot be perceived or known by the five senses—only by means of faith. That's why we need the faith God has given to each of us; it's the only means by which we can know Him. Faith is the connecting link between the visible material universe (ShadowLand) and the invisible spiritual universe, the Kingdom of God (RealRealm).

There is an entire "alter universe," so to speak, known as the Kingdom of God. It is an invisible Kingdom within us, and it is also an invisible Kingdom outside of us: a Kingdom greater, larger, and more real than the physical or material universe we know by our five senses. That unlimited, invisible Kingdom of God can be known and understood only by means of faith.

GateWay To RealRealm

Also, the Bible is the other "gateway" or connecting link through which we can "cross" back and forth between RealRealm from ShadowLand. It is the Bible "mixed" with our faith that allows us to see into the unseen, hear which cannot be heard with our physical ears, touch the untouchable, and experience that which we cannot experience with our five senses.

I tell you with all the assurance I possess after having read and interacted with the Bible daily for many years—it is unlike any other book ever written on this planet. It is really and truly **THE totally reliable, totally mistake-free Word of the Living God! But you can only know that for yourself by your use of your faith-sense.**

Also, the only means by which we can really know Jesus Christ—God the Son—is by faith, too. Look up Acts 20: 21. Jesus isn't here on earth in the flesh anymore. We can't perceive Him by means of our five senses. The only way we can believe in Him and know Him is by our faith-sense.

In our world and universe (ShadowLand)—which is a physical, material world and universe—we perceive everything by our five senses; we all grew up learning to rely almost 100% upon our five senses. Through our own life experiences, through our education, through our relationships with other people, we came to believe that if we can't know or experience something with our five senses, it either doesn't exist or isn't real. We say, *"Seeing is believing!"* meaning if we can't perceive something with our five senses then it isn't real.

That's why it's relatively difficult for many people to know and believe God, Jesus, the Holy Spirit, and the Bible. Because they can't be known by our five senses in the same way we know and perceive most material reality. We haven't been conditioned to trust our "faith-sense" like we've been conditioned to rely upon our five senses. It's not that faith isn't as real as our five senses; actually, it's more real. We simply don't know how to use our faith, rely upon it, exercise it, focus it—like we do our five senses.

When God dispenses the appropriate amount of faith to each of us, it comes to us at first in sort of a vague "form"; for most of us when we became new Jesus-believers, at first our faith is unfocused and undifferentiated. God wants us to exercise it and focus it toward Him. He wants us to train ourselves to use our faith properly.

Laser-Like Faith

Let me try to explain it this way. Natural light takes various forms. Light in a common household light bulb is unfocused; it's called radiant light, meaning it radiates out from its source equally in all directions; it's not focused in any manner. On the other hand, there is light such as laser light which is very narrowly focused into a compact, powerful beam which can be pointed or focused in a specific direction.

God wants us to learn how to focus our faith like laser light—pointed specifically at Him. He doesn't want our faith to spread out randomly in all directions (and thus lose some of it's radiant "power"). Rather, He wants our faith to be narrowly and powerfully focused towards Him.

Let's continue on with some general teaching about our faith. We know a little about how our five senses function. We know a little about auditory nerves, optic nerves, olfactory lobes, tactile nerve endings, taste buds, etc. But what do we know about how faith works and functions? More than you might think. How do we know? From the Bible. From the Holy Spirit communicating to us from within us and showing us how to apply the Bible to our lives.

For example, we have already pointed out that God gives each of us an appropriate amount of faith. The Bible teaches that we must "exercise" that faith just as we exercise our muscles and minds. We exercise our faith by "releasing" it toward God and "attaching" it to Him: by believing in Him, trusting Him, praying to Him, obeying Him, listening to Him with our "inner ears," seeing Him with our "inner eyes," etc.

As we exercise our faith in those ways, our faith is honed, sharpened, and focused; it becomes more use-able. God becomes more "responsive" (in a sense) to our prayers, to our trust, to our use of our faith. Not that we manipulate God with our faith or that He is some sort of cosmic servant who responds to our every whim; no, nothing like that!

It's just that as we open up our inner selves and use our faith more often and in a more focused manner, we become more and more aware of just how the entire, invisible, spiritual realm of faith operates. We become more aware of "spiritual laws" and how they operate, just as we have become aware of how natural laws operate in the material universe.

Just as we read, study, experience, and learn more about our physical, material universe by "exercising" our five senses, we perceive and comprehend more and more about God and our non-physical, non-material, invisible, spiritual universe (RealRealm) by exercising our faith-sense. By our five senses we are aware of our connectedness with other people, with planet earth, with the material universe. In contrast, by our faith-sense we are aware of our connectedness with another universe—the limitless expanse of the Kingdom of God—which transcends the material universe.

At this point, you may be thinking, *"Bill, didn't Jesus talk with his first disciples about having* ***little*** *faith?* (Matthew 6: 30, 8: 26, 14: 31, a6: 8, and Luke 12: 28) *If God has given every person a certain portion of faith, did He give some people just a little faith?"* Those are insightful questions. Here's the answer. In those instances where Jesus mentioned **little** faith, the original Greek word means **underdeveloped** faith, not necessarily a small portion of faith. God expects each of us to **develop** (use, exercise, strengthen) our faith so we don't have underdeveloped faith.

Uses For Our Faith

We've read that one of the things God wants us to do with the amount of faith He has given us is to have faith in Him. God has given us the appropriate amount of faith so we may direct and focus it toward Him and thus believe in Him, know Him, and trust Him—but not with our five senses. With our faith! Believing in Jesus means we have a firm, steadfast reliance upon Him—by faith.

There are other uses to which God wants us to put the faith He has given us.

First, we use our faith to believe that Jesus paid the supreme penalty for our sins and restored us to a proper relationship with God. See Romans 3: 25. What Jesus did on our behalf happened in historical time and space 2,000 years ago. We weren't there. We didn't see the event, experience it, or hear it; our five senses are unable to "prove" that Jesus gave his life and shed his blood to pay for the sins of all humankind, including you and me. Only faith can "prove" inside of us that Jesus actually did what He did; we cannot know the reality of it by any other means.

In connection with believing by faith what Jesus did for us on the cross, the only way we can know and experience the personal, indwelling, abiding presence of the living, resurrected Jesus is by faith. True, there's an empty tomb on a hillside near the city of Jerusalem; history tells us that's where Jesus was entombed after his cruel, painful death. But we weren't there personally to see Him burst forth from that tomb, alive again by the power of God's Spirit. We can believe that historical event really occurred only by means of our faith-sense.

Closely tied to that aspect of our salvation is the simple fact we could not even believe the Gospel—God's Good News for all people—without our faith. The only way we can "believe" the Gospel is by faith. God's Good News is not good news when perceived by the five senses. Actually, for the most part it is irrational and illogical nonsense to our five senses; it's foolishness. But faith makes it possible for us to understand it's the greatest, most power-full Good News ever proclaimed to humankind! (see Romans 1: 16)

Well, those are only a few examples of how we are to use our faith: to believe in God, to believe in what Jesus did for us, to believe the Bible is God's Word, and to believe, comprehend, and understand God's Good News about our full and complete, eternal salvation.

I sometimes quote poetry or music in my writings; if you were right here in our home office with me as I compose these words, I think I would probably sing you a song. Since I can't sing it to you, I'll write some of the words. Why? **This song was the precise, "divine instrument" God used to awaken my faith and cause me to give my life to Jesus** and to begin to understand the nature of faith; it's very personal to me and I sometimes cry when humming or singing it to myself. Here are some of the words of that song:

Oh, how well do I remember
how I doubted day by day
For I did not know for certain
that my sins were washed away.
When the Spirit tried to tell me
I would not the truth receive;
I endeavored to be happy and
to make myself believe.

But it's real! It's real!
Oh, I know it's real!
Praise God! The doubts are settled and
I know, I know it's real.

So I prayed to God in earnest—
And not caring what folks said—
I was hungry for God's blessings,
My poor spirit must be fed.

When at last by ***FAITH*** *I touched Him,*
Then like sparks from smitten steel—
Just that quick salvation reached me.
And Praise God, I know He's real!

Dear readers and friends, that's what faith has done for me! And I've lived by faith for many years now. Oh, there's always an interplay between my five senses and my faith. That's true of all of us. Just like there's always an interplay between ShadowLand and RealRealm. After all, we're human; we're a "blend" of both material beings and spiritual beings. But beyond my five human senses, logic, reason, education, and intellect, faith is the means of my direct connection with God and with all that comprises the limitless, boundless, eternal Kingdom of God.

We are not human beings sent here to have spiritual experiences; we are spiritual beings sent here to have human experiences!

I could teach you much more about living by faith, about reaching out to other people by faith, about "seeing" into invisible RealRealm by faith, about being "co-creators" with God by faith, about dealing with dark, unseen forces by faith, about being aware of angels by faith...yes, there's more, there's more. And it's all by faith.

I'm not suggesting that any of us demean or minimize the five senses. That's life. I use my five senses; I believe in education, the intellect, logic, reason—all of those are necessary parts of our lives and the world we live in—ShadowLand. For example, I have a great deal of formal, higher education for which I am very grateful to God; I never denigrate or minimize education. But in addition let us also determine to live and move and have our being in that realm beyond the five senses, education, reason, and logic—by means of faith!

By means of our faith-sense, we who are Jesus-believers are presently bi-locational, having mortal life here in time and space on planet earth . . . while simultaneously having immortal, eternal LIFE in the transcendent realm called the Kingdom of Heaven.

CPSIA information can be obtained at www.ICGtesting.com
Printed in the USA
236043LV00001B/76/P